Selenium WebDriver 3 Practical Guide
Second Edition

End-to-end automation testing for web and mobile browsers
with Selenium WebDriver

Unmesh Gundecha
Satya Avasarala

Packt>

BIRMINGHAM - MUMBAI

Selenium WebDriver 3 Practical Guide
Second Edition

Commissioning Editor: Kunal Chaudhari
Acquisition Editor: Divya Poojari
Content Development Editor: Deepti Thore
Technical Editor: Cymon Pereira
Copy Editor: Safis Editing
Project Coordinator: Kinjal Bari
Proofreader: Safis Editing
Indexer: Mariammal Chettiyar
Graphics: Jisha Chirayil
Production Coordinator: Arvindkumar Gupta

First published: January 2014

Second edition: July 2018

Production reference: 1300718

Published by Packt Publishing Ltd.
Livery Place
35 Livery Street
Birmingham
B3 2PB, UK.

ISBN 978-1-78899-976-2

www.packtpub.com

ʌʌMapt

`mapt.io`

Mapt is an online digital library that gives you full access to over 5,000 books and videos, as well as industry leading tools to help you plan your personal development and advance your career. For more information, please visit our website.

Why subscribe?

- Spend less time learning and more time coding with practical eBooks and Videos from over 4,000 industry professionals

- Improve your learning with Skill Plans built especially for you

- Get a free eBook or video every month

- Mapt is fully searchable

- Copy and paste, print, and bookmark content

PacktPub.com

Did you know that Packt offers eBook versions of every book published, with PDF and ePub files available? You can upgrade to the eBook version at `www.PacktPub.com` and as a print book customer, you are entitled to a discount on the eBook copy. Get in touch with us at `service@packtpub.com` for more details.

At `www.PacktPub.com`, you can also read a collection of free technical articles, sign up for a range of free newsletters, and receive exclusive discounts and offers on Packt books and eBooks.

Contributors

About the author

Unmesh Gundecha has over 16 years, experience in Agile software development, test automation, and DevOps methodologies. He is an Agile, open source, and DevOps evangelist with extensive experience in a diverse set of tools and technologies. He has extensive hands-on experience in building sustainable and repeatable test automation solutions for web and mobile platforms, APIs, and CLI apps with continuous integration and delivery pipelines, using best-of-breed open source and commercial tools to do so. He is the author of *Selenium Testing Tools Cookbook* and *Learning Selenium Testing Tools with Python*, both by Packt Publishing.

I would firstly like to thank Rushi Vesmawala, who proposed that I write this book, and Deepti Thore, who coordinated and ensured that I stayed on track. I'd like to thank Pallavi Sharma for providing valuable feedback. I would also like to thank my wife, Punam, and my children Aarav and Ira, for supporting me while I was writing this book and making sure I did things on time. Finally, a big thanks to the Selenium development and user community for building this wonderful tool.

About the reviewer

Pallavi Sharma is a founder of 5 Elements Learning. She has 12 years professional experience. She has worked in varied roles as a product/project manager, in presales team, marketing team, and test automation coach in the software testing domain. Being an avid learner, she also likes to keep herself up to date with the latest trends and technologies. She is a firm believer that there is no shortcut to success.

Packt is searching for authors like you

If you're interested in becoming an author for Packt, please visit `authors.packtpub.com` and apply today. We have worked with thousands of developers and tech professionals, just like you, to help them share their insight with the global tech community. You can make a general application, apply for a specific hot topic that we are recruiting an author for, or submit your own idea.

Table of Contents

Preface

This book is about Selenium WebDriver, that is, a browser automation tool used by software developers and QA engineers to test their web application on different web browsers. This book can be used as a reference for your day-to-day usage of WebDriver.

Selenium is a set of tools for automating browsers. It is largely used for testing applications, but its usages are not limited only to testing. It can also be used for screen scraping and automating repetitive tasks in a browser window. Selenium supports automation on all the major browsers, including Firefox, Internet Explorer, Google Chrome, Safari, and Opera. Selenium WebDriver is now a part of W3C standards, and it is supported by major browser vendors.

Who this book is for

If you are a quality assurance/testing professional, test engineer, software developer, or web application developer looking to create automated test suites for your web applications, this is the perfect guide for you! As a prerequisite, this book expects you to have a basic understanding of Java programming although any previous knowledge of WebDriver or Selenium is not needed. By the end of this book, you will have acquired a comprehensive knowledge of WebDriver, which will help you in writing your automation tests.

What this book covers

Chapter 1, *Introducing WebDriver and WebElements*, will start off with an overview of Selenium and the features. Then, we quickly jump into WebDriver by describing how it perceives a web page. We will also look at what a WebDriver's WebElement is. Then, we talk about locating WebElements on a web page and performing some basic actions on them.

Chapter 2, *Working with Browser Drivers*, will talk about various implementations of WebDriver, such as FirefoxDriver, IEDriver, and ChromeDriver. We will configure browser options to run tests in headless mode, mobile emulation, and use custom profiles. With WebDriver becoming a W3C specification, all major browser vendors now support WebDriver natively in the browser.

Chapter 3, *Using Java 8 Features along with Selenium,* will talk about prominent Java 8 features such as Streams API and Lambda expressions for processing the list of WebElements. The Stream API and Lambda expression help in applying functional programming style to create readable and fluent tests.

Chapter 4, *Exploring the Features of WebDriver,* will talk about some advanced features of WebDriver, such as taking screenshots of web pages, executing JavaScript, handling cookies, and handling Windows and Frames.

Chapter 5, *Exploring Advanced Interaction API,* will dive deeply into more advanced actions that WebDriver can perform on the WebElements of a web page, such as the dragging and dropping of elements from one frame of a page to another and right/context-clicking on WebElements. We're sure you will find this chapter interesting to read.

Chapter 6, *Understanding WebDriver Events,* will deal with the event-handling aspect of WebDriver. To state a few, events can be a value change on a WebElement, a browser back-navigation invocation, script execution completion, and so on. We will use these events to run accessibility and performance checks.

Chapter 7, *Exploring RemoteWebDriver,* will talk about using RemoteWebDriver and Selenium Standalone Server for executing tests on remote machines from your machine. You can use the RemoteWebDriver class to communicate with the Selenium Standalone Server on a remote machine to run commands on the desired browser installed on the remote machine. One of its popular use cases is browser compatibility testing.

Chapter 8, *Setting up Selenium Grid,* will talk about one important and interesting feature of Selenium named Selenium Grid. Using this, you can execute automated tests on a distributed computer network using Selenium Grid. We will configure a Hub and Nodes for cross-browser testing. This also enables running tests in parallel and in a distributed architecture.

Chapter 9, *The PageObject Pattern,* will talk about a well-known design pattern named the PageObject pattern. This is a proven pattern that will give you a better handle on your automation framework and scenarios for better maintainability.

Chapter 10, *Mobile Testing on iOS and Android Using Appium,* will take you through how WebDriver can be used to automate your test scripts for iOS and Android platform using Appium.

Chapter 11, Data-Driven Testing with TestNG, will talk about using the data-driven testing technique with TestNG. Using the data-driven testing approach, we can reuse a test with multiple sets of test data to gain additional coverage.

To get the most out of this book

The reader is expected to have a basic idea of programming, preferably using Java because we take the reader through several features of WebDriver using code examples. The following software is required for the book:

1. Oracle JDK8
2. Eclipse IDE
3. Maven 3
4. Google Chrome
5. Mozilla Firefox
6. Internet Explorer or Edge (on Windows)
7. Apple Safari
8. Appium

Installing Java

In this book, all the code examples that we show covering various features of WebDriver will be in Java. To follow these examples and write your own code, you need the Java Development Kit installed on your computer. The latest version of JDK can be downloaded from the following link:

```
http://www.oracle.com/technetwork/java/javase/downloads/jdk8-downloads-2133151.
html
```

Installing Eclipse

This book is a practical guide that expects the user to write and execute WebDriver examples. For this, it would be handy to install a Java IDE. The Eclipse IDE is a popular choice in Java user community. The Eclipse IDE can be downloaded from `https://www.eclipse.org/downloads/`.

Download the example code files

You can download the example code files for this book from your account at `www.packtpub.com`. If you purchased this book elsewhere, you can visit `www.packtpub.com/support` and register to have the files emailed directly to you.

You can download the code files by following these steps:

1. Log in or register at `www.packtpub.com`.
2. Select the **SUPPORT** tab.
3. Click on **Code Downloads & Errata**.
4. Enter the name of the book in the **Search** box and follow the onscreen instructions.

Once the file is downloaded, please make sure that you unzip or extract the folder using the latest version of:

- WinRAR/7-Zip for Windows
- Zipeg/iZip/UnRarX for Mac
- 7-Zip/PeaZip for Linux

The code bundle for the book is also hosted on GitHub at `https://github.com/PacktPublishing/Selenium-WebDriver-3-Practical-Guide-Second-Edition`. In case there's an update to the code, it will be updated on the existing GitHub repository.

We also have other code bundles from our rich catalog of books and videos available at `https://github.com/PacktPublishing/`. Check them out!

Download the color images

We also provide a PDF file that has color images of the screenshots/diagrams used in this book. You can download from `https://www.packtpub.com/sites/default/files/downloads/SeleniumWebDriver3PracticalGuideSecondEdition_ColorImages.pdf`.

Conventions used

There are a number of text conventions used throughout this book.

`CodeInText`: Indicates code words in text, database table names, folder names, filenames, file extensions, pathnames, dummy URLs, user input, and Twitter handles. Here is an example: "`beforeMethod()`, which is annotated with the `@BeforeMethod` TestNG annotation."

A block of code is set as follows:

```
<input id="search" type="search" name="q" value="" class="input-text
required-entry" maxlength="128" placeholder="Search entire store here..."
autocomplete="off">
```

When we wish to draw your attention to a particular part of a code block, the relevant lines or items are set in bold:

```
WebElement searchBox = driver.findElement(By.id("q"));
```

Bold: Indicates a new term, an important word, or words that you see onscreen. For example, words in menus or dialog boxes appear in the text like this. Here is an example: "To run the tests, right-click in the code editor and select **Run As | TestNG Test**, as shown in the following screenshot."

Warnings or important notes appear like this.

Tips and tricks appear like this.

Get in touch

Feedback from our readers is always welcome.

General feedback: Email feedback@packtpub.com and mention the book title in the subject of your message. If you have questions about any aspect of this book, please email us at questions@packtpub.com.

Errata: Although we have taken every care to ensure the accuracy of our content, mistakes do happen. If you have found a mistake in this book, we would be grateful if you would report this to us. Please visit www.packtpub.com/submit-errata, selecting your book, clicking on the Errata Submission Form link, and entering the details.

Piracy: If you come across any illegal copies of our works in any form on the Internet, we would be grateful if you would provide us with the location address or website name. Please contact us at copyright@packtpub.com with a link to the material.

If you are interested in becoming an author: If there is a topic that you have expertise in and you are interested in either writing or contributing to a book, please visit authors.packtpub.com.

Reviews

Please leave a review. Once you have read and used this book, why not leave a review on the site that you purchased it from? Potential readers can then see and use your unbiased opinion to make purchase decisions, we at Packt can understand what you think about our products, and our authors can see your feedback on their book. Thank you!

For more information about Packt, please visit packtpub.com.

1
Introducing WebDriver and WebElements

In this chapter, we will look briefly into Selenium, its various components, such as Appium, and proceed to the basic components of a web page, including the various types of WebElements. We will learn different ways to locate WebElements on a web page and execute various user actions on them. We will cover the following topics in this chapter:

- Various components of Selenium Testing Tools
- Setting up a project in Eclipse with Maven and TestNG
- Locating WebElements on a Web Page
- Actions that can be taken on the WebElements

Selenium is a set of widely popular tools used to automate browsers. It is largely used to test applications, but its usages are not limited to testing. It can also be used to perform screen scraping and automate repetitive tasks in a browser window. Selenium supports automation on all the major browsers, including Google Chrome, Mozilla Firefox, Microsoft Internet Explorer and Edge, Apple Safari, and Opera. Selenium 3.0 is now a part of W3C standards and is supported by major browser vendors.

Selenium Testing Tools

Selenium 3.0 offers three important tools, Selenium WebDriver, Selenium Server, and Selenium IDE. Each of these tools provides features to create, debug, and run tests on supported browsers and operating systems. Let's explore each of them in detail.

Selenium WebDriver

Selenium WebDriver is the successor of Selenium RC (Remote Control), which has been officially deprecated. Selenium WebDriver accepts commands using the JSON-Wire protocol (also called Client API) and sends them to a browser launched by the specific driver class (such as ChromeDriver, FirefoxDriver, or IEDriver). This is implemented through a browser-specific browser driver. It works with the following sequence:

1. The driver listens to the commands from Selenium
2. It converts these commands into the browser's native API
3. The driver takes the result of native commands and sends the result back to Selenium:

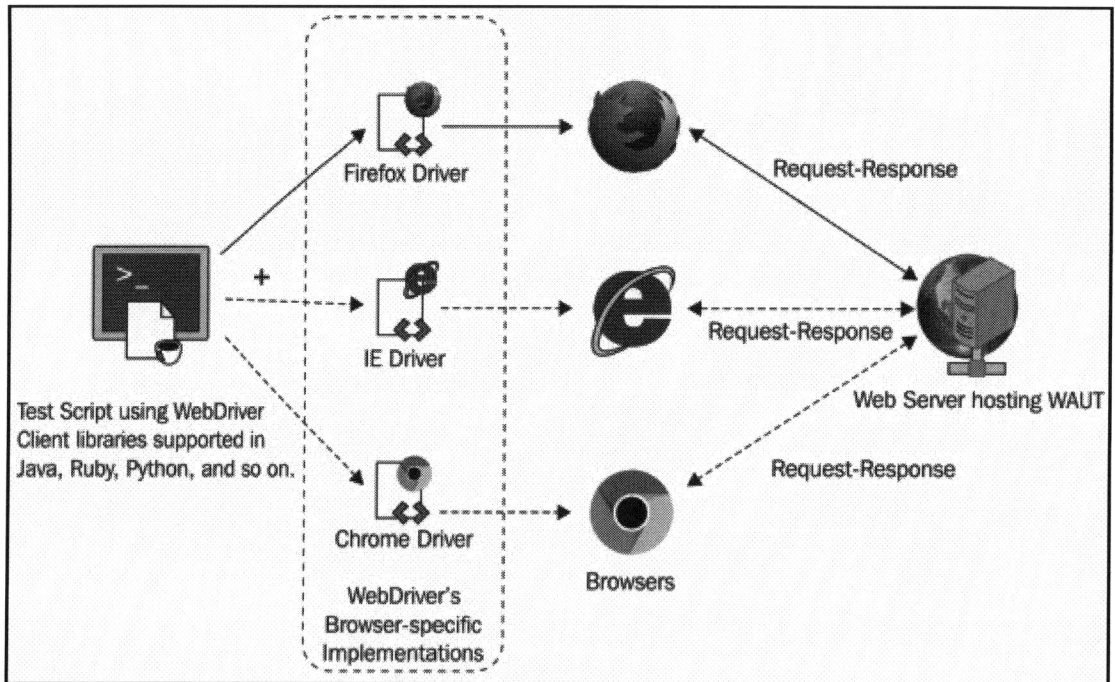

We can use Selenium WebDriver to do the following:

- Create robust, browser-based regression automation
- Scale and distribute scripts across many browsers and platforms
- Create scripts in your favourite programming language

Selenium WebDriver offers a collection of language-specific bindings (client libraries) to drive a browser. WebDriver comes with a better set of APIs that meet the expectations of most developers by being similar to object-oriented programming in its implementation. WebDriver is being actively developed over a period of time, and you can see many advanced interactions with the web as well as mobile applications.

> The Selenium Client API is a language-specific Selenium library that provides a consistent Selenium API in programming languages such as Java, C#, Python, Ruby, and JavaScript. These languages bindings let tests to launch a WebDriver session and communicate with the browser or Selenium Server.

Selenium Server

Selenium Server allows us to run tests on browser instances running on remote machines and in parallel, thus spreading a load of testing across several machines. We can create a Selenium Grid, where one server runs as the Hub, managing a pool of Nodes. We can configure our tests to connect to the Hub, which then obtains a node that is free and matches the browser we need to run the tests. The hub has a list of nodes that provide access to browser instances, and lets tests use these instances similarly to a load balancer. Selenium Grid enables us to execute tests in parallel on multiple machines by managing different types of browsers, their versions, and operating system configurations centrally.

Selenium IDE

Selenium IDE is a Firefox add-on that allows users to record, edit, debug, and play back tests captured in the *Selenese* format, which was introduced in the Selenium Core version. It also provides us with the ability to convert these tests into the Selenium RC or Selenium WebDriver format. We can use Selenium IDE to do the following:

- Create quick and simple scripts using record and replay, or use them in exploratory testing
- Create scripts to aid in automation-aided exploratory testing
- Create macros to perform repetitive tasks on Web pages

> The Selenium IDE for Firefox stopped working after the Firefox 55 moved to the WebExtension format from XPI format and it is currently no longer maintained.

Differences between Selenium 2 and Selenium 3

Before we dive further into Selenium 3, let's understand the differences between Selenium 2 and Selenium.

Handling the browser

As the Selenium WebDriver has been accepted as the W3C Standard, Selenium 3 brings a number of changes to the browser implementations. All of the major browser vendors now support WebDriver specification and provide the necessary features along with the browser. For example, Microsoft came with EdgeDriver, and Apple supports the SafariDriver implementation. We will see some of these changes later in this book.

Having better APIs

As W3C-standard WebDriver comes with a better set of APIs, which meet the expectations of most developers by being similar to the implementation of object-oriented programming.

Having developer support and advanced functionalities

WebDriver is being actively developed and is now supported by Browser vendors per W3C specification; you can see many advanced interactions with the web as well as mobile applications, such as File-Handling and Touch APIs.

Testing Mobile Apps with Appium

One of the major differences introduced in Selenium 3 was the introduction of the `Appium` project. The mobile-testing features that were part of Selenium 2 are now moved into a separate project named Appium.

`Appium` is an open source mobile-automation framework for testing native, hybrid, and web mobile apps on iOS and Android platforms using the JSON-Wire protocol with Selenium WebDriver. `Appium` replaces the iPhoneDriver and AndroidDriver APIs in Selenium 2 that were used to test mobile web applications.

`Appium` enables the use and extension of the existing Selenium WebDriver framework to build mobile tests. As it uses Selenium WebDriver to drive the tests, we can use any programming language to create tests for a Selenium client library.

Setting up a project in Eclipse with Maven and TestNG using Java

Selenium WebDriver is a library that helps you automate browsers. However, much more is needed when using it for testing and building a test framework or automating browsers for non-testing purposes. You will need an Integrated Development Environment (**IDE**) or a code editor to create a new Java project and add Selenium WebDriver and other dependencies in order to build a testing framework.

In the Java development community, Eclipse is a widely-used IDE, as well as IntelliJ IDEA and NetBeans. Eclipse provides a feature-rich environment for Selenium WebDriver test-development.

Along with Eclipse, Apache Maven provides support for managing the life cycle of a test project. Maven is used to define the project structure, dependencies, build, and test-management.

We can use Eclipse and Maven to build our Selenium WebDriver test framework from a single window. Another important benefit of using Maven is that we can get all the Selenium library files and their dependencies by configuring the pom.xml file. Maven automatically downloads the necessary files from the repository while building the project.

In this section, we will learn how to configure Eclipse and Maven for the Selenium WebDriver test development. Most of the code in this book has been developed in Eclipse and Maven.

You will need Eclipse and Maven to set up the test-development environment. Download and set up Maven from `http://maven.apache.org/download.html`. Follow the instructions on the Maven download page (see the Installation Instructions section of the page).

Download and set up Eclipse IDE for Java Developers from `https://eclipse.org/downloads/`

Along with Eclipse and Maven, we will also use TestNG as a testing framework for our project. The TestNG library will help us define test cases, test fixtures, and assertions. We need to install the TestNG plugin for Eclipse via Eclipse Marketplace.

Let's configure Eclipse with Maven to develop Selenium WebDriver tests using the following steps:

1. Launch the **Eclipse IDE**.
2. Create a new project by selecting **File** | **New** | **Other** from the Eclipse **Main Menu**.
3. On the **New** dialog, select **Maven** | **Maven Project**, as shown in the following screenshot, and click **Next**:

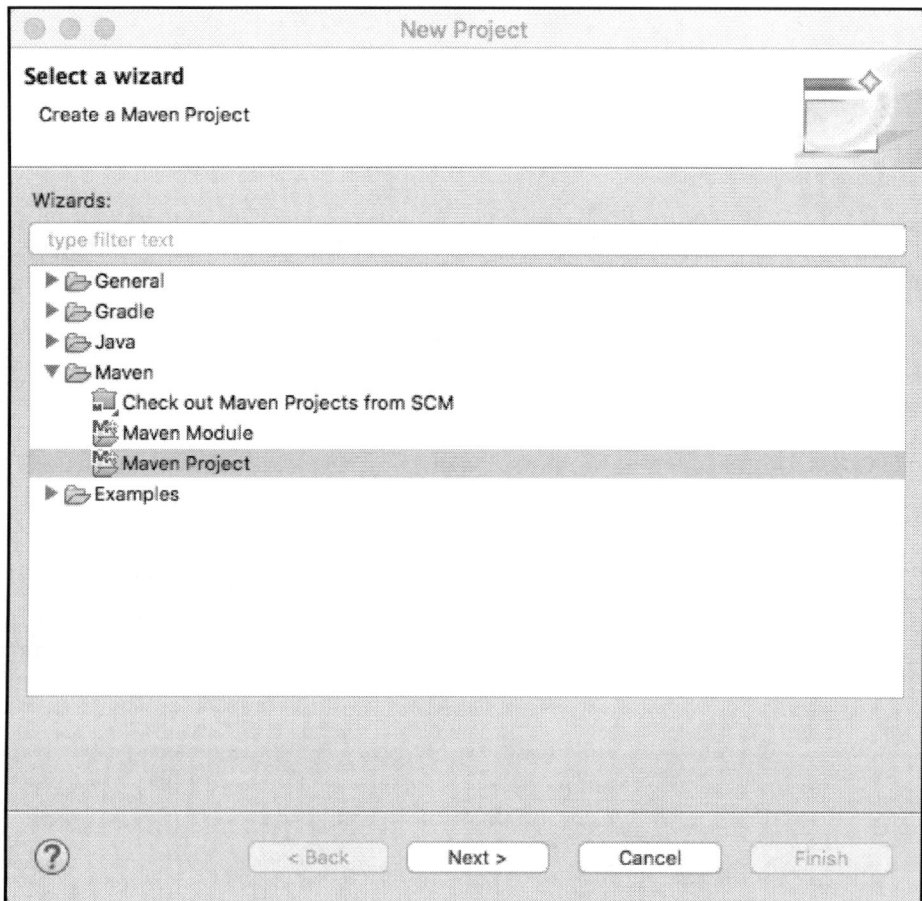

4. The **New Maven Project** dialog will be displayed. Select the **Create a simple project (skip archetype selection) checkbox** and click on the **Next** button, as shown in the following screenshot:

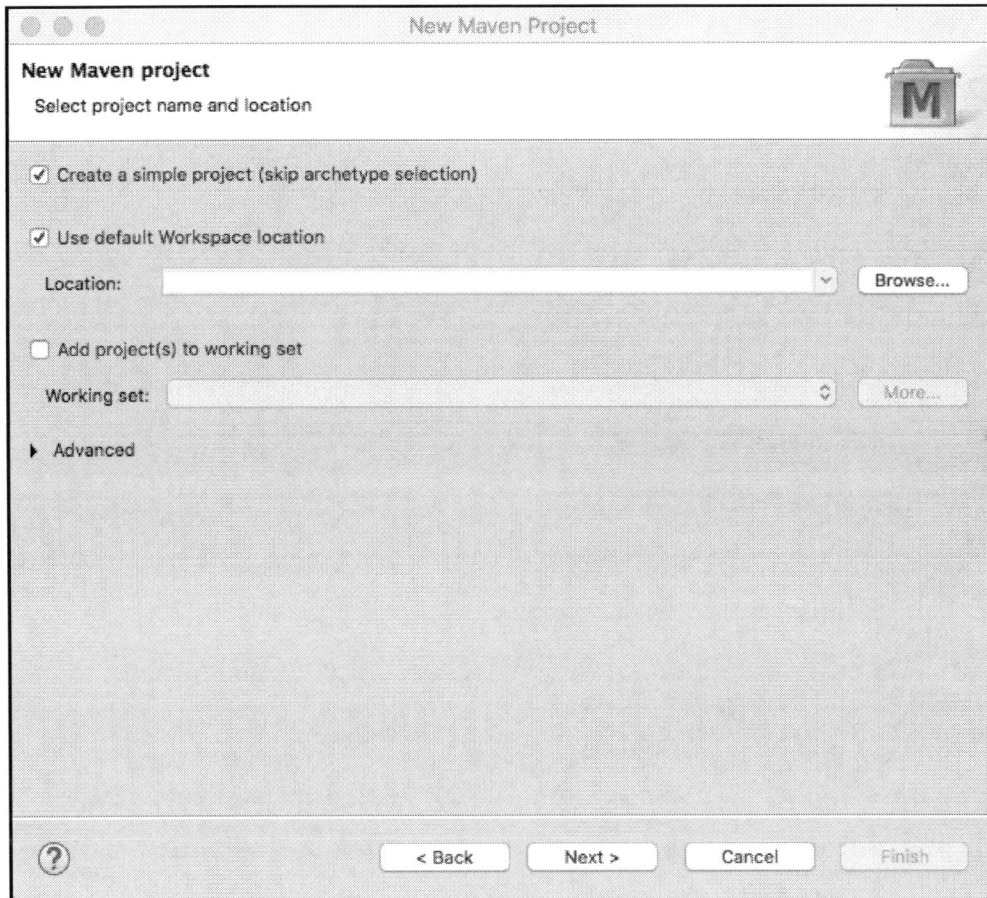

5. On the **New Maven Project** dialog box, enter *com.example* in the **Group Id:** textbox and *chapter1* in the **Artifact Id:** textbox. You can also add a name and description. Click on the **Finish** button, as shown in the following screenshot:

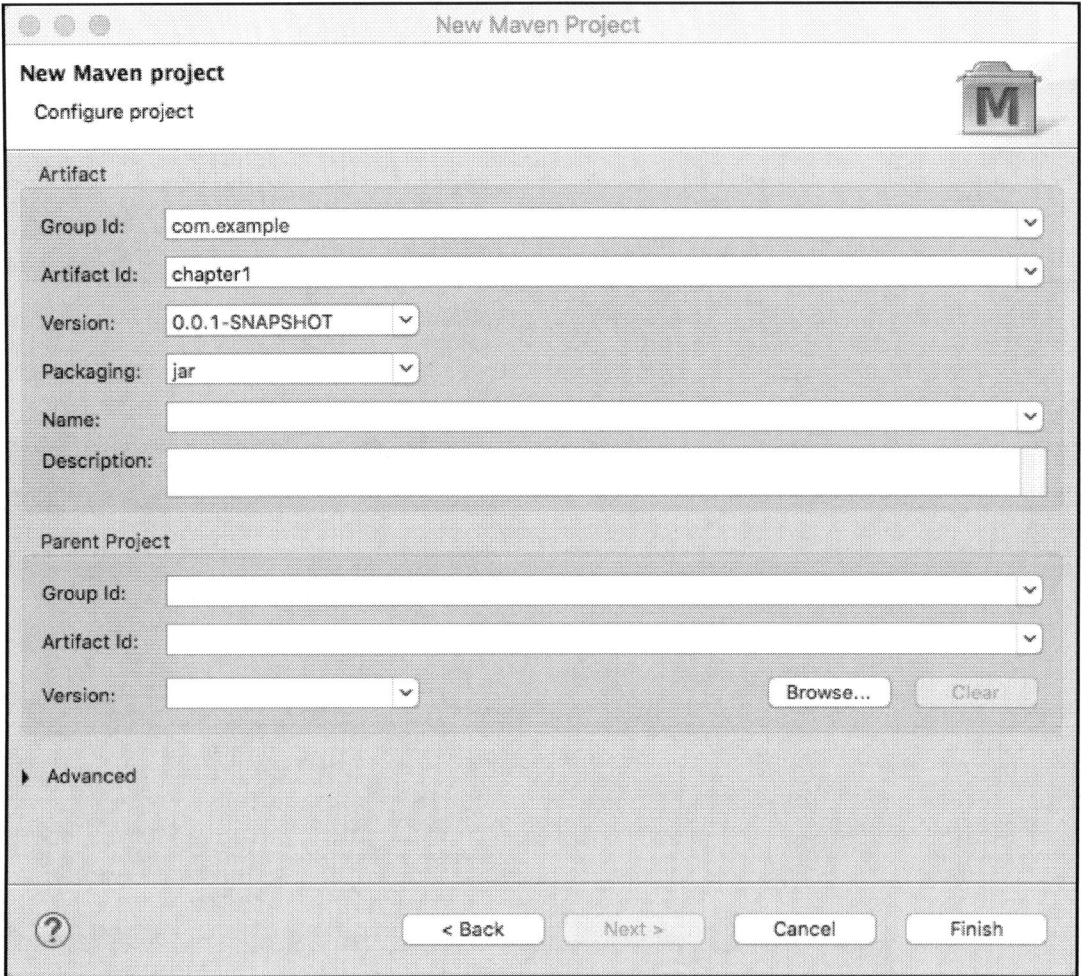

6. Eclipse will create the *chapter1* project with a structure (in **Package Explorer**) similar to the one shown in the following screenshot:

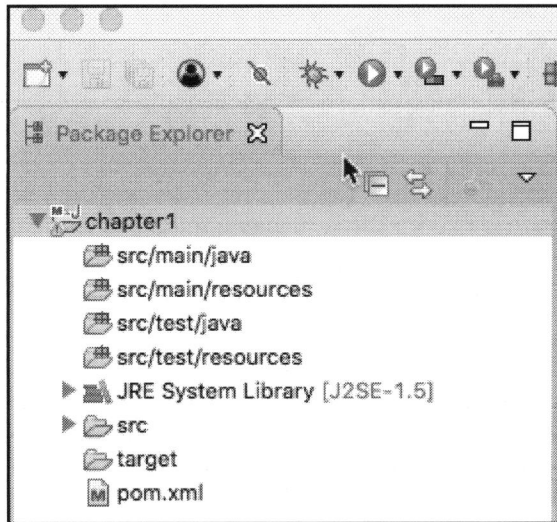

7. Select **pom.xml** from **Package Explorer**. This will open the **pom.xml** file in the editor area with the **Overview** tab open. Select the **pom.xml** tab next to the **Overview** tab, as shown in the following screenshot:

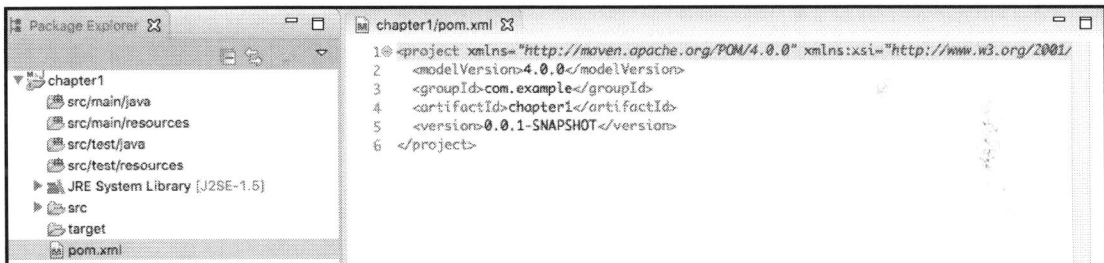

8. Add the Selenium WebDriver and TestNG dependencies highlighted in the following code snippet to **pom.xml** in the between `project` node:

```xml
<properties>
 <java.version>1.8</java.version>
 <selenium.version>3.13.0</selenium.version>
 <testng.version>6.13.1</testng.version>
 <maven.compiler.version>3.7.0</maven.compiler.version>
</properties>

<dependencies>
 <dependency>
 <groupId>org.seleniumhq.selenium</groupId>
 <artifactId>selenium-java</artifactId>
 <version>${selenium.version}</version>
 </dependency>
 <dependency>
 <groupId>org.testng</groupId>
 <artifactId>testng</artifactId>
 <version>${testng.version}</version>
 </dependency>
</dependencies>

<build>
 <plugins>
 <plugin>
 <groupId>org.apache.maven.plugins</groupId>
 <artifactId>maven-compiler-plugin</artifactId>
 <version>${maven.compiler.version}</version>
 <configuration>
 <source>${java.version}</source>
 <target>${java.version}</target>
 </configuration>
 </plugin>
 </plugins>
</build>
```

9. Select **src/test/java** in **Package Explorer** and right-click on it to show the menu. Select **New | Other**, as shown in the following screenshot:

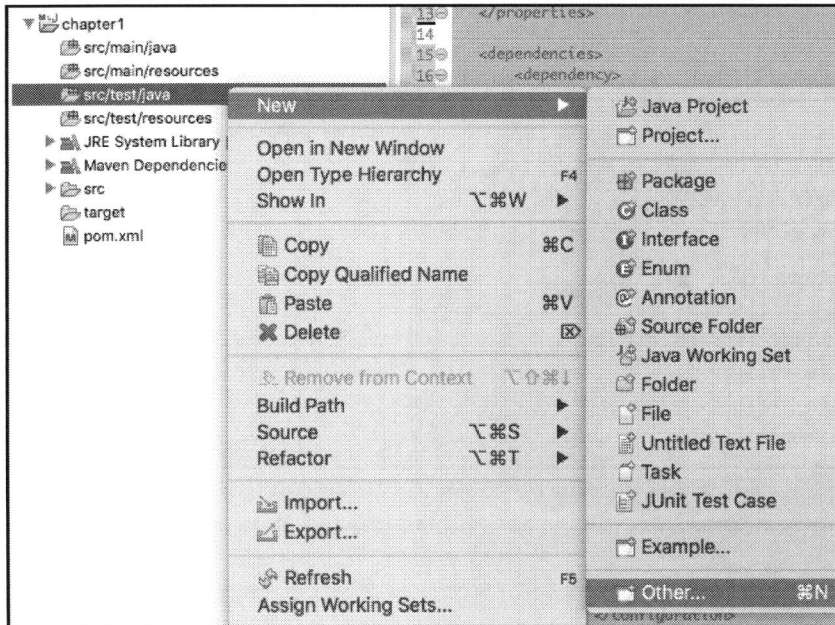

10. Select the **TestNG** | **TestNG** class from the **Select a wizard** dialog, as shown in the following screenshot:

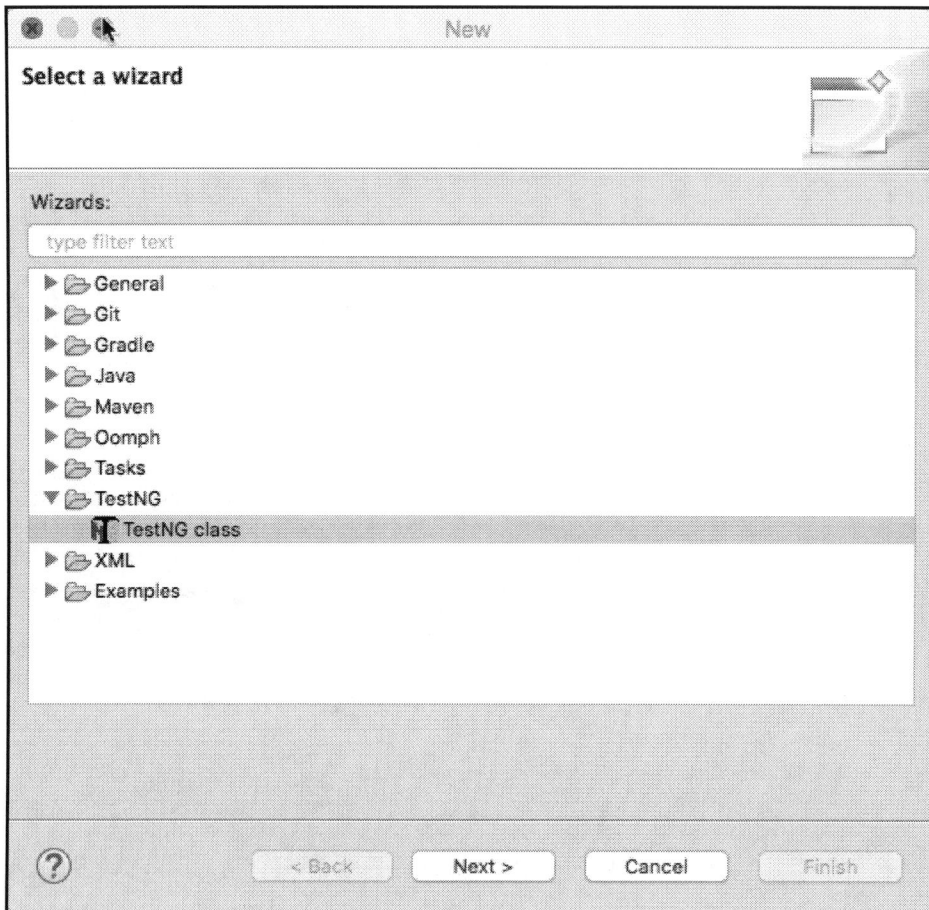

11. On the **New TestNG class** dialog box, enter */chapter1/src/test/java* in the **Source folder:** field. Enter **com.example** in the **Package name:** field. Enter **NavigationTest** in the **Class name:** field. Select the **@BeforeMethod** and **@AfterMethod** checkboxes and add `src/test/resources/suites/testng.xml` in the **XML suite file:** field. Click on the **Finish** button:

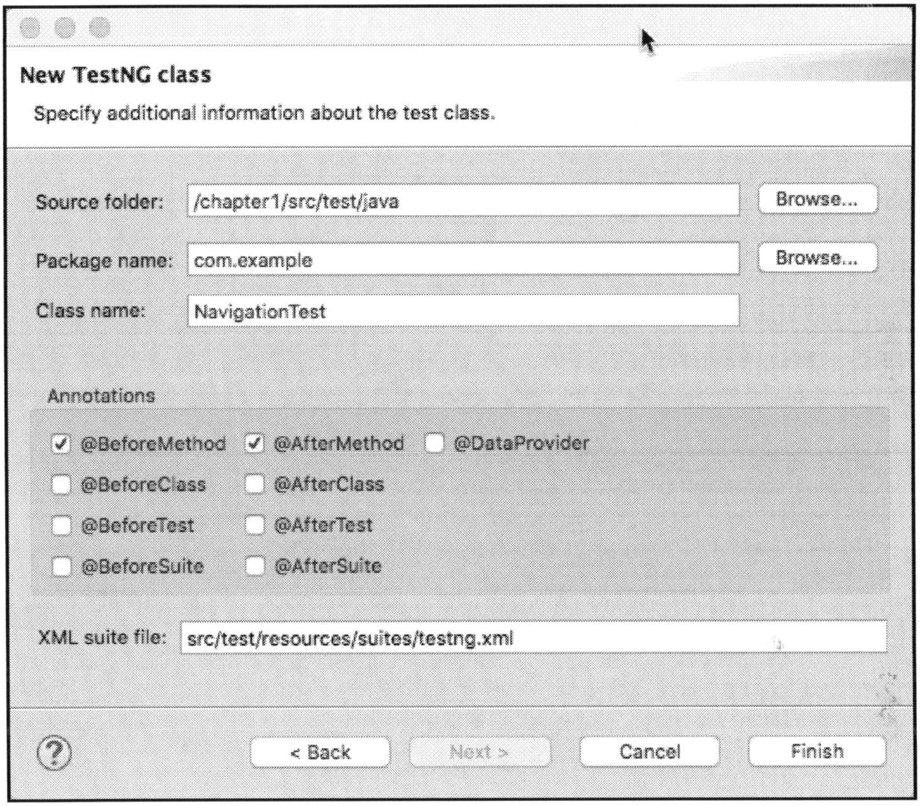

New TestNG class

Specify additional information about the test class.

Source folder:	/chapter1/src/test/java	Browse...
Package name:	com.example	Browse...
Class name:	NavigationTest	

Annotations

☑ @BeforeMethod ☑ @AfterMethod ☐ @DataProvider

☐ @BeforeClass ☐ @AfterClass

☐ @BeforeTest ☐ @AfterTest

☐ @BeforeSuite ☐ @AfterSuite

XML suite file: src/test/resources/suites/testng.xml

< Back Next > Cancel Finish

12. This will create the **NavigationTest.java** class in the **com.example** package with TestNG annotations such as @Test, @BeforeMethod, and @AfterMethod, and the beforeMethod and afterMethod methods:

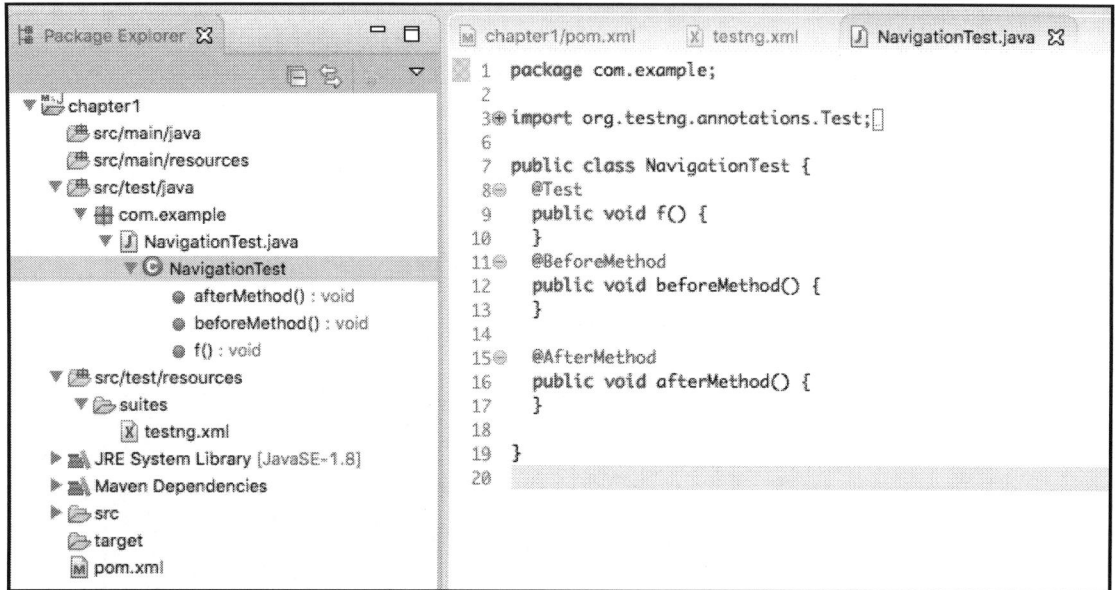

```
Package Explorer 🔀                                chapter1/pom.xml      testng.xml      NavigationTest.java 🔀
                                         1   package com.example;
                              📄 📚   ▽   2
                                         3⊖ import org.testng.annotations.Test;⬚
▼ 📁 chapter1                              6
   📁 src/main/java                        7   public class NavigationTest {
   📁 src/main/resources                   8⊖    @Test
   ▼ 📁 src/test/java                       9      public void f() {
      ▼ 🏛 com.example                      10     }
         ▼ 📄 NavigationTest.java           11⊖    @BeforeMethod
            ▼ ⓒ NavigationTest            12      public void beforeMethod() {
               ● afterMethod() : void     13     }
               ● beforeMethod() : void    14
               ● f() : void               15⊖    @AfterMethod
   ▼ 📁 src/test/resources                  16      public void afterMethod() {
      ▼ 📂 suites                          17     }
         📄 testng.xml                     18
   ▶ 📚 JRE System Library [JavaSE-1.8]    19  }
   ▶ 📚 Maven Dependencies                 20
   ▶ 📂 src
      📂 target
      📄 pom.xml
```

13. Modify the NavigationTest class with following code:

```java
package com.example;
import org.openqa.selenium.WebDriver;
import org.openqa.selenium.chrome.ChromeDriver;
import org.testng.Assert;
import org.testng.annotations.*;

public class NavigationTest {

    WebDriver driver;

    @BeforeMethod
    public void beforeMethod() {

        // set path of Chromedriver executable
        System.setProperty("webdriver.chrome.driver",
                "./src/test/resources/drivers/chromedriver");

        // initialize new WebDriver session
        driver = new ChromeDriver();
```

```
        }

        @Test
        public void navigateToAUrl() {
            // navigate to the web site
            driver.get("http://demo-store.seleniumacademy.com/");
            // Validate page title
            Assert.assertEquals(driver.getTitle(), "Madison
Island");
        }
        @AfterMethod
        public void afterMethod() {

            // close and quit the browser
            driver.quit();
        }
    }
```

In the preceding code, three methods are added as part of the NavigationTest class. We also declared a WebDriver driver; instance variable, which we will use later in the test to launch a browser and navigate to the site.

beforeMethod(), which is annotated with the @BeforeMethod TestNG annotation, will execute before the test method. It will set the path of the *chromedriver* executable required by Google Chrome. It will then instantiate the driver variable using the ChromeDriver() class. This will launch a new Google Chrome window on the screen.

The next method, navigateToAUrl(), annotated with the @Test annotation is the test method. We will call the get() method of the WebDriver interface passing the URL of the application. This will navigate to the site in the browser. We will check the title of the page by calling TestNG's Assert.assertEquals method and the getTitle() method of the WebDriver interface.

Lastly, afterMethod() is annotated with the @AfterMethod TestNG annotation will close the browser window.

> We need to download and copy the chromedriver executable
> from https://sites.google.com/a/chromium.org/chromedriver/
> downloads. Download the appropriate version based on the Google
> Chrome browser version installed on your computer as well as the
> operating system. Copy the executable file in
> the /src/test/resources/ drivers folder.

To run the tests, right-click in the code editor and select **Run As | TestNG Test**, as shown in the following screenshot:

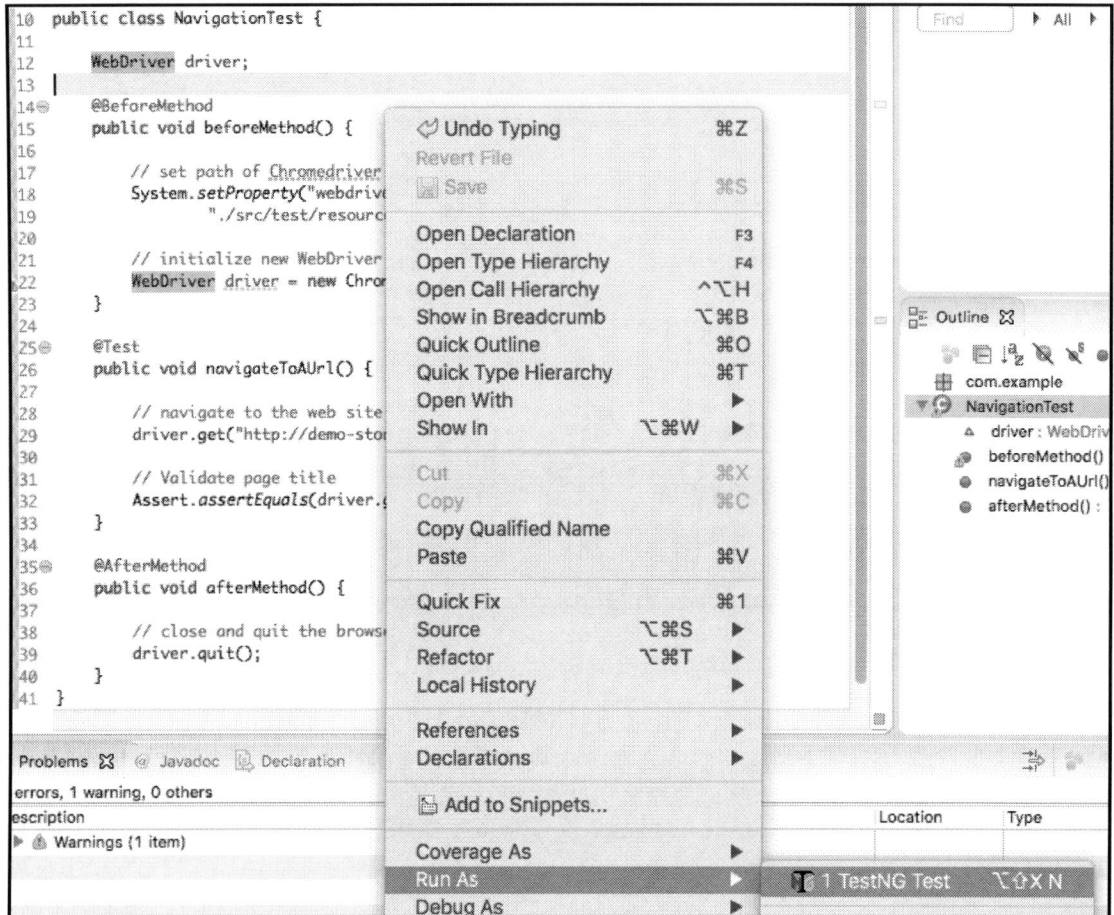

This will launch a new Google Chrome browser window and navigate to the site. The test will validate the page title and the browser window will be closed at the end of the test. The TestNG Plugin will display results in Eclipse:

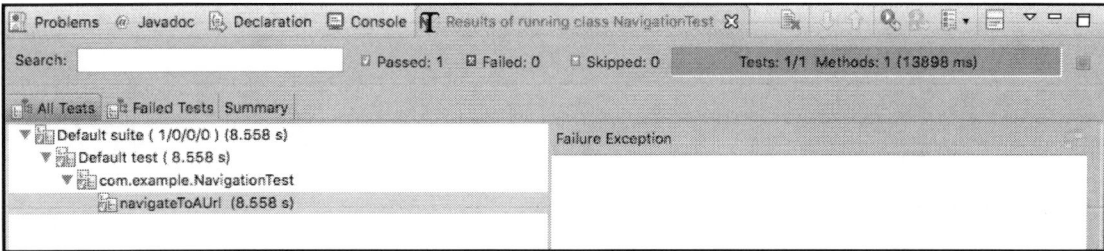

> You can download the example code files for all the Packt books you have purchased from your account at http://www.packtpub.com. If you have purchased this book elsewhere, you can visit http://www.packtpub.com/support and register to have the files emailed directly to you. The example code is also hosted at https://github.com/PacktPublishing/Selenium-WebDriver-3-Practical-Guide-Second-Edition

WebElements

A web page is composed of many different types of HTML elements, such as links, textboxes, dropdown buttons, a body, labels, and forms. These are called WebElements in the context of WebDriver. Together, these elements on a web page will achieve the user functionality. For example, let's look at the HTML code of the login page of a website:

```html
<html>
<body>
    <form id="loginForm">
        <label>Enter Username: </label>
        <input type="text" name="Username"/>
        <label>Enter Password: </label>
        <input type="password" name="Password"/>
        <input type="submit"/>
    </form>
    <a href="forgotPassword.html">Forgot Password ?</a>
</body>
</html>
```

In the preceding HTML code, there are different types of WebElements, such as `<html>`, `<body>`, `<form>`, `<label>`, `<input>`, and `<a>`, which together make a web page provide the Login feature for the user. Let's analyze the following WebElement:

```html
<label>Enter Username: </label>
```

Here, `<label>` is the start tag of the WebElement label. `Enter Username:` is the text present on the `label` element. Finally, `</label>` is the end tag, which indicates the end of a WebElement.

Similarly, take another WebElement:

```
<input type="text" name="Username"/>
```

In the preceding code, `type` and `name` are the attributes of the WebElement `input` with the `text` and `Username` values, respectively.

UI-automation using Selenium is mostly about locating these WebElements on a web page and executing user actions on them. In the rest of the chapter, we will use various methods to locate WebElements and execute relevant user actions on them.

Locating WebElements using WebDriver

Let's start this section by automating the Search feature from the Homepage of the demo application, `http://demo-store.seleniumacademy.com/`, which involves navigating to the homepage, typing the search text in the textbox, and executing the search. The code is as follows:

```java
import org.openqa.selenium.By;
import org.openqa.selenium.WebDriver;
import org.openqa.selenium.WebElement;
import org.openqa.selenium.chrome.ChromeDriver;
import org.testng.annotations.AfterMethod;
import org.testng.annotations.BeforeMethod;
import org.testng.annotations.Test;

import static org.assertj.core.api.AssertionsForClassTypes.assertThat;

public class SearchTest {

    WebDriver driver;

    @BeforeMethod
    public void setup() {
        System.setProperty("webdriver.chrome.driver",
                "./src/test/resources/drivers/chromedriver");
        driver = new ChromeDriver();
        driver.get("http://demo-store.seleniumacademy.com/");
    }
```

```
@Test
public void searchProduct() {
    // find search box and enter search string
    WebElement searchBox = driver.findElement(By.name("q"));
    searchBox.sendKeys("Phones");
    WebElement searchButton =
            driver.findElement(By.className("search-button"));
    searchButton.click();
    assertThat(driver.getTitle())
            .isEqualTo("Search results for: 'Phones'");
}

@AfterMethod
public void tearDown() {
    driver.quit();
}
}
```

As you can see, there are three new things that are highlighted, as follows:

```
WebElement searchBox = driver.findElement(By.name("q"));
```

They are the findElement() method, the By.name() method, and the WebElement interface. The findElement() and By() methods instruct WebDriver to locate a WebElement on a web page, and once found, the findElement() method returns the WebElement instance of that element. Actions, such as click and type, are performed on a returned WebElement using the methods declared in the WebElement interface, which will be discussed in detail in the next section.

The findElement method

In UI automation, locating an element is the first step before executing any user actions on it. WebDriver's findElement() method is a convenient way to locate an element on the web page. According to WebDriver's Javadoc (http://selenium.googlecode.com/git/docs/api/java/index.html), the method declaration is as follows:

```
WebElement findElement(By by)
```

So, the input parameter for the findElement() method is the By instance. The By instance is a WebElement-locating mechanism. There are eight different ways to locate a WebElement on a web page. We will see each of these eight methods later in the chapter.

The return type of the findElement() method is the WebElement instance that represents the actual HTML element or component of the web page. The method returns the first WebElement that the driver comes across that satisfies the locating-mechanism condition. This WebElement instance will act as a handle to that component from then on. Appropriate actions can be taken on that component by the test-script developer using this returned WebElement instance.

If WebDriver doesn't find the element, it throws a runtime exception named NoSuchElementException, which the invoking class or method should handle.

The findElements method

For finding multiple elements matching the same locator criteria on a web page, the findElements() method can be used. It returns a list of WebElements found for a given locating mechanism. The method declaration of the findElements() method is as follows:

```
java.util.List findElements(By by)
```

The input parameter is the same as the findElement() method, which is an instance of the By class. The difference lies in the return type. Here, if no element is found, an empty list is returned and if there are multiple WebElements present that satisfy the locating mechanism, all of them are returned to the caller in a list.

Inspecting Elements with Developer Tools

Before we start exploring how to find elements on a page and what locator mechanism to use, we need to look at the HTML code of the page to understand the Document Object Model (**DOM**) tree, what properties or attributes are defined for the elements displayed on the page, and how JavaScript or AJAX calls are made from the application. browsers use the HTML code written for the page to render visual elements in the browser window. It uses other resources, including JavaScript, CSS, and images, to decide on the look, feel, and behavior of these elements.

Here is an example of a login page of the demo application and the HTML code written to render this page in a browser, as displayed in the following screenshot:

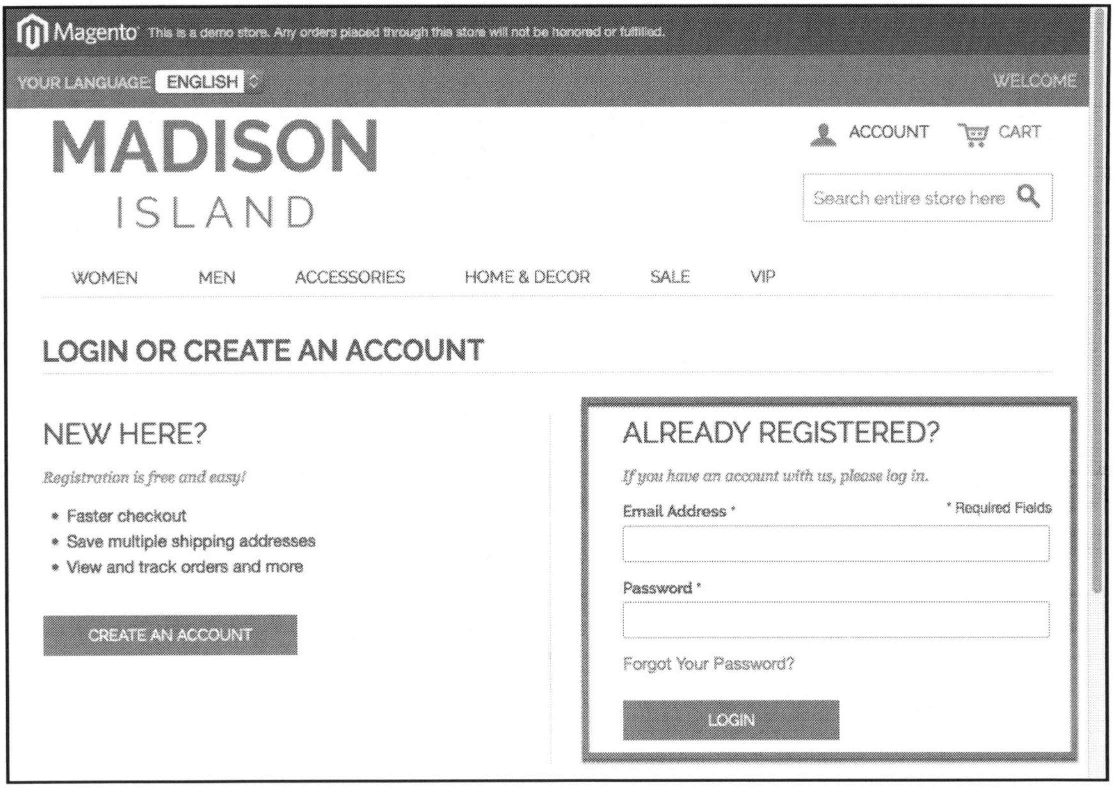

We need tools that can display the HTML code of the page in a structured and easy-to-understand format. Almost all browsers now offer Developer tools to inspect the structure of the page and associated resources.

Inspecting pages and elements with Mozilla Firefox

The newer versions of Mozilla Firefox provide built-in ways to inspect the page and elements. To inspect an element from the page, move the mouse over the desired element and right-click to open the pop-up menu. Select the **Inspect Element** option, as shown in the following screenshot:

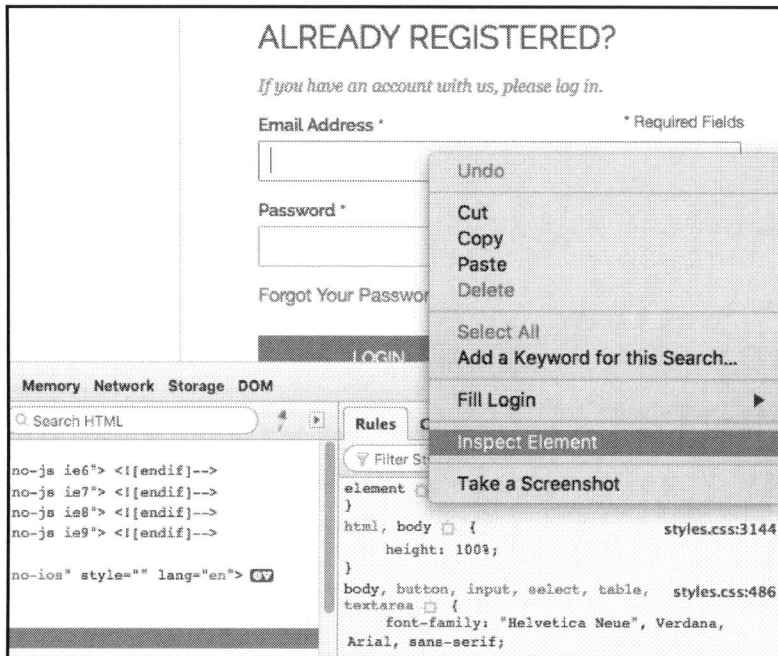

This will display the **Inspector** tab with the HTML code in a tree format with the selected element highlighted, as shown in the following screenshot:

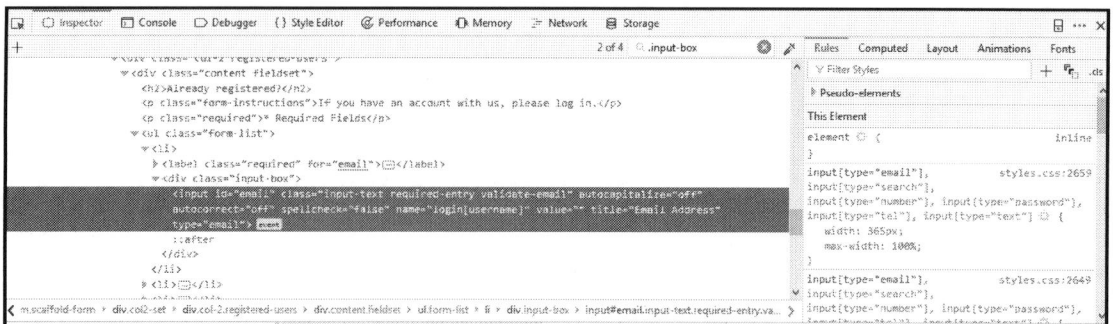

Using **Inspector**, we can also validate the XPath or CSS Selectors using the search box shown in the **Inspector** section. Just enter the XPath or CSS Selector and **Inspector** will highlight the elements that match the expression, as shown in the following screenshot:

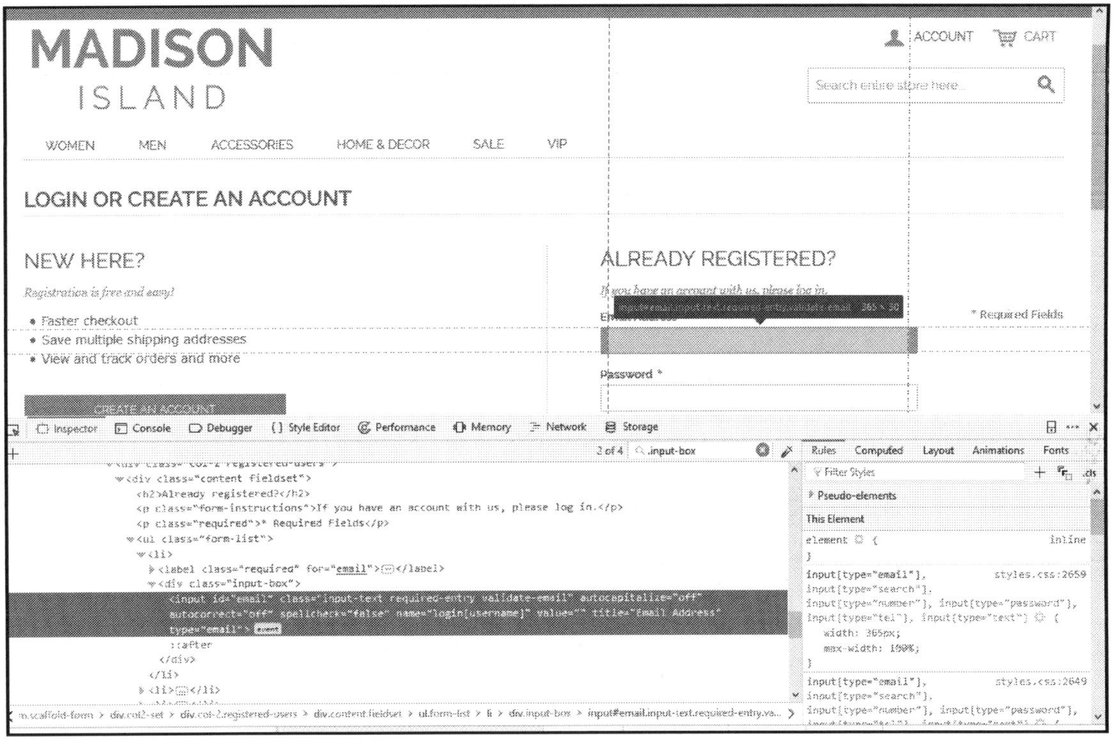

The Developer tools provide various other debugging features. It also generates XPath and CSS selectors for elements. For this, select the desired element in the tree, right-click, and select the **Copy > XPath** or **Copy > CSS Path** option from the pop-up menu, as shown in the following screenshot:

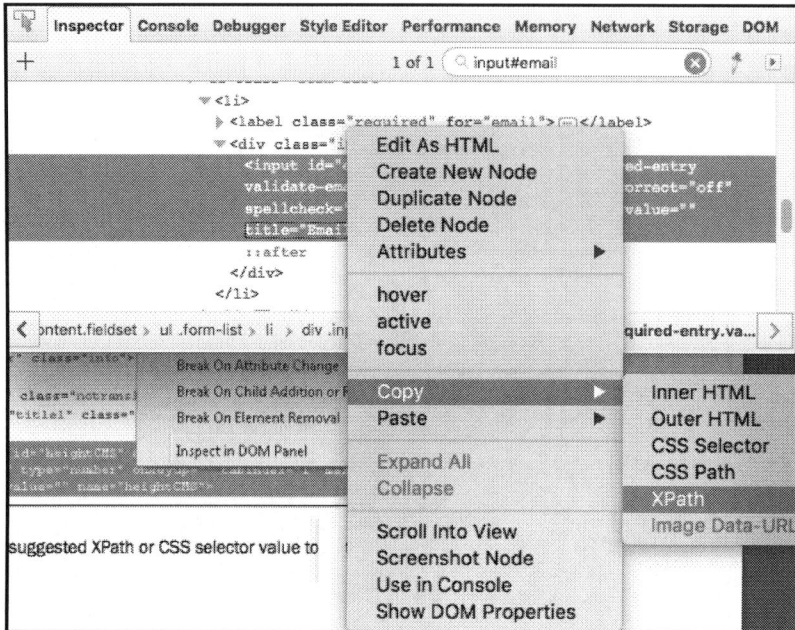

This will paste the suggested XPath or CSS selector value to the clipboard to be used later with the `findElement()` method.

Inspecting pages and elements in Google Chrome with Developer Tools

Similar to Mozilla Firefox, Google Chrome also provides a built-in feature to inspect pages and elements. We can move the mouse over a desired element on the page, right-click to open the pop-up menu, and then select the **Inspect element** option. This will open Developer tools in the browser, which displays information similar to that of Firefox, as shown in the following screenshot:

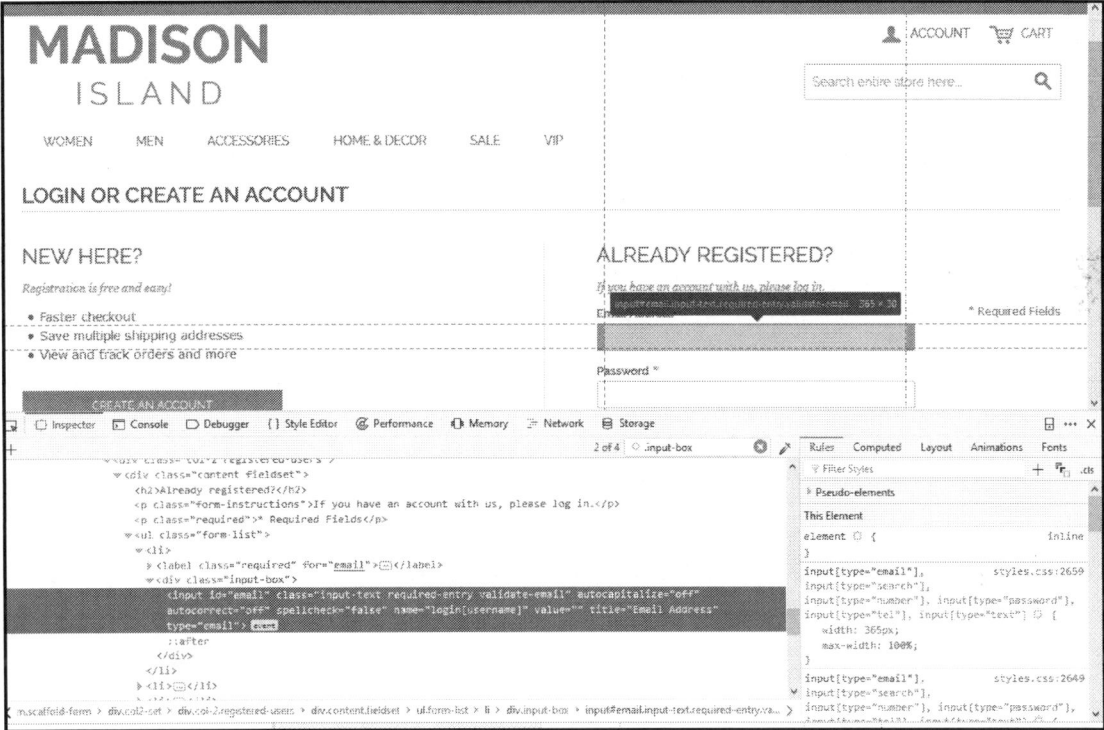

Similar to Firefox, we can also test XPath and CSS Selectors in Google Chrome Developer tools. Press *Ctrl + F* (on Mac, use *Command + F*) in the **Elements** tab. This will display a search box. Just enter *XPath* or *CSS Selector*, and matching elements will be highlighted in the tree, as shown in the following screenshot:

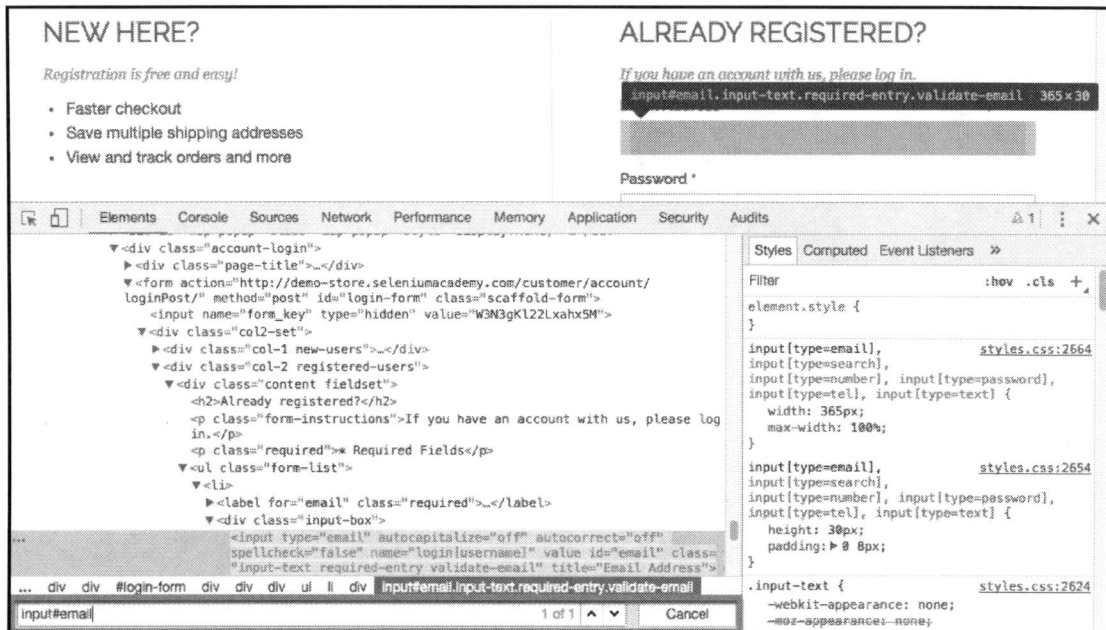

Chrome Developer Tools also provides a feature where you can get the XPath for an element by right-clicking on the desired element in the tree and selecting the **Copy XPath** option from the pop-up menu.

> Similar to Mozilla Firefox and Google Chrome, you will find similar Developer tools in any major browser, including Microsoft Internet Explorer and Edge.

Browser developer tools come in really handy during the test-script development. These tools will help you to find the locator details for the elements with which you need to interact as part of the test. These tools parse the code for a page and display the information in a hierarchal tree.

TIP

WebElements on a web page may not have all the attributes declared. It is up to the developer of the test script to select the attribute that uniquely identifies the WebElement on the web page for the automation.

Using the By locating mechanism

By is the locating mechanism passed to the `findElement()` method or the `findElements()` method to fetch the respective WebElement(s) on a web page. There are eight different locating mechanisms; that is, eight different ways to identify

an HTML element on a web page. They are located by **ID**, **Name**, **ClassName**, **TagName**, **LinkText**, **PartialLinkText**, **XPath**, and **CSS** Selector.

The By.id() method

On a web page, each element is uniquely identified by an ID attribute, which is optionally provided. An ID can be assigned manually by the developer of the web application or left to be dynamically generated by the application. Dynamically-generated IDs can be changed on every page refresh or over a period of time. Now, consider the HTML code of the Search box:

```
<input id="search" type="search" name="q" value="" class="input-text
required-entry" maxlength="128" placeholder="Search entire store here..."
autocomplete="off">
```

In the preceding code, the `id` attribute value of the search box is `search`.

Let's see how to use the ID attribute as a locating mechanism to find the Search box:

```
@Test
public void byIdLocatorExample() {
    WebElement searchBox = driver.findElement(By.id("search"));
    searchBox.sendKeys("Bags");
    searchBox.submit();
    assertThat(driver.getTitle())
            .isEqualTo("Search results for: 'Bags'");
}
```

In preceding code, we used the `By.id()` method and the search box's `id` attribute value to find the element.

Here, try to use the `By.id` identifier, and use the name value (that is, q) instead of the `id` value (that is, `search`). Modify line three as follows:

```
WebElement searchBox = driver.findElement(By.id("q"));
```

The test script will fail to throw an exception, as follows:

```
Exception in thread "main" org.openqa.selenium.NoSuchElementException:
Unable to locate element: {"method":"id","selector":"q"}
```

WebDriver couldn't find an element by `id` whose value is q. Thus, it throws an exception saying `NoSuchElementException`.

The By.name() method

As seen earlier, every element on a web page has many attributes. Name is one of them. For instance, the HTML code for the Search box is:

```
<input id="search" type="search" name="q" value="" class="input-text
required-entry" maxlength="128" placeholder="Search entire store here..."
autocomplete="off">
```

Here, `name` is one of the many attributes of the search box, and its value is q. If we want to identify this search box and set a value in it in your test script, the code will look as follows:

```
@Test
public void searchProduct() {
    // find search box and enter search string
    WebElement searchBox = driver.findElement(By.name("q"));
    searchBox.sendKeys("Phones");
    searchBox.submit();
    assertThat(driver.getTitle())
            .isEqualTo("Search results for: 'Phones'");
}
```

If you observe line four, the locating mechanism used here is `By.name` and the name is q. So, where did we get this name from? As discussed in the previous section, it is the browser developer tools that helped us get the name of the button. Launch Developer tools and use the inspect elements widget to get the attributes of an element.

The By.className() method

Before we discuss the `className()` method, we have to talk a little about style and CSS. Every HTML element on a web page, generally, is styled by the web page developer or designer. It is not mandatory that each element should be styled, but they generally are to make the page appealing to the end user.

So, in order to apply styles to an element, they can be declared directly in the element tag, or placed in a separate file called the CSS file and can be referenced in the element using the `class` attribute. For instance, a style attribute for a button can be declared in a CSS file as follows:

```
.buttonStyle{
    width: 50px;
    height: 50px;
    border-radius: 50%;
    margin: 0% 2%;
}
```

Now, this style can be applied to the button element in a web page as follows:

```
<button name="sampleBtnName" id="sampleBtnId" class="buttonStyle">I'm
Button</button>
```

So, `buttonStyle` is used as the value for the `class` attribute of the button element, and it inherits all the styles declared in the CSS file. Now, let's try this on our Homepage. We will try to make WebDriver identify the search button using its class name and click on it.

First, in order to get the class name of the search button, as we know, we will use Developers tools to fetch it. After getting it, change the location mechanism to `By.className` and specify the class attribute value in it. The code for that is as follows:

```
@Test
public void byClassNameLocatorExample() {
    WebElement searchBox = driver.findElement(By.id("search"));
    searchBox.sendKeys("Electronics");
    WebElement searchButton =
            driver.findElement(By.className("search-button"));
    searchButton.click();
    assertThat(driver.getTitle())
            .isEqualTo("Search results for: 'Electronics'");
}
```

In the preceding code, we have used the `By.className` locating mechanism by passing the class attribute value to it.

Sometimes, an element might have multiple values given for the `class` attribute. For example, the Search button has *button* and *search-button* values specified in the `class` attribute in the following HTML snippet:

```
<button type="submit" title="Search" class="button search-
button"><span><span>Search</span></span></button>
```

We have to use one of the values of the `class` attribute with the `By.className` method. In this case, we can either use *button* or *search-button*, whichever uniquely identifies the element.

The By.linkText() method

As the name suggests, the `By.linkText` locating mechanism can only be used to identify the HTML links. Before we start discussing how WebDriver can be commanded to identify a link element using link text, let's see what an HTML link element looks like. The HTML link elements are represented on a web page using the `<a>` tag, an abbreviation for the anchor tag. A typical anchor tag looks like this:

```
<a href="http://demo-store.seleniumacademy.com/customer/account/" title="My
Account">My Account</a>
```

Here, `href` is the link to a different page where your web browser will take you when you click on the link. So, the preceding HTML code when rendered by the browser looks like this:

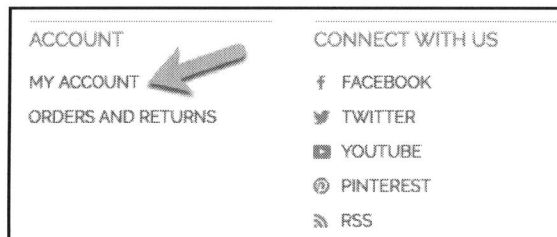

This **MY ACCOUNT** is the link text. So the `By.linkText` locating mechanism uses this text on an anchor tag to identify the WebElement. The code would look like this:

```
@Test
public void byLinkTextLocatorExample() {
    WebElement myAccountLink =
```

```
        driver.findElement(By.linkText("MY ACCOUNT"));
    myAccountLink.click();
    assertThat(driver.getTitle())
            .isEqualTo("Customer Login");
}
```

Here, the `By.linkText` locating mechanism is used to identify the **MY ACCOUNT** link.

> The `linkText` and `partialLinkText` methods are case-sensitive.

The By.partialLinkText() method

The `By.partialLinkText` locating mechanism is an extension of the `By.linkText` locator. If you are not sure of the entire link text or want to use only part of the link text, you can use this locator to identify the link element. So, let's modify the previous example to use only partial text on the link; in this case, we will use Privacy from the Privacy Policy link in the site footer:

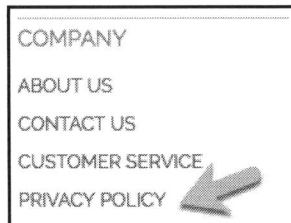

The code would look like this:

```
@Test
public void byPartialLinkTextLocatorExample() {
    WebElement orderAndReturns =
            driver.findElement(By.partialLinkText("PRIVACY"));
    orderAndReturns.click();
    assertThat(driver.getTitle())
            .isEqualTo("Privacy Policy");
}
```

What happens if there are multiple links whose text has *Privacy* in it? That is a question for the findElement() method rather than the locator. Remember when we discussed the findElement() method earlier, it will return only the first WebElement that it comes across. If you want all the WebElements that contain *Privacy* in its link text, use the findElements() method, which will return a list of all those elements.

> Use WebDriver's findElements() method if you think you need all the WebElements that satisfy a locating-mechanism condition.

The By.tagName() method

Locating an element by tag name is slightly different from the locating mechanisms we saw earlier. For example, on a Homepage, if you search for an element with the button tag name, it will result in multiple WebElements because there are nine buttons present on the Homepage. So, it is always advisable to use the findElements() method rather than the findElement() method when trying to locate elements using tag names.

Let's see how the code looks when a search for the number of links present on a Homepage is made:

```
@Test
public void byTagNameLocatorExample() {

    // get all links from the Home page
    List<WebElement> links = driver.findElements(By.tagName("a"));

    System.out.println("Found links:" + links.size());

    // print links which have text using Java 8 Streams API
    links.stream()
            .filter(elem -> elem.getText().length() > 0)
            .forEach(elem -> System.out.println(elem.getText()));
}
```

In the preceding code, we have used the `By.tagName` locating mechanism and the `findElements()` method, which return a list of all the links, that is, the `a` anchor tags defined on the page. On line five, we printed the size of the list, and then printed text of only links where the text has been provided. We use the Java 8 Stream API to filter the element list and output the text value by calling the `getText()` method. This will generate the following output:

Found links:88
 ACCOUNT
 CART
 WOMEN
 ...

The By.xpath() method

WebDriver uses **XPath** to identify a WebElement on the web page. Before we see how it does that, let's quickly look at the syntax for XPath. XPath is a short name for the XML path, the query language used for searching XML documents. The HTML for our web page is also one form of the XML document. So, in order to identify an element on an HTML page, we need to use a specific XPath syntax:

- The root element is identified as `//`.
- To identify all the div elements, the syntax will be `//div`.
- To identify the link tags that are within the div element, the syntax will be `//div/a`.
- To identify all the elements with a tag, we use *. The syntax will be `//div/*`.
- To identify all the div elements that are at three levels down from the root, we can use `//*/*/div`.
- To identify specific elements, we use attribute values of those elements, such as `//*/div/a[@id='attrValue']`, which will return the anchor element. This element is at the third level from the root within a `div` element and has an `id` value of `attrValue`.

So, we need to pass the XPath expression to the `By.xpath` locating mechanism to make it identify our target element.

Now, let's see the code example and how WebDriver uses this XPath to identify the element:

```
@Test
public void byXPathLocatorExample() {
    WebElement searchBox =
            driver.findElement(By.xpath("//*[@id='search']"));
    searchBox.sendKeys("Bags");
    searchBox.submit();
    assertThat(driver.getTitle())
            .isEqualTo("Search results for: 'Bags'");
}
```

In the preceding code, we are using the `By.xpath` locating mechanism and passing the XPath of the WebElement to it.

One disadvantage of using XPath is that it is costly in terms of time. For every element to be identified, WebDriver actually scans through the entire page, which is very time consuming, and too much usage of XPath in your test script will actually make it too slow to execute.

The By.cssSelector() method

The `By.cssSelector()` method is similar to the `By.xpath()` method in its usage, but the difference is that it is slightly faster than the `By.xpath` locating mechanism. The following are the commonly used syntaxes to identify elements:

- To identify an element using the div element with the `#flrs` ID, we use the `#flrs` syntax
- To identify the child anchor element, we use the `#flrs > a` syntax, which will return the link element
- To identify the anchor element with its attribute, we use the `#flrs > a[a[href="/intl/en/about.html"]]` syntax

Let's try to modify the previous code, which uses the XPath locating mechanism to use the `cssSelector` mechanism:

```
@Test
public void byCssSelectorLocatorExample() {
    WebElement searchBox =
            driver.findElement(By.cssSelector("#search"));
    searchBox.sendKeys("Bags");
    searchBox.submit();
    assertThat(driver.getTitle())
```

```
            .isEqualTo("Search results for: 'Bags'");
    }
```

The preceding code uses the `By.cssSelector` locating mechanism, which uses the css selector ID of the Search box.

Let's look at a slightly complex example. We will try to identify the About Us on the Homepage:

```
@Test
public void byCssSelectorLocatorComplexExample() {

    WebElement aboutUs =
            driver.findElement(By
                    .cssSelector("a[href*='/about-magento-demo-store/']"));

    aboutUs.click();

    assertThat(driver.getTitle())
            .isEqualTo("About Us");
}
```

The preceding code uses the `cssSelector()` method to find the anchor element identified by its `href` attribute.

Interacting with WebElements

In the previous section, we saw how to locate WebElements on a web page by using different locator methods. Here, we will see all the different user actions that can be performed on a WebElement. Different WebElements will have different actions that can be taken on them. For example, in a textbox element, we can type in some text or clear the text that is already typed in it. Similarly, for a button, we can click on it, get the dimensions of it, and so on, but we cannot type into a button, and for a link, we cannot type into it. So, though all the actions are listed in one WebElement interface, it is the test script developer's responsibility to use the actions that are supported by the target element. In case we try to execute the wrong action on a WebElement, we don't see any exception or error thrown and we don't see any action get executed; WebDriver ignores such actions silently.

Now, let's get into each of the actions individually by looking at their Javadocs and a code example.

Getting element properties and attributes

In this section, we will learn the various methods to retrieve value and properties from the WebElement interface.

The getAttribute() method

The `getAttribute` method can be executed on all the WebElements. Remember, we have seen attributes of WebElement in the WebElements section. The HTML attributes are modifiers of HTML elements. They are generally key-value pairs that appear in the start tag of an element. For example:

```
<label name="Username" id="uname">Enter Username: </label>
```

In the preceding code, `name` and `id` are the attributes or attribute keys and `Username` and `uname` are the attribute values.

The API syntax of the `getAttribute()` method is as follows:

```
java.lang.String getAttribute(java.lang.String name)
```

In the preceding code, the input parameter is `String`, which is the name of the attribute. The return type is again `String`, which is the value of the attribute.

Now let's see how we can get all the attributes of a WebElement using WebDriver. Here, we will make use of the Search box from the example application. This is what the element looks like:

```
<input id="search" type="search" name="q" value="" class="input-text
required-entry" maxlength="128" placeholder="Search entire store here..."
autocomplete="off">
```

We will list all the attributes of this WebElement using WebDriver. The code for that is as follows:

```
@Test
public void elementGetAttributesExample() {
    WebElement searchBox = driver.findElement(By.name("q"));
    System.out.println("Name of the box is: "
            + searchBox.getAttribute("name"));
    System.out.println("Id of the box is: " +
searchBox.getAttribute("id"));
    System.out.println("Class of the box is: "
            + searchBox.getAttribute("class"));
    System.out.println("Placeholder of the box is: "
```

```
        + searchBox.getAttribute("placeholder"));
}
```

In the preceding code, the last four lines of code use the getAttribute() method to fetch the attribute values of the name, id, class, and placeholder attributes of the WebElement search box. The output of the preceding code will be following:

```
Name of the box is: q
Id of the box is: search
Class of the box is: input-text required-entry
Placeholder of the box is: Search entire store here...
```

Going back to the By.tagName() method of the previous section, if the search by a locating mechanism, By.tagName, results in more than one result, you can use the getAttribute() method to further filter the results and get to your exact intended element.

The getText() method

The getText method can be called from all the WebElements. It will return visible text if the element contains any text on it, otherwise it will return nothing. The API syntax for the getText() method is as follows:

```
java.lang.String getText()
```

There is no input parameter for the preceding method, but it returns the visible innerText string of the WebElement if anything is available, otherwise it will return an empty string.

The following is the code to get the text present on the Site notice element present on the example application Homepage:

```
@Test
public void elementGetTextExample() {
    WebElement siteNotice = driver.findElement(By
            .className("global-site-notice"));
    System.out.println("Complete text is: "
            + siteNotice.getText());
}
```

The preceding code uses the getText() method to fetch the text present on the Site notice element, which returns the following:

```
Complete text is: This is a demo store. Any orders placed through this
store will not be honored or fulfilled.
```

The getCssValue() method

The `getCssValue` method can be called on all the WebElements. This method is used to fetch a CSS property value from a WebElement. CSS properties can be `font-family`, `background-color`, `color`, and so on. This is useful when you want to validate the CSS styles that are applied to your WebElements through your test scripts. The API syntax for the `getCssValue()` method is as follows:

```
java.lang.String getCssValue(java.lang.String propertyName)
```

In the preceding code, the input parameter is the String value of the CSS property name, and the return type is the value assigned to that property name.

The following is the code example to retrieve `font-family` of the text from the Search box:

```
@Test
public void elementGetCssValueExample() {
    WebElement searchBox = driver.findElement(By.name("q"));
    System.out.println("Font of the box is: "
            + searchBox.getCssValue("font-family"));
}
```

The preceding code uses the `getCssValue()` method to find `font-family` of the text visible in the Search box. The output of the method is shown here:

```
Font of the box is: Raleway, "Helvetica Neue", Verdana, Arial, sans-serif
```

The getLocation() method

The `getLocation` method can be executed on all the WebElements. This is used to get the relative position of an element where it is rendered on the web page. This position is calculated relative to the top-left corner of the web page of which the (x, y) coordinates are assumed to be (0, 0). This method will be of use if your test script tries to validate the layout of your web page.

The API syntax of the `getLocation()` method is as follows:

```
Point getLocation()
```

The preceding method obviously doesn't take any input parameters, but the return type is a `Point` class that contains the (x, y) coordinates of the element.

The following is the code to retrieve the location of the Search box:

```
WebElement searchBox = driver.findElement(By.name("q"));
System.out.println("Location of the box is: "
        + searchBox.getLocation());
```

The output for the preceding code is the (x, y) location of the Search box, as shown in the following screenshot:

```
Location of the box is: (873, 136)
```

The getSize() method

The getSize method can also be called on all the visible components of HTML. It will return the width and height of the rendered WebElement. The API syntax of the getSize() method is as follows:

```
Dimension getSize()
```

The preceding method doesn't take any input parameters, and the return type is a class instance named Dimension. This class contains the width and height of the target WebElement. The following is the code to get the width and height of the Search box:

```
WebElement searchBox = driver.findElement(By.name("q"));
System.out.println("Size of the box is: "
        + searchBox.getSize());
```

The output for the preceding code is the width and height of the Search box, as shown in the following screenshot:

```
Size of the box is: (281, 40)
```

The getTagName() method

The getTagName method can be called from all the WebElements. This will return the HTML tag name of the WebElement. For example, in the following HTML code, the button is the tag name of the HTML element:

```
<button id="gbqfba" class="gbqfba" name="btnK" aria-label="Google Search">
```

In the preceding code, the button is the tag name of the HTML element.

The API syntax for the get TagName () method is as follows:

```
java.lang.String getTagName()
```

The return type of the preceding method is String, and it returns the tag name of the target element.

The following is the code that returns the tag name of the Search button:

```
@Test
public void elementGetTagNameExample() {
    WebElement searchButton = driver.findElement(By.className("search-
button"));
    System.out.println("Html tag of the button is: "
            + searchButton.getTagName());
}
```

The preceding code uses the getTagName () method to get the tag name of the Search button element. The output of the code is as expected:

```
Html tag of the button is: button
```

Performing actions on WebElements

In the previous section, we saw how to retrieve values or properties of WebElements. In this section, we will see how to perform actions on WebElements, which is the most crucial part of automation. Let's explore the various methods available in the WebElement interface.

The sendKeys() method

ThesendKeys action is applicable for textbox or textarea HTML elements. This is used to type text into the textbox. This will simulate the user keyboard and types text into WebElements exactly as a user would. The API syntax for the sendKeys () method is as follows:

```
void sendKeys(java.lang.CharSequence...keysToSend)
```

The input parameter for the preceding method is `CharSequence` of text that has to be entered into the element. This method doesn't return anything. Now, let's see a code example of how to type a search text into the Search box using the `sendKeys()` method:

```
@Test
public void elementSendKeysExample() {
    WebElement searchBox = driver.findElement(By.name("q"));
    searchBox.sendKeys("Phones");
    searchBox.submit();
    assertThat(driver.getTitle())
            .isEqualTo("Search results for: 'Phones'");
}
```

In the preceding code, the `sendKeys()` method is used to type the required text in the textbox element of the web page. This is how we deal with normal keys, but if you want to type in some special keys, such as *Backspace, Enter, Tab,* or *Shift,* we need to use a special enum class of WebDriver, named `Keys`. Using the `Keys` enumeration, you can simulate many special keys while typing into a WebElement.

Now let's see some code example, which uses the *Shift* key to type the text in uppercase in the Search Box:

```
@Test
public void elementSendKeysCompositeExample() {
    WebElement searchBox = driver.findElement(By.name("q"));
    searchBox.sendKeys(Keys.chord(Keys.SHIFT, "phones"));
    searchBox.submit();
    assertThat(driver.getTitle())
            .isEqualTo("Search results for: 'PHONES'");
}
```

In the preceding code, the `chord()` method from the `Keys` enum is used to type the key, while the text specified is being given as an input to be the textbox. Try this in your environment to see all the text being typed in uppercase.

The clear() method

The clear action is similar to the `sendKeys()` method, which is applicable for the `textbox` and `textarea` elements. This is used to erase the text entered in a WebElement using the `sendKeys()` method. This can be achieved using the `Keys.BACK_SPACE` enum, but WebDriver has given us an explicit method to clear the text easily. The API syntax for the `clear()` method is as follows:

```
void clear()
```

This method doesn't take any input and doesn't return any output. It is simply executed on the target text-entry element.

Now, let's see how we can clear text that is entered in the Search box. The code example for it is as follows:

```
@Test
public void elementClearExample() {
    WebElement searchBox = driver.findElement(By.name("q"));
    searchBox.sendKeys(Keys.chord(Keys.SHIFT,"phones"));
    searchBox.clear();
}
```

We have used the WebElement's `clear()` method to clear the text after typing `phones` into the Search box.

The submit() method

The `submit()` action can be taken on a `Form` or on an element, which is inside a `Form` element. This is used to submit a form of a web page to the server hosting the web application. The API syntax for the `submit()` method is as follows:

```
void submit()
```

The preceding method doesn't take any input parameters and doesn't return anything. But a `NoSuchElementException` is thrown when this method is executed on a WebElement that is not present within the form.

Now, let's see a code example to submit the form on a Search page:

```
@Test
public void elementSubmitExample() {
    WebElement searchBox = driver.findElement(By.name("q"));
    searchBox.sendKeys(Keys.chord(Keys.SHIFT,"phones"));
    searchBox.submit();
}
```

In the preceding code, toward the end is where the Search form is submitted to the application servers using the `submit()` method. Now, try to execute the `submit()` method on an element, let's say the About link, which is not a part of any form. We should see `NoSuchElementException` is thrown. So, when you use the `submit()` method on a WebElement, make sure it is part of the `Form` element.

Checking the WebElement state

In the previous sections, we saw how to retrieve values and perform actions on WebElements. Now, we will see how to check the state of a WebElement. We will explore methods to check whether the WebElement is displayed in the Browser window, whether it is editable, and if the WebElement is Radio Button of Checkbox, we can determine whether it's selected or unselected. Let's see how we can use the methods available in the WebElement interface.

The isDisplayed() method

The `isDisplayed` action verifies whether an element is displayed on the web page and can be executed on all the WebElements. The API syntax for the `isDisplayed()` method is as follows:

```
boolean isDisplayed()
```

The preceding method returns a `Boolean` value specifying whether the target element is displayed on the web page. The following is the code to verify whether the Search box is displayed, which obviously should return true in this case:

```
@Test
public void elementStateExample() {
    WebElement searchBox = driver.findElement(By.name("q"));
    System.out.println("Search box is displayed: "
            + searchBox.isDisplayed());
}
```

The preceding code uses the `isDisplayed()` method to determine whether the element is displayed on a web page. The preceding code returns `true` for the Search box:

```
Search box is displayed: true
```

The isEnabled() method

The `isEnabled` action verifies whether an element is enabled on the web page and can be executed on all the WebElements. The API syntax for the `isEnabled()` method is as follows:

```
boolean isEnabled()
```

The preceding method returns a `Boolean` value specifying whether the target element is enabled on the web page. The following is the code to verify whether the Search box is enabled, which obviously should return true in this case:

```
@Test
public void elementStateExample() {
    WebElement searchBox = driver.findElement(By.name("q"));
    System.out.println("Search box is enabled: "
            + searchBox.isEnabled());
}
```

The preceding code uses the `isEnabled()` method to determine whether the element is enabled on a web page. The preceding code returns true for the Search box:

```
Search box is enabled: true
```

The isSelected() method

The `isSelected` method returns a `boolean` value if an element is selected on the web page and can be executed only on a radio button, options in **select**, and checkbox WebElements. When executed on other elements, it will return false. The API syntax for the `isSelected()` method is as follows:

```
boolean isSelected()
```

The preceding method returns a `Boolean` value specifying whether the target element is selected on the web page. The following is the code to verify whether the Search box is selected on a search page:

```
@Test
public void elementStateExample() {
    WebElement searchBox = driver.findElement(By.name("q"));
    System.out.println("Search box is selected: "
            + searchBox.isSelected());
}
```

The preceding code uses the `isSelected()` method. It returns false for the Search box, because this is not a radio button, options in select, or a checkbox. The preceding code returns `false` for the Search box:

```
Search box is selected: false
```

> **TIP**
>
> To select a Checkbox or Radio button, we need to call the `WebElement.click()` method, which toggles the state of the element. We can use the `isSelected()` method to see whether it's selected.

Summary

In this chapter, we covered a brief overview of the Selenium testing tools, and the architecture of WebDriver, WebElements. We learned how to set up a test-development environment using Eclipse, Maven, and TestNG. This will provide us with the foundation to build a testing framework using Selenium. Then, we saw how to locate elements, and the actions that can be taken on them. This is the most important aspect when automating Web Applications. In this chapter, we used ChromeDriver to run our tests. In the next chapter, we will learn how to configure and run tests on Mozilla Firefox, Microsoft IE and Edge, and Apple Safari.

Questions

1. True or false: Selenium is a browser automation library.
2. What are the different types of locator mechanisms provided by Selenium?
3. True or false: With the `getAttribute()` method, we can read CSS attributes as well?
4. What actions can be performed on a WebElement?
5. How can we determine whether the checkbox is checked or unchecked?

Further information

You can check out the following links for more information on the topics covered in this chapter:

- Read the WebDriver Specification at `https://www.w3.org/TR/webdriver/`
- Read more about using TestNG and Maven in `Chapter 1`, *Creating a Faster Feedback Loop* from *Mastering Selenium WebDriver* By Mark Collin, Packt Publishing
- Read more about element interaction in *Chapter 2, Finding Elements* and *Chapter 3, Working with Elements* from *Selenium Testing Tools Cookbook*, 2nd Edition, by Unmesh Gundecha, Packt Publishing

Different Available WebDrivers

2

The previous chapter introduced the Selenium WebDriver architecture and WebDriver interface. We used Google Chrome with ChromeDriver to create a simple test. In this chapter, we will explore the WebDriver implementation for Mozilla Firefox, Microsoft Internet Explorer, Microsoft Edge, and Safari. With WebDriver becoming a W3C specification, all of the major browser vendors now support WebDriver natively. In this chapter, we will look at the following:

- Using driver-specific implementations for Mozilla Firefox, Google Chrome, Microsoft Internet Explorer and Edge, and Apple Safari
- Using the browser options class to execute tests in headless mode and use custom profiles
- Using mobile emulation with Google Chrome

Firefox Driver

The implementation of Firefox Driver has been changed in Selenium 3.0. Starting with Firefox version 47.0+, we need to use separate a driver that will interact with the Firefox browser similarly to ChromeDriver. The new driver for Firefox is called Geckodriver.

The Geckodriver provides the HTTP API described by the W3C WebDriver Protocol to communicate with Gecko browsers, such as Firefox. It translates calls into the Firefox Remote Protocol (Marionette) by acting as a proxy between the local and remote ends.

Using GeckoDriver

In this section, we will see how to configure and use **Geckodriver** for Firefox in our tests. First of all, we need to download the **Geckodriver** executable from `https://github.com/mozilla/geckodriver/releases`

Download the appropriate version of **Geckodriver** based on the Firefox version installed on your computer as well as the operating system. Copy the executable file into the `/src/test/resources/drivers` folder.

We will use the Search Test we created in Chapter 1 and modify the test to use the **Geckodriver**. For this, we need to modify the `setup()` method, provide the path of the **Geckodriver** binary in the `webdriver.gecko.driver` property, and instantiate the `FirefoxDriver` class:

```java
public class SearchTest {

    WebDriver driver;

    @BeforeMethod
    public void setup() {

        System.setProperty("webdriver.gecko.driver",
                "./src/test/resources/drivers/geckodriver.exe");

        driver = new FirefoxDriver();
        driver.get("http://demo-store.seleniumacademy.com/");
    }

    @Test
    public void searchProduct() {

        // find search box and enter search string
        WebElement searchBox = driver.findElement(By.name("q"));

        searchBox.sendKeys("Phones");

        WebElement searchButton =
                driver.findElement(By.className("search-button"));

        searchButton.click();

        assertThat(driver.getTitle())
                .isEqualTo("Search results for: 'Phones'");
    }

    @AfterMethod
    public void tearDown() {
        driver.quit();
    }
}
```

Now execute the test, and you will see **Geckodriver** running in the console:

```
1532165868138 geckodriver INFO geckodriver 0.21.0
1532165868147 geckodriver INFO Listening on 127.0.0.1:36466
```

It will launch a new Firefox window and execute the test. The Firefox window will be closed at the end of the execution.

Using Headless Mode

Headless mode is a very useful way to run Firefox for automated testing with Selenium WebDriver. In headless mode, Firefox runs as normal only you don't see the UI components. This makes Firefox faster and tests run more efficiently, especially in the CI (Continuous Integration) environment.

We can run Selenium tests in headless mode by configuring the `FirefoxOptions` class, as shown in the following code snippet:

```
@BeforeMethod
public void setup() {


        System.setProperty("webdriver.gecko.driver",
                "./src/test/resources/drivers/geckodriver 2");

        FirefoxOptions firefoxOptions = new FirefoxOptions();
        firefoxOptions.setHeadless(true);

        driver = new FirefoxDriver(firefoxOptions);

        driver.get("http://demo-store.seleniumacademy.com/");
}
```

In the preceding code, we first created an instance of the `FirefoxOptions` class, called the `setHeadless()` method, that passes the value as `true` to launch the Firefox browser in headless mode. You will see a long message indicating the browser instance has been launched in headless mode, as shown in the following console output:

```
1532194389309 geckodriver INFO geckodriver 0.21.0
1532194389317 geckodriver INFO Listening on 127.0.0.1:21734
1532194390907 mozrunner::runner INFO Running command:
"/Applications/Firefox.app/Contents/MacOS/firefox-bin" "-marionette" "-
headless" "-foreground" "-no-remote" "-profile"
"/var/folders/zr/rdwhsjk54k5bj7yr34rfftrh0000gn/T/rust_mozprofile.DmJCQRKVV
Rs6"
  *** You are running in headless mode.
```

During the execution, you will not see the Firefox window on the screen but the test will be executed in headless mode.

Understanding the Firefox profile

A Firefox profile is a folder that the Firefox browser uses to store all your passwords, bookmarks, settings, and other user data. A Firefox user can create any number of profiles with different custom settings and use it accordingly. According to Mozilla, the following are the different attributes that can be stored in the profiles:

- Bookmarks and browsing history
- Passwords
- Site-specific preferences
- Search engines
- A personal dictionary
- Autocomplete history
- Download history
- Cookies
- DOM Storage
- Security certificate settings
- Security device settings
- Download actions
- Plugin MIME types
- Stored sessions
- Toolbar customizations
- User styles

To create, rename, or delete a profile, you have to perform the following steps:

1. Open the Firefox profile manager. To do that, in the command prompt terminal, navigate to the install directory of Firefox; typically, it is in **Program Files** if you are on Windows. Navigate to the location where you can find the `firefox` binary file, and execute the following command:

```
/path/to/firefox -p
```

   It will open the profile manager, which will look like the following screenshot:

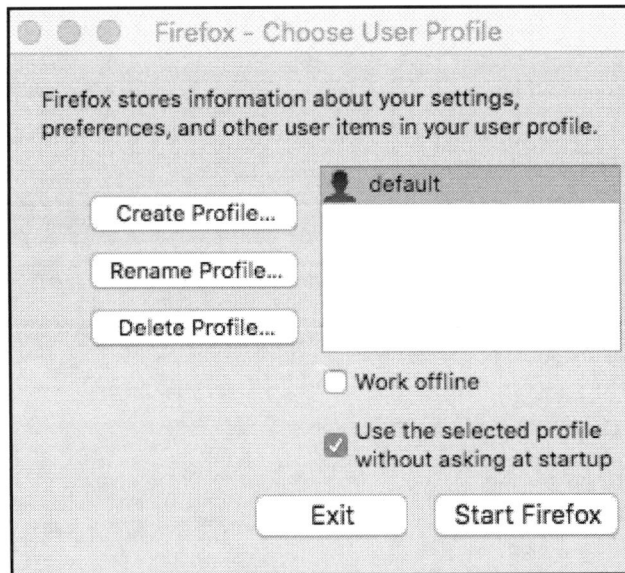

   Note that before executing the preceding command, you need to make sure you close all your currently-running Firefox instances.

2. Use the **Create Profile...** button to create another profile, the **Rename Profile...** button to rename an existing profile, and the **Delete Profile...** button to delete one.

So, coming back to our WebDriver, whenever we create an instance of `FirefoxDriver`, a temporary profile is created and used by the WebDriver. To see the profile that is currently being used by a Firefox instance, navigate to **Help | Troubleshooting Information**.

This will launch all the details of the particular Firefox instance of which the profile is a part. It will look similar to the following screenshot:

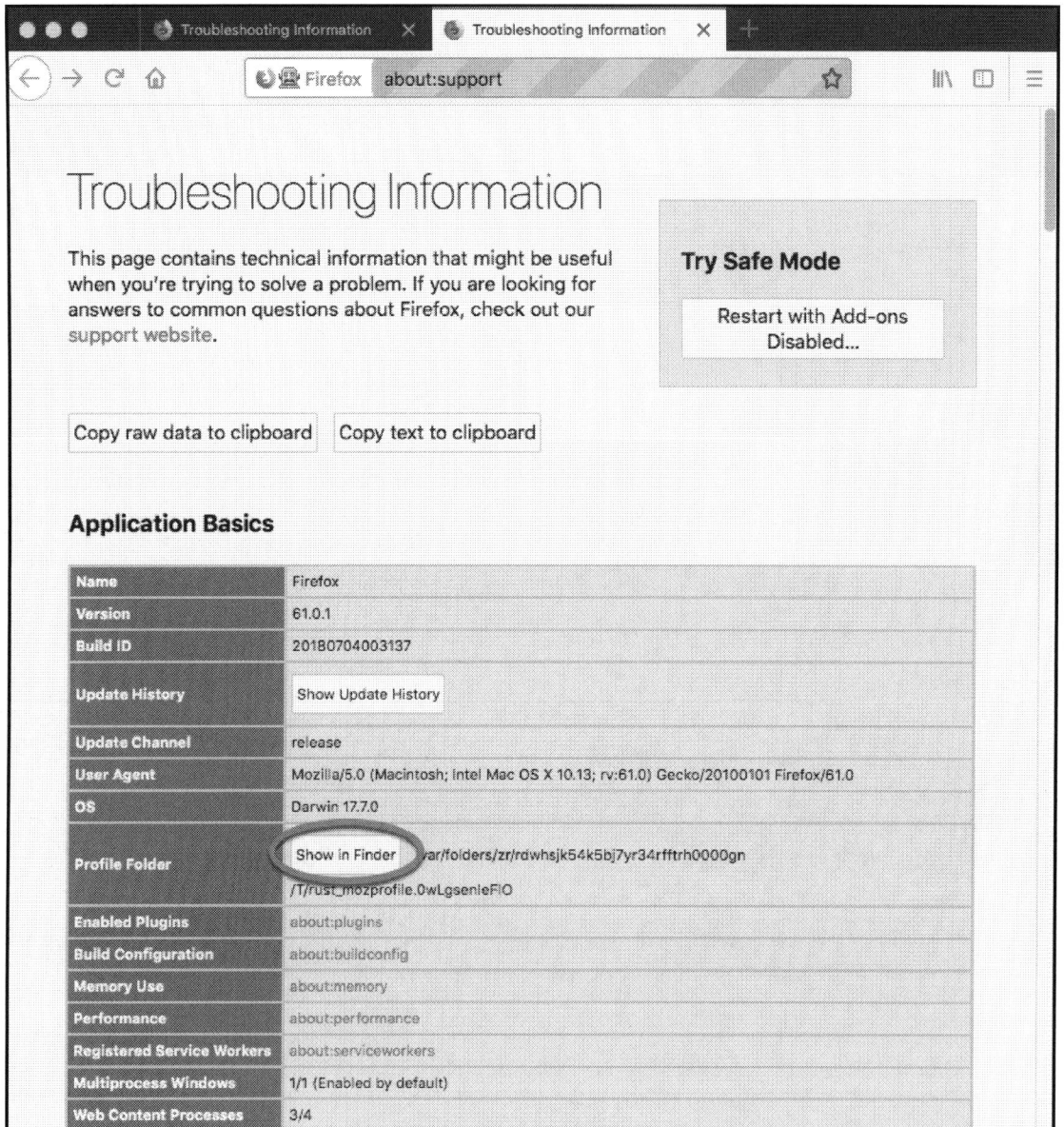

The highlighted oval in the preceding screenshot shows the profile folder. Click on the **Show Folder** button; it should open the location of the profile corresponding to that of your current Firefox instance. Now, let's launch a Firefox browser instance using our FirefoxDriver, and verify its profile location.

Let's launch a Firefox browser using the following code:

```
public class FirefoxProfile {
  public static void main(String... args) {
  System.setProperty("webdriver.gecko.driver",
  "./src/test/resources/drivers/geckodriver 2");
  FirefoxDriver driver = new FirefoxDriver();
  driver.get("http://www.google.com");
  }
}
```

This will launch a browser instance. Now, navigate to **Help** | **Troubleshooting Information**, and once the info is launched, click the **Show Folder** button. This will open the current WebDriver's profile directory. Every time you launch a Firefox instance using Firefox Driver, it will create a new profile for you. If you go one level above this directory, you will see the profiles created by your **FirefoxDriver**, as shown in the following screenshot:

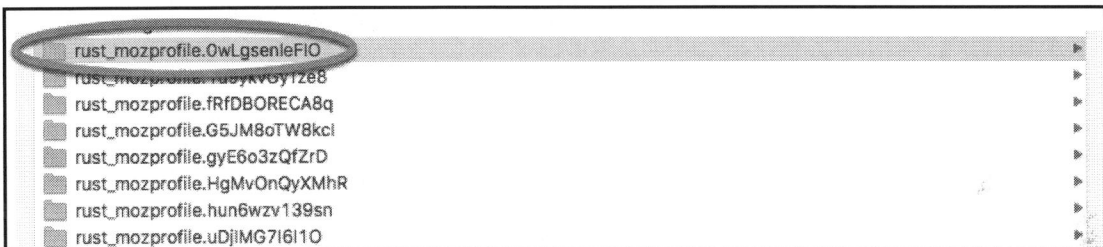

All the preceding folders correspond to each of the Firefox instances launched by the FirefoxDriver.

So far, we have seen what Firefox profiles are and how WebDriver creates one every time it launches the browser. Now, let's see how we can create our own custom profiles using WebDriver APIs. The following is the code example to create your own Firefox profile using the WebDriver library and set the options you want your browser to have, overriding what FirefoxDriver gives you:

```
public class FirefoxCustomProfile {
    public static void main(String... args) {

        System.setProperty("webdriver.gecko.driver",
```

```
                    "./src/test/resources/drivers/geckodriver 2");

        FirefoxProfile profile = new FirefoxProfile();

        FirefoxOptions firefoxOptions = new FirefoxOptions();
        firefoxOptions.setProfile(profile);

        FirefoxDriver driver = new FirefoxDriver(firefoxOptions);
        try {
            driver.get("http://www.google.com");
        } finally {
            driver.quit();
        }
    }
}
```

In the preceding code, `FirefoxProfile` is the class that has been instantiated to create a custom profile for the Firefox browser launched from the test. Now, having an instance of that class, we can set various options and preferences in it, which we will discuss shortly. First, there are two overloaded versions of constructors for `FirefoxProfile`. One creates an empty profile and moulds it according to requirements. This is seen in the preceding code. The second version creates a profile instance from an existing profile directory, as follows:

```
public FirefoxProfile(java.io.File profileDir)
```

Here, the `profileDir` input parameter is the directory location of an existing profile. The profile directory is the one we saw in the preceding screenshot. Let's discuss some interesting customizations that we can do to our Firefox browser using Firefox profiles.

Adding the extension to Firefox

In this section, we will see how we can extend our Firefox browser with some additional capabilities using Profiles. Whenever WebDriver launches a new Firefox browser, it creates a new profile on the disk, and this profile doesn't contain any of the installed Firefox extensions in it. We will add an extension using the Profiles every time WebDriver creates an instance of the Firefox browser.

Now, let's change the profile using the `addExtension()` method provided by `FirefoxProfile`. This method is used to add extensions to the Firefox browser.

The following is the API syntax for the method:

```
public void addExtension(java.io.File extensionToInstall) throws
java.io.IOException
```

The input parameter is the XPI file that has to be installed on the Firefox browser. If WebDriver doesn't find the file in the specified location, it will raise `IOException`. The following is the code to override the default profile and extend the Firefox browser to have an extension named Xpath Finder:

```
public class FirefoxCustomProfile {
    public static void main(String... args) {

        System.setProperty("webdriver.gecko.driver",
                "./src/test/resources/drivers/geckodriver 2");

        FirefoxProfile profile = new FirefoxProfile();
        profile.addExtension(
                new
File("./src/test/resources/extensions/xpath_finder.xpi"));

        FirefoxOptions firefoxOptions = new FirefoxOptions();
        firefoxOptions.setProfile(profile);

        FirefoxDriver driver = new FirefoxDriver(firefoxOptions);
        try {
            driver.get("http://www.google.com");
        } finally {
            //driver.quit();
        }
    }
}
```

Now, if you see the Firefox browser that is launched by the FirefoxDriver, you will find the Xpath Finder extension installed on it. In the console log, you will see a message indicating the extension has been added to the browser:

1532196699704 addons.xpi-utils DEBUG New add-on xPathFinder@0.9.3 installed in app-profile

Storing and retrieving a profile

We can also write the profile information of the browser to the JSON file and later instantiate new browsers with the same profile. The FirefoxProfile class provides a method to export the profile information as JSON. The following is its API syntax:

```
public String toJson()
```

The output or return type is a String, which contains the JSON information in it.

Now, to create a browser with the same profile, the FirefoxProfile class provides a static method that takes the JSON string as the input. The following is the API syntax:

```
public static FirefoxProfile fromJson(java.lang.String json) throws
java.io.IOException
```

This is a static method in the FirefoxProfile class that takes the JSON string to create a profile from. The following is the code example for that:

```
FirefoxProfile profile = new FirefoxProfile();
profile.addExtension(
        new File("./src/test/resources/extensions/xpath_finder.xpi"));
String json = profile.toJson();
FirefoxOptions firefoxOptions = new FirefoxOptions();
firefoxOptions.setProfile(FirefoxProfile.fromJson(json));
```

In the preceding code, we have exported the profile as a JSON string. In your test case, you can write that JSON information to a file and store it. Later, you can read the JSON file using FirefoxOptions and create FirefoxDriver from that.

Dealing with Firefox preferences

So far, we have learned about Firefox profiles, and how we can create our own customized profiles for Firefox Driver. Now, let's see how we can set our preferences in the profiles we create and where FirefoxDriver stores them.

According to Mozilla, a Firefox Preference is any value or defined behavior that can be set by a user. These values are saved to the preference files. If you open the profile directory by navigating to **Help | Troubleshooting Information** and clicking on the **Show Folder** button, you will see two preference files: `prefs.js` and `user.js`. All the user preferences are written to the `prefs.js` file by the Firefox application during the launch. A user can override those values for their chosen values, and they are stored in the `user.js` file. The value in `user.js` for a preference takes precedence over all the other values set for that particular preference. So, your FirefoxDriver overwrites all the default preferences of Firefox in the `user.js` file for you. When you add a new preference, FirefoxDriver writes that to the `user.js` preference file, and the Firefox browser behaves accordingly.

Open the `user.js` file in the profile directory. The following are the list of all the preferences that FirefoxDriver sets for you by default:

```
user_pref("app.normandy.api_url", "");
user_pref("app.update.auto", false);
user_pref("app.update.enabled", false);
user_pref("browser.EULA.3.accepted", true);
user_pref("browser.EULA.override", true);
user_pref("browser.displayedE10SNotice", 4);
user_pref("browser.dom.window.dump.enabled", true);
user_pref("browser.download.manager.showWhenStarting", false);
user_pref("browser.laterrun.enabled", false);
user_pref("browser.link.open_external", 2);
user_pref("browser.link.open_newwindow", 2);
user_pref("browser.newtab.url", "about:blank");
user_pref("browser.newtabpage.enabled", false);
user_pref("browser.offline", false);
user_pref("browser.reader.detectedFirstArticle", true);
user_pref("browser.safebrowsing.blockedURIs.enabled", false);
user_pref("browser.safebrowsing.downloads.enabled", false);
user_pref("browser.safebrowsing.enabled", false);
user_pref("browser.safebrowsing.malware.enabled", false);
user_pref("browser.safebrowsing.passwords.enabled", false);
user_pref("browser.safebrowsing.phishing.enabled", false);
user_pref("browser.search.update", false);
user_pref("browser.selfsupport.url", "");
user_pref("browser.sessionstore.resume_from_crash", false);
user_pref("browser.shell.checkDefaultBrowser", false);
user_pref("browser.showQuitWarning", false);
user_pref("browser.snippets.enabled", false);
user_pref("browser.snippets.firstrunHomepage.enabled", false);
user_pref("browser.snippets.syncPromo.enabled", false);
user_pref("browser.startup.homepage", "about:blank");
user_pref("browser.startup.homepage_override.mstone", "ignore");
user_pref("browser.startup.page", 0);
```

```
user_pref("browser.tabs.closeWindowWithLastTab", false);
user_pref("browser.tabs.warnOnClose", false);
user_pref("browser.tabs.warnOnOpen", false);
user_pref("browser.uitour.enabled", false);
user_pref("browser.usedOnWindows10.introURL", "about:blank");
user_pref("browser.warnOnQuit", false);
user_pref("datareporting.healthreport.about.reportUrl",
"http://%(server)s/dummy/abouthealthreport/");
user_pref("datareporting.healthreport.documentServerURI",
"http://%(server)s/dummy/healthreport/");
user_pref("datareporting.healthreport.logging.consoleEnabled", false);
user_pref("datareporting.healthreport.service.enabled", false);
user_pref("datareporting.healthreport.service.firstRun", false);
user_pref("datareporting.healthreport.uploadEnabled", false);
user_pref("datareporting.policy.dataSubmissionEnabled", false);
user_pref("datareporting.policy.dataSubmissionPolicyAccepted", false);
user_pref("datareporting.policy.dataSubmissionPolicyBypassNotification",
true);
user_pref("devtools.errorconsole.enabled", true);
user_pref("dom.disable_open_during_load", false);
user_pref("dom.ipc.reportProcessHangs", false);
user_pref("dom.max_chrome_script_run_time", 30);
user_pref("dom.max_script_run_time", 30);
user_pref("dom.report_all_js_exceptions", true);
user_pref("extensions.autoDisableScopes", 10);
user_pref("extensions.blocklist.enabled", false);
user_pref("extensions.checkCompatibility.nightly", false);
user_pref("extensions.enabledScopes", 5);
user_pref("extensions.installDistroAddons", false);
user_pref("extensions.logging.enabled", true);
user_pref("extensions.shield-recipe-client.api_url", "");
user_pref("extensions.showMismatchUI", false);
user_pref("extensions.update.enabled", false);
user_pref("extensions.update.notifyUser", false);
user_pref("focusmanager.testmode", true);
user_pref("general.useragent.updates.enabled", false);
user_pref("geo.provider.testing", true);
user_pref("geo.wifi.scan", false);
user_pref("hangmonitor.timeout", 0);
user_pref("javascript.enabled", true);
user_pref("javascript.options.showInConsole", true);
user_pref("marionette.log.level", "INFO");
user_pref("marionette.port", 51549);
user_pref("network.captive-portal-service.enabled", false);
user_pref("network.http.phishy-userpass-length", 255);
user_pref("network.manage-offline-status", false);
user_pref("network.sntp.pools", "%(server)s");
user_pref("offline-apps.allow_by_default", true);
```

```
user_pref("plugin.state.flash", 0);
user_pref("prompts.tab_modal.enabled", false);
user_pref("security.csp.enable", false);
user_pref("security.fileuri.origin_policy", 3);
user_pref("security.fileuri.strict_origin_policy", false);
user_pref("services.settings.server",
"http://%(server)s/dummy/blocklist/");
user_pref("signon.rememberSignons", false);
user_pref("startup.homepage_welcome_url", "");
user_pref("startup.homepage_welcome_url.additional", "about:blank");
user_pref("toolkit.networkmanager.disable", true);
user_pref("toolkit.startup.max_resumed_crashes", -1);
user_pref("toolkit.telemetry.enabled", false);
user_pref("toolkit.telemetry.prompted", 2);
user_pref("toolkit.telemetry.rejected", true);
user_pref("toolkit.telemetry.server",
"https://%(server)s/dummy/telemetry/");
user_pref("webdriver_accept_untrusted_certs", true);
user_pref("webdriver_assume_untrusted_issuer", true);
user_pref("xpinstall.signatures.required", false);
user_pref("xpinstall.whitelist.required", false);
```

This Firefox Driver treats them as `Frozen Preferences` and doesn't allow the test-script developer to change them. However, there are a few preferences in the preceding list that FirefoxDriver allows you to change, which we will see shortly.

Setting preferences

Now we will learn how to set our own preferences. As an example, we will see how to change the user agent of your browser. These days, many web applications have a main site as well as a mobile site/m. site. The application will validate the user agent of the incoming request and decide whether to act as a server for a normal site or mobile site. So, in order to test your mobile site from your laptop or desktop browser, you just have to change your user agent. Let's see a code example where we can change the user-agent preference of our Firefox browser using FirefoxDriver, and send a request to the Facebook homepage. But before that, let's see the `setPreference()` method provided by the FirefoxProfile class:

```
public void setPreference(java.lang.String key, String value)
```

The input parameters are `key`, which is a string and represents your preference, and `value`, which has to be set to the preference.

There are two other overloaded versions of the preceding method shown; one of which is as follows:

```
public void setPreference(java.lang.String key, int value)
```

Here is the other overloaded version:

```
public void setPreference(java.lang.String key,boolean value)
```

Now, using the preceding setPreference() method, we will try to change the user agent of our browser using the following code:

```
public class SettingPreferences {
    public static void main(String... args) {

        System.setProperty("webdriver.gecko.driver",
                "./src/test/resources/drivers/geckodriver 2");

        FirefoxProfile profile = new FirefoxProfile();
        profile.setPreference("general.useragent.override",
          "Mozilla/5.0 (iPhone; CPU iPhone OS 11_0 like Mac OS X) " +
          "AppleWebKit/604.1.38 (KHTML, like Gecko) Version/11.0 " +
          "Mobile/15A356 Safari/604.1");
        FirefoxOptions firefoxOptions = new FirefoxOptions();
        firefoxOptions.setProfile(profile);
        FirefoxDriver driver = new FirefoxDriver(firefoxOptions);
        driver.get("http://facebook.com");
    }
}
```

In the preceding code for the setPreference() method, general.useragent.override is set as the name of the preference, and the second parameter is the value for that preference, which represents the iPhone user agent. Now open the user.js file for this particular Firefox instance, and you will see the entry for this preference. You should use the following preference in your user.js file:

```
user_pref("general.useragent.override", "Mozilla/5.0 (iPhone; CPU iPhone OS
11_0 like Mac OS X) AppleWebKit/604.1.38 (KHTML, like Gecko) Version/11.0
Mobile/15A356 Safari/604.1");
```

Apart from this, you will observe that the mobile version of the Facebook homepage has been served to you.

Understanding frozen preferences

Now, let's go back to the big list of frozen preferences that user.js contains, which we saw earlier. The Firefox Driver thinks that a test-script developer doesn't have to deal with them and doesn't allow those values to be changed. Let's pick one frozen preference and try to change its values in our code. Let's consider the browser.shell.checkDefaultBrowser preference, whose value FirefoxDriver implementers thought should be set to false so that the Firefox browser does not ask you whether to make Firefox your default browser, if it is not already, when you are busy executing your test cases. Ultimately, you don't have to deal with the pop-up itself in your test scripts. Apart from setting the preference value to false, the implementers of FirefoxDriver also thought of freezing this value so that users don't alter these values. That is the reason these preferences are called frozen preferences. Now, what happens if you try to modify these values in your test scripts? Let's see a code example:

```
public class FirefoxFrozenPreferences {
    public static void main(String... args) {

        System.setProperty("webdriver.gecko.driver",
                "./src/test/resources/drivers/geckodriver 2");

        FirefoxProfile profile = new FirefoxProfile();
        profile.setPreference("browser.shell.checkDefaultBrowser", true);
        FirefoxOptions firefoxOptions = new FirefoxOptions();
        firefoxOptions.setProfile(profile);
        FirefoxDriver driver = new FirefoxDriver(firefoxOptions);
        driver.get("http://facebook.com");
    }
}
```

Now when you execute your code, you will immediately see an exception saying you're not allowed to override these values. The following is the exception stack trace you will see:

```
Exception in thread "main" java.lang.IllegalArgumentException: Preference
browser.shell.checkDefaultBrowser may not be overridden: frozen
value=false, requested value=true
```

This is how FirefoxDriver mandates a few preferences that are not to be touched. However, there are a few preferences of the frozen list that FirefoxDriver allows to alter through code. For that, it explicitly exposes methods in the FirefoxProfile class. Those exempted preferences are for dealing with SSL certificates and native events. Here, we will see how we can override the SSL certificates' preferences.

Let's use a code example that tries to override the default Firefox behavior to handle SSL certificates. The `FirefoxProfile` class has two methods to handle the SSL certificates; the first one is as follows:

```
public void setAcceptUntrustedCertificates(boolean acceptUntrustedSsl)
```

This lets Firefox know whether to accept SSL certificates that are untrusted. By default, it is set to true, that is, Firefox accepts SSL certificates that are untrusted. The second method is as follows:

```
public void setAssumeUntrustedCertificateIssuer(boolean untrustedIssuer)
```

This lets Firefox assume that the untrusted certificates are issued by untrusted or self-signed certification agents. Firefox, by default, assumes the issuer to be untrusted. That assumption is particularly useful when you test an application in the test environment while using the certificate from the production environment.

The preferences, `webdriver_accept_untrusted_certs` and `webdriver_assume_untrusted_issuer`, are the ones related to the SSL certificates. Now, let's create a Java code to modify the values for these two values. By default, the values are set to true, as seen in the `user.js` file. Let's mark them as false with the following code:

```java
public static void main(String... args) {

    System.setProperty("webdriver.gecko.driver",
            "./src/test/resources/drivers/geckodriver 2");

    FirefoxProfile profile = new FirefoxProfile();

    profile.setAssumeUntrustedCertificateIssuer(false);
    profile.setAcceptUntrustedCertificates(false);
    FirefoxOptions firefoxOptions = new FirefoxOptions();
    firefoxOptions.setProfile(profile);

    FirefoxDriver driver = new FirefoxDriver(firefoxOptions);
    driver.get("http://facebook.com");
}
```

Here, we have set the values to false, and now if we open the `user.js` file in the profile directory of this instance of Firefox, you will see the values set to false, as follows:

```
user_pref("webdriver_accept_untrusted_certs", false);
user_pref("webdriver_assume_untrusted_issuer", false);
```

Chrome Driver

The ChromeDriver works similar to the Geckodriver and implements the W3C WebDriver protocol. We saw how to set up and use ChromeDriver in Chapter 1. In this section, we will focus on the ChromeDriver options to run tests in headless mode, use mobile emulation, and use custom profiles.

Using Headless Mode

Similar to Firefox, we can run tests in headless mode with ChromeDriver. This makes Chrome tests run faster and tests run more efficiently, especially in the CI (Continuous Integration) environment.

We can run Selenium tests in headless mode by configuring the ChromeOptions class as shown in the following code snippet:

```java
@BeforeMethod
public void setup() {
  System.setProperty("webdriver.chrome.driver",
  "./src/test/resources/drivers/chromedriver");

  ChromeOptions chromeOptions = new ChromeOptions();
  chromeOptions.setHeadless(true);

  driver = new ChromeDriver(chromeOptions);

  driver.get("http://demo-store.seleniumacademy.com/");

}
```

In the preceding code, we first created an instance of the ChromeOptions class, called the setHeadless() method, that passes the value as true to launch the Chrome browser in headless mode. During the execution, you will not see the Chrome window on the screen but the test will be executed in headless mode.

Using Mobile Emulation for testing mobile web applications

The Chrome browser allows users to emulate Chrome on mobile devices, such as Pixel 2, Nexus 7, iPhone, or iPad, from the desktop version of Chrome via DevTools. The following screenshot shows how our sample application will be seen in Chrome for iPhone. We can start the mobile emulation in Chrome browser with the following steps:

1. Navigate to the sample web application in the Chrome Browser:

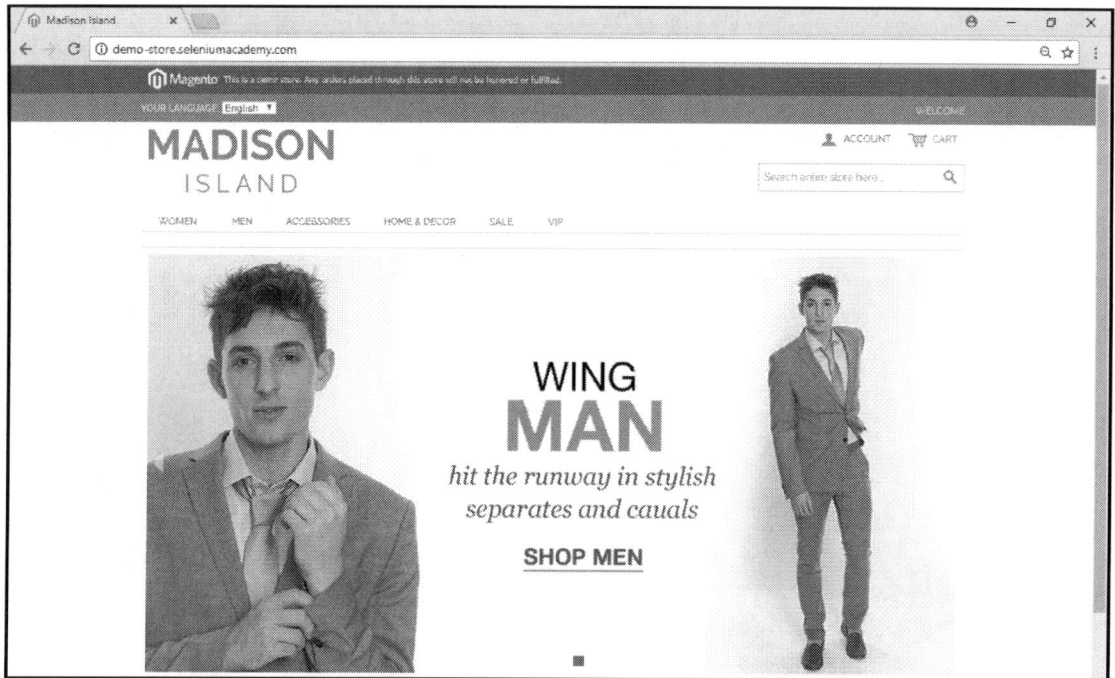

2. Open the Developer Tools. Select the blue Mobile device icon and then select the device. In this example, we selected iPhone X. The Chrome browser will reload according to the selected device:

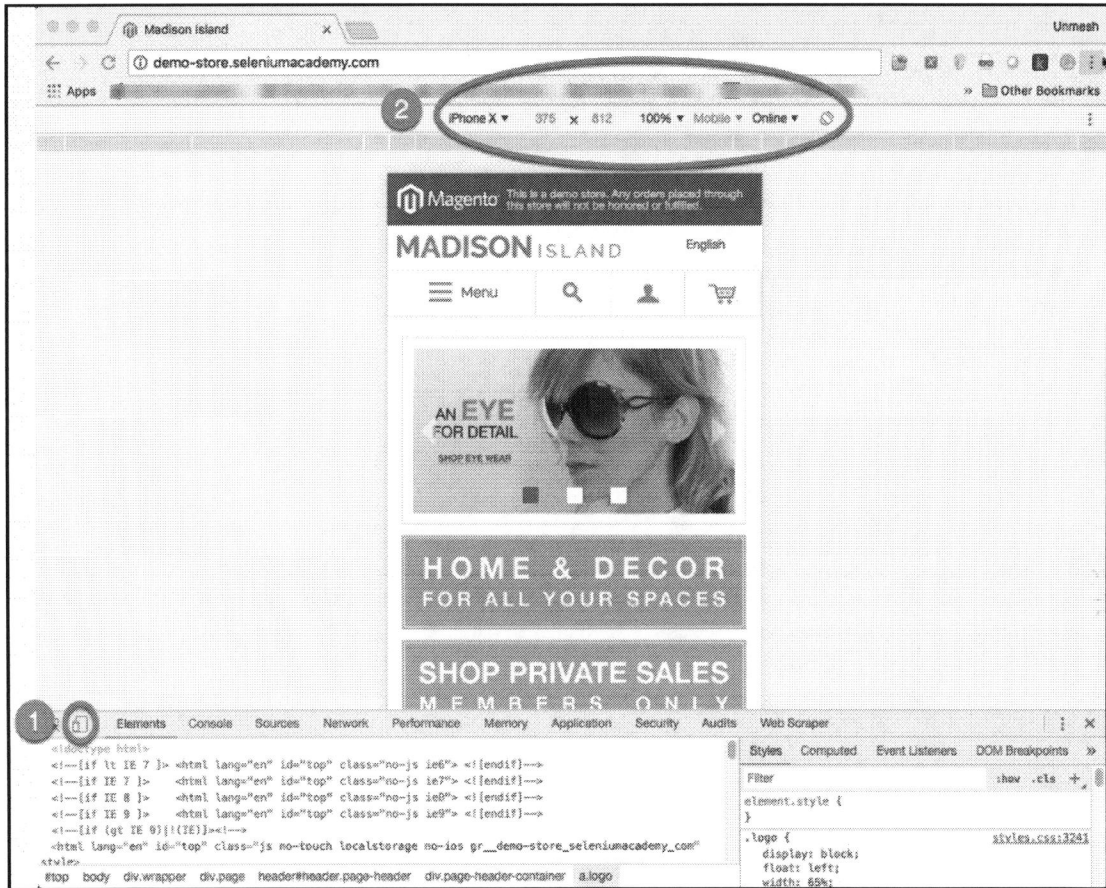

The mobile-emulation feature allows developers and testers to quickly test how a website will be displayed on a mobile device, without requiring a real device and speed up the development process.

We can also use mobile emulation with our Selenium WebDriver tests by configuring ChromeOptions. Let's modify the search test to test on Google Pixel 2:

```
@BeforeMethod
public void setup() {

    System.setProperty("webdriver.chrome.driver",
            "./src/test/resources/drivers/chromedriver");

    Map<String, Object> deviceMetrics = new HashMap<>();
    deviceMetrics.put("width", 411);
    deviceMetrics.put("height", 823);
```

```
        deviceMetrics.put("pixelRatio", 3.0);


    Map<String, Object> mobileEmulation = new HashMap<>();
    mobileEmulation.put("deviceMetrics", deviceMetrics);
    mobileEmulation.put("userAgent", "Mozilla/5.0 (Linux; Android 8.0.0;" +
            "Pixel 2 XL Build/OPD1.170816.004) AppleWebKit/537.36 (KHTML,
like Gecko) " +
            "Chrome/67.0.3396.99 Mobile Safari/537.36");

    ChromeOptions chromeOptions = new ChromeOptions();
    chromeOptions.setExperimentalOption("mobileEmulation",
mobileEmulation);

    driver = new ChromeDriver(chromeOptions);
    driver.get("http://demo-store.seleniumacademy.com/");


}
```

The preceding code will enable the Mobile emulation in Chrome during the execution, and will load the mobile version of the Website. This is done by first configuring the Device metrics, such as width and height, using a Java HashMap. In this example, we configured the deviceMetrics hashmap as shown in the following code:

```
Map<String, Object> deviceMetrics = new HashMap<>();
    deviceMetrics.put("width", 411);
    deviceMetrics.put("height", 823);
    deviceMetrics.put("pixelRatio", 3.0);
```

Next, we need to create another Hashmap, named mobileEmulation, that will hold the deviceMetrics and userAgent Strings. The userAgent string specifies which Mobile device should be used, such as Pixel 2 XL, and the rendering engine versions:

```
    Map<String, Object> mobileEmulation = new HashMap<>();
    mobileEmulation.put("deviceMetrics", deviceMetrics);
    mobileEmulation.put("userAgent", "Mozilla/5.0 (Linux; Android 8.0.0;" +
            "Pixel 2 XL Build/OPD1.170816.004) AppleWebKit/537.36 (KHTML,
like Gecko) " +
            "Chrome/67.0.3396.99 Mobile Safari/537.36");
```

Finally, we need to pass the mobileEmulation hashmap to the ChromeOptions class, and call the setExperimentalOption() method that passes the mobileEmulation hashmap:

```
ChromeOptions chromeOptions = new ChromeOptions();
chromeOptions.setExperimentalOption("mobileEmulation", mobileEmulation);

driver = new ChromeDriver(chromeOptions);
```

This will load the mobile version of the application and Selenium will run the test as usual.

We can get the `userAgent` string after configuring the mobile device. Go to the **Network** tab in the Chrome Developer tools. Reload the page, select the first request from the list, and copy the value of the **User-Agent** key from the **Headers** tab, as shown in the following screenshot:

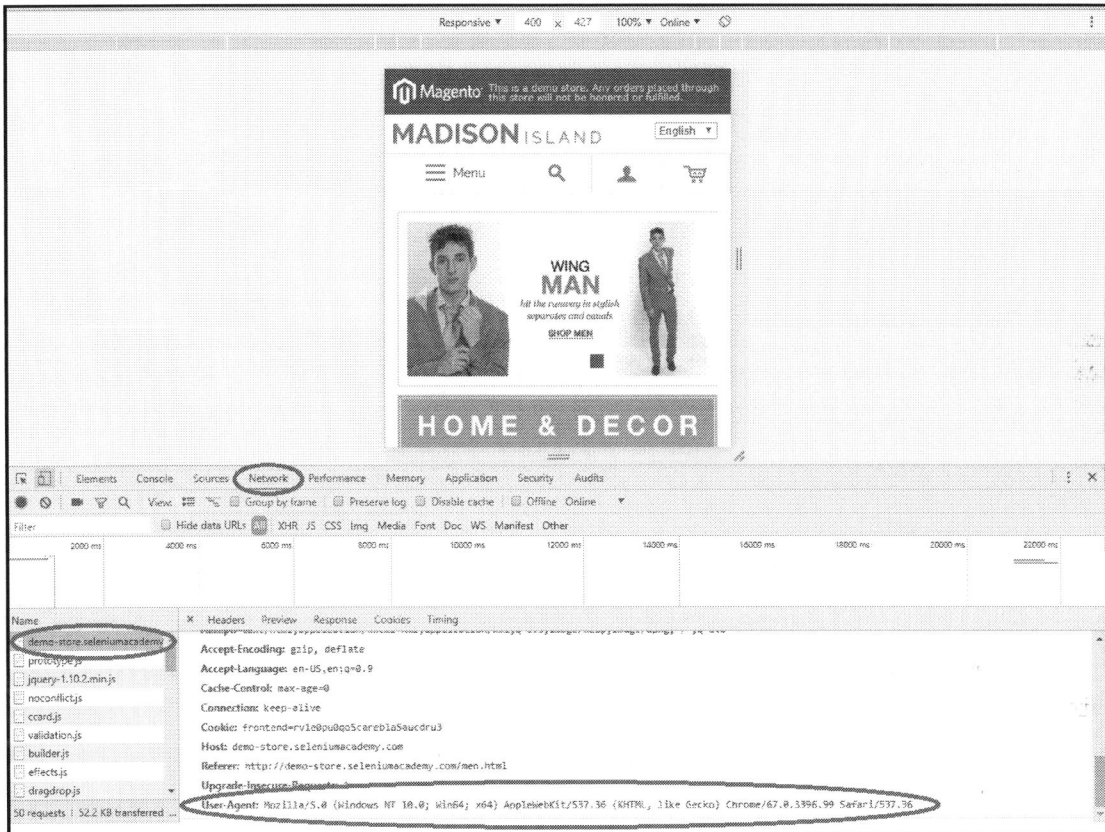

> We can set a number of Chrome preferences using the `setExperimentalOptions()` method and the `ChromeOptions` class.

Adding ChromeExtensions

Similar to Firefox, we can add extensions to the Chrome browser by specifying the location of the extension. We can add **Packed** (.crx file) or **Unpacked** (folder) extensions using the ChromeOptions class.

To add a **Packed** extension, we need to call the `addExtension()` method:

```
ChromeOptions chromeOptions = new ChromeOptions();
chromeOptions.addExtensions(new File("/path/to/extension.crx"));
ChromeDriver driver = new ChromeDriver(chromeOptions);
```

To add an Unpacked extension, we need to use the `addArguments()` method, which will load the extension reading the specified folder while launching the Chrome binary. This is done as follows:

```
ChromeOptions chromeOptions = new ChromeOptions();
chromeOptions.addArguments("load-extension=/path/to/extension");
ChromeDriver driver = new ChromeDriver(chromeOptions);
```

Similarly, you can use Chrome options to add more extensions, arguments, and Binaries to your Chrome browser.

InternetExplorerDriver

In order to execute your test scripts on the Internet Explorer browser, you need WebDriver's InternetExplorerDriver. Similar to Google Chrome and Firefox, we need to download the **IEDriver Server** executable from `https://www.seleniumhq.org/download/` for Internet Explorer.

The IEDriver server then uses its IEThreadExplorer class, which is written in C++, to drive the IE browser using the Component Object Model framework.

Writing your first test script for the IE browser

Now you are all set to write test scripts that run on the Internet Explorer browser. The following is the code that instantiates InternetExplorerDriver:

```
public class SearchTest {

    WebDriver driver;
```

```
@BeforeMethod
public void setup() {

    System.setProperty("webdriver.ie.driver",
            "./src/test/resources/drivers/IEDriverServer.exe");

    driver = new InternetExplorerDriver();
    driver.get("http://demo-store.seleniumacademy.com/");
}

@Test
public void searchProduct() {

    // find search box and enter search string
    WebElement searchBox = driver.findElement(By.name("q"));

    searchBox.sendKeys("Phones");

    WebElement searchButton =
            driver.findElement(By.className("search-button"));

    searchButton.click();

    assertThat(driver.getTitle())
            .isEqualTo("Search results for: 'Phones'");
}

@AfterMethod
public void tearDown() {
    driver.quit();
}
}
```

Understanding IEDriver capabilities

In this section, we will discuss some of the important capabilities of InternetExplorerDriver. This is where we have set the IEDriver capability to ignore the security domains. The code is as follows:

```
DesiredCapabilities ieCapabilities = DesiredCapabilities
.internetExplorer();
ieCapabilities.setCapability(InternetExplorerDriver.INTRODUCE_FLAK
INESS_BY_IGNORING_SECURITY_DOMAINS,true);
```

Similar to `INTRODUCE_FLAKINESS_BY_IGNORING_SECURITY_DOMAINS`, IEDriver has many other capabilities. The following is a list with an explanation on why it is used:

Capability	Value to be Set	Purpose
INITIAL_BROWSER_URL	URL, for example, `http://www. google. com`	This capability is set with the URL value that the driver should navigate the browser to as soon as it opens up.
INTRODUCE_ FLAKINESS_BY_ IGNORING_SECURITY_ DOMAINS	True or False	This defines whether the IEDriverServer should ignore the browser security domain settings.
NATIVE_EVENTS	True or False	This tells the IEDriver server whether to use native events or JavaScript events for executing mouse or keyboard actions.
REQUIRE_WINDOW_ FOCUS	True or False	If the value is set to True, the IE browser window will get the focus. This is especially useful when executing native events.
ENABLE_PERSISTENT_ HOVERING	True or False	If set to True, IEDriver will persistently fire a mouse-hovering event. This is especially important in overcoming issues with how IE handles mouse-over events.
IE_ENSURE_CLEAN_ SESSION	True or False	If True, it clears all the cookies, cache, history, and saved form data of all the instances of IE.
IE_SET_PROXY_BY_ SERVER	True or False	If True, the proxy server settings for the IEDriver server is used. If False, WindowsProxyManager is used to determine the proxy server.

Edge Driver

Microsoft Edge is the latest web browser launched with Microsoft Windows 10. Microsoft Edge was one of the first browsers to implement the W3C WebDriver standard and provides built-in support for Selenium WebDriver.

Similar to Internet Explorer, in order to execute test scripts on the Microsoft Edge browser, we need to use the EdgeDriver class and a standalone Microsoft WebDriver Server executable. The Microsoft WebDriver Server is maintained by the Microsoft Edge development team. You can find more information at `https://docs.microsoft.com/en-gb/microsoft-edge/webdriver`

Writing your first test script for the Edge browser

Let's set up the Microsoft WebDriver Server and create a test for testing the search feature on Microsoft Edge. We need to download and install Microsoft WebDriver Server on Windows 10 (https://developer.microsoft.com/en-us/microsoft-edge/tools/webdriver/):

```java
public class SearchTest {

    WebDriver driver;

    @BeforeMethod
    public void setup() {

        System.setProperty("webdriver.edge.driver",
                "./src/test/resources/drivers/MicrosoftWebDriver.exe");

        EdgeOptions options = new EdgeOptions();
        options.setPageLoadStrategy("eager");
        driver = new EdgeDriver(options);
        driver.get("http://demo-store.seleniumacademy.com/");
    }

    @Test
    public void searchProduct() {

        // find search box and enter search string
        WebElement searchBox = driver.findElement(By.name("q"));

        searchBox.sendKeys("Phones");

        WebElement searchButton =
                driver.findElement(By.className("search-button"));

        searchButton.click();

        assertThat(driver.getTitle())
                .isEqualTo("Search results for: 'Phones'");
    }

    @AfterMethod
    public void tearDown() {
        driver.quit();
    }
}
```

The Microsoft WebDriver Server is a standalone server executable that implements WebDriver's JSON-wire protocol, which works as a glue between the test script and the Microsoft Edge browser. In the preceding code, we need to specify the path of the executable using the `webdriver.edge.driver` property similarly to other browser configurations we saw earlier in the chapter.

We also set the Page Load Strategy to eager, using the `EdgeOptions` class:

```
EdgeOptions options = new EdgeOptions();
options.setPageLoadStrategy("eager");
```

When navigating to a new page URL, Selenium WebDriver, by default, waits until the page has fully loaded before passing the control to the next command. This works well in most cases but can cause long wait times on pages that have to load a large number of third-party resources. Using the `eager` page-load strategy can make test execution faster. The eager page-load strategy will wait until the `DOMContentLoaded` event is complete, that is, the HTML content is downloaded and parsed only, but other resources, such as images, may still be loading. However, this may introduce flakiness where elements are dynamically loaded.

Safari Driver

With Selenium 3.0 and WebDriver becoming the W3C standard, Apple now provides SafariDriver built into the browser. We do not have to download it separately. However, in order to work it with Selenium WebDriver, we have to set a **Develop | Allow Remote Automation** option from Safari's main menu, as shown in the following screenshot:

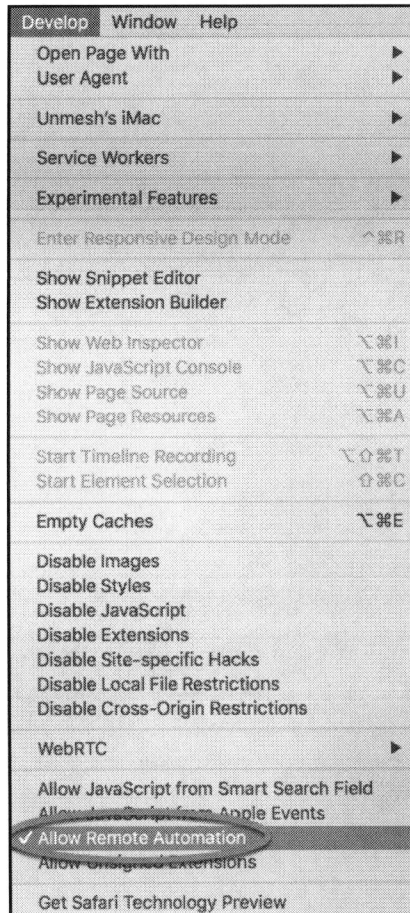

Allowing remote automation

Writing your first test script for the Safari browser

This is as straight forward. The following is the test script using the Safari Driver:

```
public class SearchTest {

    WebDriver driver;

    @BeforeMethod
```

```
public void setup() {

    driver = new SafariDriver();
    driver.get("http://demo-store.seleniumacademy.com/");
}

@Test
public void searchProduct() {

    // find search box and enter search string
    WebElement searchBox = driver.findElement(By.name("q"));

    searchBox.sendKeys("Phones");

    WebElement searchButton =
            driver.findElement(By.className("search-button"));

    searchButton.click();

    assertThat(driver.getTitle())
            .isEqualTo("Search results for: 'Phones'");
}

@AfterMethod
public void tearDown() {
    driver.quit();
}
}
```

In the preceding code, we created an instance of the `SafariDriver` class to launch and execute tests on the Safari browser.

Summary

In this chapter, you have seen some of the major implementations of WebDriver that are widely used in the industry. We looked at some of the key configuration options for each browser and how to use them for custom profiles and mobile emulation. The underlying technology for every driver is JSONWire Protocol, which is fundamental for all the implementations. In the next chapter, we will learn how to use the Java 8 Stream API and Lambda functions with the Selenium WebDriver API.

Questions

1. What is the significance of WebDriver becoming W3C Specification?
2. True or False: WebDriver is an interface?
3. Which browsers support Headless testing?
4. How can we test mobile websites with Chrome?

Further information

You can check out the following links for more information about the topics covered in this chapter:

- Read the WebDriver Specification at `https://www.w3.org/TR/webdriver/`
- You can find more details about GeckoDriver and its capabilities at `https://github.com/mozilla/geckodriver`
- Read more about the ChromeDriver capabilities at `http://chromedriver.chromium.org/capabilities` and mobile emulation at `http://chromedriver.chromium.org/capabilities`
- Read more about EdgeDriver capabilities at `https://docs.microsoft.com/en-gb/microsoft-edge/webdriver`

Using Java 8 Features with Selenium

3

With Selenium 3.0 moving to Java 8, we can use some of the new features of Java 8, such as Stream API and Lambda or Anonymous functions to create scripts in a functional programming style. We do so by reducing the number of lines of code as well as reaping the benefits of the newer features of the language. In this chapter, we will cover these topics:

- Introducing Java 8 Stream API
- Using Stream API to collect and filter data
- Using Stream API with Selenium WebDriver

Introducing Java 8 Stream API

The Stream API is a new addition to the Collections API in Java 8. The Stream API brings new ways to process collections of objects. A stream represents a sequence of elements and supports different kinds of operations (**filter**, **sort**, **map**, and **collect**) from a collection. We can chain these operations together to form a pipeline to query the data, as shown in this diagram:

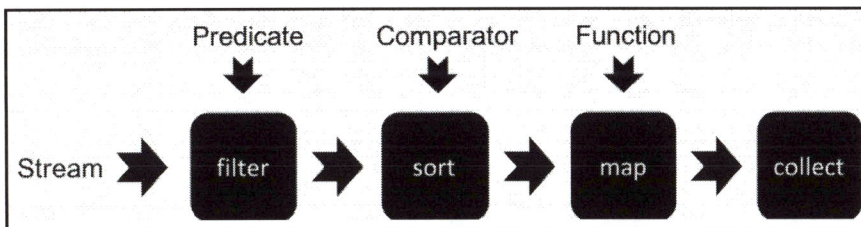

We can obtain a Stream from a collection using the `.stream()` method. For example, we have a dropdown of languages supported by the sample web application displayed in the header section. Let's capture this in an `Array list`, as follows:

```
List<String> languages = new ArrayList<String>();
languages.add("English");
languages.add("German");
languages.add("French");
```

If we have to print the list members, we will use a `for` loop in the following way:

```
for(String language : languages) {
    System.out.println(language);
}
```

Using the streams **API** we can obtain the stream by calling the `.stream()` method on the `languages` array list and print the members in the following way:

```
languages.stream().forEach(System.out::println);
```

After obtaining the stream, we called the `forEach()` method, passing the action we wanted to take on each element, that is, output the member value on the console, using the `System.out.println` method.

Once we have obtained a Stream from a collection, we can use that stream to process the elements or members of the collection.

Stream.filter()

We can filter a stream using the `filter()` method. Let's filter the stream obtained from the `languages` list to filter items starting with **E**, as shown in the following code:

```
stream.filter( item -> item.startsWith("E") );
```

The `filter()` method takes a Predicate as a parameter. The `predicate` interface contains a function called `boolean test(T t)` that takes a single parameter and returns a boolean. In the preceding example, we passed the lambda expression `item -> item.startsWith("E")` to the `test()` function.

When the `filter()` method is called on a Stream, the filter passed as a parameter to the `filter()` function is stored internally. The items are not filtered immediately.

The parameter passed to the `filter()` function determines what items in the stream should be processed and what should be excluded. If the `Predicate.test()` function returns `true` for an item, that means it should be processed. If `false` is returned, the item is not processed. In the preceding example, the `test()` function will return true for all items starting with the character E.

Stream.sort()

We can sort a stream by calling the `sort()` function. Let's use the `sort()` function on the `languages` list, as shown in the following code:

```
languages.stream().sorted();
```

This will sort the elements in alphabetical order. We can provide a lambda expression to sort the elements using custom comparison logic.

Stream.map()

Streams provide a map() method to map the elements of a stream into another form. We can map the elements into a new object. Let's take the previous example and convert the elements of languages list to uppercase, as shown here:

```
languages.stream().map(item -> item.toUpperCase());
```

This will map all elements that are strings in the language collection to their uppercase equivalents. Again, this doesn't actually perform the mapping; it only configures the stream for mapping. Once one of the stream processing methods is invoked, the mapping (and filtering) will be performed.

Stream.collect()

Streams provide the collect() method, among the other methods, for stream processing on the Stream interface. When the collect() method is invoked, filtering and mapping will take place, and the object resulting from those actions will be collected. Let's take the previous example and obtain a new list of languages in uppercase, as shown in the following code:

```
List<String> upperCaseLanguages = languages.stream()
        .map(item -> item.toUpperCase())
        .collect(Collectors.toList());

System.out.println(upperCaseLanguages);
```

This example creates a stream, adds a map to convert the strings to uppercase, and collects all objects in a new list. We can also use the filter or sort method and collect the resulting list based on conditions applied in the filter method.

Stream.min() and Stream.max()

The Streams API provides min() and max() methods—stream processing for finding the minimum or maximum value in the stream respectively.

Let's take an example in the context of the sample application we're testing. We will create a simple Java class called Product that stores the name and price of products returned by the search. We want to find the product that has the minimum price and the one that has the maximum price. Our product class will have two members, as shown in the following code:

```
class Product {
    String name;
    Double price;

    public Product(String name, double price) {
        this.name = name;
        this.price = price;
    }

    public String getName() {
        return name;
    }

    public Double getPrice() {
        return price;
    }
}
```

Let's create a list of products returned by the search result, as shown here:

```
List<Product> searchResult = new ArrayList<>();
searchResult.add(new Product("MADISON OVEREAR HEADPHONES", 125.00));
searchResult.add(new Product("MADISON EARBUDS", 35.00));
searchResult.add(new Product("MP3 PLAYER WITH AUDIO", 185.00));
```

We can call the `.min()` function by passing the comparison attribute, in this case, price, using the `.getPrice()` method. The `.min()` function will use the price attribute and return the element that has the lowest price, as shown in this code:

```
Product product = searchResult.stream()
        .min(Comparator.comparing(item -> item.getPrice()))
        .get();

System.out.println("The product with lowest price is " +
product.getName());
```

The `get()` method will return the object returned by the `min()` function. We will store this in an instance of Product. The `min()` function finds **MADISON EARBUDS** as the lowest-priced product, as shown in the following console output:

```
The product with lowest price is MADISON EARBUDS
```

As opposed to the `min()` function, the `max()` function will return the product with the highest price, as shown in the following code:

```
product = searchResult.stream()
        .max(Comparator.comparing(item -> item.getPrice()))
        .get();
System.out.println("The product with highest price is " +
product.getName());
```

The `max()` function finds **MP3 PLAYER WITH AUDIO** as the highest-priced product:

```
The product with highest price is MP3 PLAYER WITH AUDIO
```

The `min()` and `max()` functions return an optional instance, which has a `get()` method to obtain the object. The `get()` method will return null if the stream has no elements.

Both the functions take a comparator as a parameter. The `Comparator.comparing()` method creates a comparator based on the lambda expression passed to it.

Stream.count()

The streams API provides a count method that returns the number of elements in the stream after filtering has been applied. Let's take the previous example to get a count of Products from the MADISON brand:

```
long count = searchResult.stream()
        .filter(item -> item.getName().startsWith("MADISON"))
        .count();
System.out.println("The number of products from MADISON are: " + count);
```

The `count()` method returns a `long`, which is the count of elements matching with the filter criteria. In this example, the following output will be displayed on the console:

```
The number of products from MADISON are: 2
```

Using Stream API with Selenium WebDriver

Now that we have introduced Streams API and its various functions, let's see how we can use them in our tests.

Filtering and counting WebElements

Let's start with a simple test to determine the links displayed on the home page of the sample application. We get all the links from the home page and print their count, followed by the count of links that are visible on the page, as shown in the following code:

```
@Test
public void linksTest() {

    List<WebElement> links = driver.findElements(By.tagName("a"));
    System.out.println("Total Links : " + links.size());

    long count = links.stream().filter(item -> item.isDisplayed()).count();
    System.out.println("Total Link visible " + count);
}
```

In the preceding code, we used the `findElements()` method along with `By.tagName` to get all the links from the home page. However, for finding out the visible links out of them, we used the `filter()` function with a predicate to test whether the links are displayed. This is done by calling the `isDisplayed()` method of the `WebElement` interface. The `isDisplayed` method will return `true` if the link is displayed; otherwise it will return `false`. Finally, we called the `count()` method to get the count of links returned by the `filter()` function. This will show the following output on the console:

```
Total Links : 88
Total Link visible 37
```

Filtering element attributes

In the example code, we will filter a list of images that have an empty `alt` attribute defined. This is useful if you want to check the accessibility of images displayed on the page. As per the accessibility guidelines, all images should have the `alt` attribute defined. This is done by filtering images, by testing the `getAttribute("alt")` method; it returns an empty string, as shown in the following code:

```java
@Test
public void imgAltTest() {

    List<WebElement> images = driver.findElements(By.tagName("img"));

    System.out.println("Total Images : " + images.size());

    List<WebElement> imagesWithOutAlt = images.stream()
            .filter(item -> item.getAttribute("alt") == "")
            .collect(Collectors.toList());
    System.out.println("Total images without alt attribute " +
imagesWithOutAlt);
}
```

The `filter()` function will return the list of all image elements that have an empty `alt` attribute defined.

Using the Map function to get the text value from elements

In this example, we will modify the search test we created in earlier chapters to test the results containing the list of expected products, as shown in the following code:

```java
@Test
public void searchProduct() {

    // find search box and enter search string
    WebElement searchBox = driver.findElement(By.name("q"));

    searchBox.sendKeys("Phones");

    WebElement searchButton =
            driver.findElement(By.className("search-button"));

    searchButton.click();

    assertThat(driver.getTitle())
            .isEqualTo("Search results for: 'Phones'");


    List<WebElement> searchItems = driver
            .findElements(By.cssSelector("h2.product-name a"));

    List<String> expectedProductNames =
            Arrays.asList("MADISON EARBUDS",
                    "MADISON OVEREAR HEADPHONES",
                    "MP3 PLAYER WITH AUDIO");

    List<String> productNames = searchItems.stream()
            .map(WebElement::getText)
            .collect(Collectors.toList());

    assertThat(productNames).
            isEqualTo(expectedProductNames);

}
```

In the preceding code, we created a list of all the matching products returned by the findElements() method. We then retrieved the text of each element by calling the map() function and mapped the return values to a list of strings. This is compared with the expectedProductNames list.

Filtering and performing actions on WebElements

Let's further modify the search test and find a product matching with a given name. We will then click on the product to open the product details page, as shown in this code:

```
@Test
 public void searchAndViewProduct() {

        // find search box and enter search string
        WebElement searchBox = driver.findElement(By.name("q"));

        searchBox.sendKeys("Phones");

        WebElement searchButton =
                driver.findElement(By.className("search-button"));

        searchButton.click();

        assertThat(driver.getTitle())
                .isEqualTo("Search results for: 'Phones'");

        List<WebElement> searchItems = driver
                .findElements(By.cssSelector("h2.product-name a"));

        WebElement product = searchItems.stream()
                .filter(item -> item.getText().equalsIgnoreCase("MADISON
EARBUDS"))
                .findFirst()
                .get();

        product.click();

        assertThat(driver.getTitle())
                .isEqualTo("Madison Earbuds");
 }
```

In the preceding code, we used the `filter()` function to find a specific product from the list of WebElements. We retrieved the first matching product, using the `findFirst()` function. This will return a `WebElement` representing the link element. We then clicked on the element to open the product details page in the browser.

Thus, we can use Streams API in a number of ways to create functional, readable code with just a few lines.

Summary

In this short chapter, we learned how to use Selenium 8 Stream API and Lambda functions to simplify the Selenium WebDriver code. This helps you to write code in a functional programming style, which is more fluent and readable. Streams are useful for working with the list of WebElements. We can collect and filter data with a stream easily.

In the next `chapter`, we will explore the features of WebDriver for taking screenshots, handling Windows and Frames, synchronization, and managing cookies.

Questions

1. Which version of Java Streams API is introduced?
2. Explain the filter function of Streams API.
3. Which method of Streams API will return the number of matching elements from the filter() function?
4. We can use the map() function to filter a list of WebElements by attribute values: True or false?

Further information

You can check out the following links for more information about the topics covered in this chapter:

- Read more about Stream API at `https://www.oracle.com/technetwork/articles/java/ma14-java-se-8-streams-2177646.html` and `https://docs.oracle.com/javase/8/docs/api/java/util/stream/Stream.html`
- Read more about Lambda expressions at `https://docs.oracle.com/javase/tutorial/java/javaOO/lambdaexpressions.html`

4
Exploring the Features of WebDriver

So far, we have looked at various basic and advanced interactions that a user can perform on a web page using WebDriver. In this chapter, we will discuss the different capabilities and features of WebDriver that enable test script developers to have better control over WebDriver, and consequently of the web application that is being tested. The features that we are going to cover in this chapter are as follows:

- Taking screenshots
- Locating target windows and iFrames
- Exploring Navigate
- Waiting for WebElements to load
- Handling cookies

Let's get started without any further delay.

Taking screenshots

Taking a screenshot of a web page is a very useful capability of WebDriver. This is very handy when your test case fails, and you want to see the state of the application when the test case failed. The TakesScreenShot interface in the WebDriver library is implemented by all of the different variants of WebDriver, such as Firefox Driver, Internet Explorer Driver, Chrome Driver, and so on.

The TakesScreenShot capability is enabled in all of the browsers by default. Because this is a read-only capability, a user cannot toggle it. Before we see a code example that uses this capability, we should look at an important method of the TakesScreenShot interface—getScreenshotAs().

The API syntax for `getScreenshotAs()` is as follows:

```
public X getScreenshotAs(OutputType target)
```

Here, `OutputType` is another interface of the WebDriver library. We can ask WebDriver to output the screenshot in three different formats : `BASE64`, `BYTES` (raw data), and `FILE`. If you choose the `FILE` format, it writes the data into a `.png` file, which will be deleted once the JVM is killed. So, you should always copy that file into a safe location so that it can be used for later reference.

The return type is a specific output that depends on the selected `OutputType`. For example, selecting `OutputType.BYTES` will return a `byte` array, and selecting `OutputType.FILE` will return a file object.

Depending on the browser used, the output screenshot will be one of the following, in order of preference:

- The entire page
- The current window
- A visible portion of the current frame
- The screenshot of the entire display containing the browser

For example, if you are using Firefox Driver, `getScreenshotAs()` takes a screenshot of the entire page, but Chrome Driver returns only the visible portion of the current frame.

It's time to take a look at the following code example:

```
@BeforeMethod
public void setup() throws IOException {
    System.setProperty("webdriver.chrome.driver",
            "./src/test/resources/drivers/chromedriver");
    driver = new ChromeDriver();
    driver.get("http://demo-store.seleniumacademy.com/");

    File scrFile = ((TakesScreenshot)
driver).getScreenshotAs(OutputType.FILE);
    FileUtils.copyFile(scrFile, new File("./target/screenshot.png"));

}
```

In the preceding code, we used the `getScreenshotAs()` method to take the screenshot of the web page and save it to a file format. We can open the saved image from the target folder and examine it.

Locating target windows and Frames

WebDriver enables the developers to switch between multiple child windows, browser tabs, and frames used in the application. For example, when you click on an internet banking link on a bank web application, it will open the internet banking application in a separate window or Tab. At this point, you may want to switch back to the original window to handle some events. Similarly, you may have to deal with a web application that is divided into two frames on the web page. The frame on the left may contain navigation items, and the frame on the right displays the appropriate web page, based on what is selected in the frame on the left. Using WebDriver, you can develop test cases that can easily handle such complex situations.

The `WebDriver.TargetLocator` interface is used to locate a given frame or window. In this section, we will see how WebDriver handles switching between browser windows and between two frames in the same window.

Switching among windows

First, we will see a code example for handling multiple windows. For this chapter, there is an HTML file provided with this book named `Window.html`. It is a very basic web page that links to Google's search page. When you click on the link, the Google's search page is opened in a different window. Every time you open a web page using WebDriver in a browser window, WebDriver assigns a window handle to that. WebDriver uses the window handle to identify the window. At this point, in WebDriver, there are two window handles registered. Now, on the screen, you can see that the Google's search page is in the front and has the focus. At this point, if you want to switch to the first browser window, you can use WebDriver's `switchTo()` method to do that.

The API syntax for `TargetLocator` is as follows:

```
WebDriver.TargetLocator switchTo()
```

This method returns the `WebDriver.TargetLocator` instance, where you can tell the WebDriver whether to switch between browser windows or frames. Let's see how WebDriver deals with this:

```
public class WindowHandlingTest {

    WebDriver driver;

    @BeforeMethod
    public void setup() throws IOException {
```

```
        System.setProperty("webdriver.chrome.driver",
                "./src/test/resources/drivers/chromedriver");
        driver = new ChromeDriver();
        driver.get("http://guidebook.seleniumacademy.com/Window.html");
    }

    @Test
    public void handleWindow() {

        String firstWindow = driver.getWindowHandle();
        System.out.println("First Window Handle is: " + firstWindow);

        WebElement link = driver.findElement(By.linkText("Google Search"));
        link.click();

        String secondWindow = driver.getWindowHandle();
        System.out.println("Second Window Handle is: " + secondWindow);
        System.out.println("Number of Window Handles so for: "
                + driver.getWindowHandles().size());

        driver.switchTo().window(firstWindow);
    }

    @AfterMethod
    public void tearDown() {
        driver.quit();
    }
}
```

Observe the following line in the preceding code:

```
String firstWindow = driver.getWindowHandle();
```

Here, the driver returns the assigned identifier for the window. Now, before we move on to a different window, it is better to store this value so that if we want to switch back to this window, we can use this handle or identifier. To retrieve all the window handles that are registered with your driver so far, you can use the following method:

```
driver.getWindowHandles()
```

This will return the set of identifiers of all of the browser window handles opened in the driver session so far. Now, in our example, after we open Google's search page, the window corresponding to it is shown in front with the focus. If you want to go back to the first window, you have to use the following code:

```
driver.switchTo().window(firstWindow);
```

This will bring the first window into focus.

Switching between frames

Let's now see how we can handle switching between the frames of a web page. In the HTML files supplied with this book, you will see a file named `Frames.html`. If you open that, you will see two HTML files loaded in two different frames. Let's see how we can switch between them and type into the text boxes available in each frame:

```
public class FrameHandlingTest {
    WebDriver driver;

    @BeforeMethod
    public void setup() throws IOException {
        System.setProperty("webdriver.chrome.driver",
                "./src/test/resources/drivers/chromedriver");
        driver = new ChromeDriver();
        driver.get("http://guidebook.seleniumacademy.com/Frames.html");
    }

    @Test
    public void switchBetweenFrames() {

        // First Frame
        driver.switchTo().frame(0);
        WebElement firstField = driver.findElement(By.name("1"));
        firstField.sendKeys("I'm Frame One");
        driver.switchTo().defaultContent();

        // Second Frame
        driver.switchTo().frame(1);
        WebElement secondField = driver.findElement(By.name("2"));
        secondField.sendKeys("I'm Frame Two");
    }

    @AfterMethod
    public void tearDown() {
        driver.quit();
    }
}
```

In the preceding code, we have used `switchTo().frame` instead of `switchTo().window` because we are moving across frames.

The API syntax for `frame` is as follows:

```
WebDriver frame(int index)
```

This method takes the index of the frame that you want to switch to. If your web page has three frames, WebDriver indexes them as 0, 1, and 2, where the zero index is assigned to the first frame encountered in the DOM. Similarly, you can switch between frames using their names by using the previous overloaded method. The API syntax is as follows:

```
WebDriver frame(String frameNameOrframeID)
```

You can pass the name of the frame or its ID. Using this, you can switch to the frame if you are not sure about the index of the target frame. The other overloaded method is as follows:

```
WebDriver frame(WebElement frameElement)
```

The input parameter is the WebElement of the frame. Let's consider our code example: First, we have switched to our first frame and typed into the text field. Then, instead of directly switching to the second frame, we have come to the main or default content and then switched to the second frame. The code for that is as follows:

```
driver.switchTo().defaultContent();
```

This is very important. If you don't do this and try to switch to the second frame while you are still in the first frame, your WebDriver will complain, saying that it couldn't find a frame with index 1. This is because the WebDriver searches for the second frame in the context of the first frame, which is obviously not available. So, you have to first come to the top-level container and switch to the frame you are interested in.

After switching to the default content, you can now switch to the second frame using the following code:

```
driver.switchTo().frame(1);
```

Thus, you can switch between the frames and execute the corresponding WebDriver actions.

Handling alerts

Apart from switching between windows and frames, you may have to handle various modal dialogs in a web application. For this, WebDriver provides an API to handle alert dialogs. The API for that is as follows:

```
Alert alert()
```

The preceding method will switch to the currently active modal dialog on the web page. This returns an `Alert` instance, where appropriate actions can be taken on that dialog. If there is no dialog currently present, and you invoke this API, it throws back a `NoAlertPresentException`.

The `Alert` interface contains a number of APIs to execute different actions. The following list discusses them, one after the other:

- `void accept()`: This is equivalent to the **OK** button action on the dialog. The corresponding **OK** button actions are invoked when the `accept()` action is taken on a dialog.
- `void dismiss()`: This is equivalent to clicking on the **CANCEL** action button.
- `java.lang.String getText()`: This will return the text that appears on the dialog. This can be used if you want to evaluate the text on the modal dialog.
- `void sendKeys(java.lang.String keysToSend)`: This will allow the developer to type in some text into the alert if the alert has some provision for it.

Exploring Navigate

As we know, WebDriver talks to individual browsers natively. This way it has better control, not just over the web page, but over the browser itself. **Navigate** is one such feature of WebDriver that allows the test script developer to work with the browser's back, forward, and refresh controls. As users of a web application, quite often, we use the browser's back and forward controls to navigate between the pages of a single application, or, sometimes, multiple applications. As a test-script developer, you may want to develop tests that observe the behavior of the application when browser navigation buttons are clicked, especially the **back** button. For example, if you use your navigation button in a banking application, the session should expire and the user should be logged out. So, using the WebDriver's navigation feature, you can emulate those actions.

The method that is used for this purpose is `navigate()`. The following is its API syntax:

```
WebDriver.Navigation navigate()
```

Obviously, there is no input parameter for this method, but the return type is the `WebDriver.Navigation` interface, which contains all of the browser navigation options that help you navigate through your browser's history.

Now let's see a code example and then analyze the code:

```
@Test
public void searchProduct() {
    driver.navigate().to("http://demo-store.seleniumacademy.com/");

    // find search box and enter search string
    WebElement searchBox = driver.findElement(By.name("q"));

    searchBox.sendKeys("Phones");

    WebElement searchButton =
            driver.findElement(By.className("search-button"));

    searchButton.click();

    assertThat(driver.getTitle())
            .isEqualTo("Search results for: 'Phones'");

    driver.navigate().back();
    driver.navigate().forward();
    driver.navigate().refresh();
}
```

The preceding code opens the demo application's Homepage, and, at first, searches for `Phone`; then, after the search results are loaded. Now that we have a navigation history created in the browser, it uses WebDriver navigation to go back in the browser history, and then go forward and refresh the page.

Let's analyze the navigation methods used in the preceding code. The line of code that initially loads the demo application's Homepage uses the `to()` method of the `Navigation` class, as follows:

```
driver.navigate().to("http://demo-store.seleniumacademy.com/");
```

Here, the `driver.navigate()` method returns the `WebDriver.Navigation` interface on which the `to()` method is used to navigate to a web URL.

The API syntax is as follows:

```
void to(java.lang.String url)
```

The input parameter for this method is the `url` string that has to be loaded in the browser. This method will load the page in the browser by using the HTTP GET operation, and it will block everything else until the page is completely loaded. This method is the same as the `driver.get(String url)` method.

The `WebDriver.Navigation` interface also provides an overloaded method of this `to()` method to make it easy to pass the URL. The API syntax for it is as follows:

```
void to(java.net.URL url)
```

Next, in the code example, we did a search for `Phone`. Then, we tried to use Navigation's `back()` method to emulate our browser's **back** button, using the following line of code:

```
driver.navigate().back();
```

This will take the browser to the home page. The API syntax for this method is pretty straightforward; it's as follows:

```
void back()
```

This method doesn't take any input and doesn't return anything as well, but it takes the browser one level back in its history.

Then, the next method in the navigation is the `forward()` method, which is pretty much similar to the `back()` method, but it takes the browser one level in the opposite direction. In the preceding code example, the following is invoked:

```
driver.navigate().forward();
```

The API syntax for the method is as follows:

```
void forward()
```

This method doesn't take any input, and doesn't return anything either, but it takes the browser one level forward in its history.

The last line of code in the code example uses the `refresh()` method of WebDriver's navigation:

```
driver.navigate().refresh();
```

This method will reload the current URL to emulate the browser's *refresh* (*F5* key) action. The API syntax is as follows:

```
void refresh()
```

As you can see, the syntax is very similar to the `back()` and `forward()` methods, and this method will reload the current URL. Hence, these are the various methods WebDriver provides developers to emulate some browser actions.

Waiting for WebElements to load

If you have a previous UI automation experience, I'm sure you would have come across a situation where your test script couldn't find an element on the web page because the web page was still loading. This could happen due to various reasons. One classic example is when the application server or web server is serving the page too slowly due to resource constraints; the other could be when you are accessing the page on a very slow network. The reason could be that the element on the web page is not loaded by the time your test script tries to find it. This is where you have to calculate and configure the average wait time for your test scripts to wait for WebElements to load on the web page.

WebDriver provides test-script developers with a very handy feature to manage wait time. *Wait time* is the time your driver will wait for the WebElement to load, before it gives up and throws `NoSuchElementException`. **Remember, in** `Chapter 1`, *Introducing WebDriver and WebElements*, we discussed the `findElement(By by)` method that throws a `NoSuchElementException` when it cannot find the target WebElement.

There are two ways by which you can make the WebDriver wait for WebElement. They are **Implicit Wait Time** and **Explicit Wait Time**. Implicit timeouts are common to all the WebElements and have a global timeout period associated with them, but the explicit timeouts can be configured to individual WebElements. Let's discuss each of them here.

Implicit wait time

Implicit wait time is used when you want to configure the WebDriver's wait time as a whole for the application under test. Imagine you have hosted a web application on a local server and on a remote server. Obviously, the time to load for a web page hosted on a local server would be less than the time for the same page hosted on a remote server, due to network latency. Now, if you want to execute your test cases against each of them, you may have to configure the wait time accordingly, such that your test case doesn't end up spending more time waiting for the page, or spend nowhere near enough time, and timeout. To handle these kinds of wait-time issues, WebDriver provides an option to set the implicit wait time for all of the operations that the driver does using the `manage()` method.

Let's see a code example of implicit wait time:

```
driver = new ChromeDriver();
driver.navigate().to("http://demo-store.seleniumacademy.com/");
driver.manage().timeouts().implicitlyWait(10, TimeUnit.SECONDS);
```

Let's analyze the following highlighted line of code:

```
driver.manage().timeouts().implicitlyWait(10, TimeUnit.SECONDS);
```

Here, `driver.manage().timeouts()` returns the `WebDriver.Timeouts` interface, which declares a method named `implicitlyWait`, which is where you specify the amount of time the driver should wait when searching for a WebElement on a web page if it is not immediately present. Periodically, the WebDriver will poll for the WebElement on the web page, until the maximum wait time specified to the previous method is over. In the preceding code, 10 seconds is the maximum wait time your driver will wait for any WebElement to load on your browser. If it loads within this time period, WebDriver proceeds with the rest of the code; otherwise, it will throw `NoSuchElementException`.

Use this method when you want to specify a maximum wait time, which is generally common for most of the WebElements on your web application. The various factors that influence the performance of your page are network bandwidth, server configuration, and so on. Based on those conditions, as a developer of your WebDriver test cases, you have to arrive at a value for the maximum implicit wait time, such that your test cases don't take too long to execute, and, at the same time, don't timeout very frequently.

Explicit wait time

Implicit timeout is generic to all the WebElements of a web page. But, if you have one specific WebElement in your application, where you want to wait for a very long time, this approach may not work. Setting the implicit wait time to the value of this very long time period will delay your entire test suite execution. So, you have to make an exception for only a particular case, such as this WebElement. To handle such scenarios, WebDriver has an explicit wait time for a WebElement.

So, let's see how you can wait for a particular WebElement using WebDriver, with the following code:

```
WebElement searchBox = (new WebDriverWait(driver, 20))
        .until((ExpectedCondition<WebElement>) d ->
d.findElement(By.name("q")));
```

The highlighted code is where we have created a conditional wait for a particular WebElement. The `ExpectedCondition` interface can be used to apply the conditional wait to a WebElement. Here, WebDriver will wait for a maximum of 20 seconds for this particular WebElement. The implicit timeout doesn't get applied for this WebElement. If the WebElement doesn't load within the 20 seconds maximum wait time, as we know, the driver throws a `NoSuchElementException`. Thus, you can override the implicit wait time exclusively for the WebElements you think will take more time, by using this handy explicit wait time.

Handling cookies

Let's say you are automating the demo application. There could be many scenarios you want to automate, such as searching for products, adding products to the shopping cart, checkout, returns, and so on. For all these actions, one common thing is to have to log into the demo application in each of the test cases. So, logging into the application in every test case of yours will increase the overall test execution time significantly. To reduce the execution time of your test cases, you can actually skip signing in for every test case. This can be done by signing in once and writing all the cookies of that domain into a file. From the next login onward, you can actually load the cookies from the file and add them to the driver.

To fetch all the cookies that are loaded for a web page, WebDriver provides the following method:

```
driver.manage().getCookies()
```

This will return all the cookies that the web page stores in the current session. Each cookie is associated with a name, value, domain, path, expiry, and the status of whether it is secure or not. The server to validate a client cookie parses all of these values. Now, we will store all of this information for each cookie in a file so that our individual test cases read from this file and load that information into the driver. Hence, you can skip the login, because once your driver session has this information in it, the application server treats your browser session as authenticated and directly takes you to your requested URL. The following is a quick code to store the cookie information:

```
public class StoreCookieInfo {
    WebDriver driver;

    @BeforeMethod
    public void setup() throws IOException {
        System.setProperty("webdriver.chrome.driver",
                "./src/test/resources/drivers/chromedriver");
```

```
        driver = new ChromeDriver();
driver.get("http://demo-
store.seleniumacademy.com/customer/account/login/");
    }

    @Test
    public void storeCookies() {
driver.findElement(By.id("email")).sendKeys("user@seleniumacademy.com");
        driver.findElement(By.id("pass")).sendKeys("tester");
        driver.findElement(By.id("send2")).submit();

        File dataFile = new File("./target/browser.data");
        try {
            dataFile.delete();
            dataFile.createNewFile();
            FileWriter fos = new FileWriter(dataFile);
            BufferedWriter bos = new BufferedWriter(fos);
            for (Cookie ck : driver.manage().getCookies()) {
                bos.write((ck.getName() + ";" + ck.getValue() + ";" + ck.
                    getDomain()
                    + ";" + ck.getPath() + ";" + ck.getExpiry() + ";" +
ck.

                    isSecure()));
                bos.newLine();
            }
            bos.flush();
            bos.close();
            fos.close();
        } catch (Exception ex) {
            ex.printStackTrace();
        }
    }

    @AfterMethod
    public void tearDown() {
        driver.quit();
    }
}
```

From now on, for every test case or a set of test cases, load the cookie information from the `browser.data` file, and add it to the driver using the following method:

```
driver.manage().addCookie(ck);
```

After you add this information to your browser session and go to the dashboard page, it will automatically redirect you to the home page, without asking for a login, thus avoiding a login every time, for every test case. The code that adds all of the previous cookies to the driver is as follows:

```
public class LoadCookieInfo {
    WebDriver driver;

    @BeforeMethod
    public void setup() throws IOException {
        System.setProperty("webdriver.chrome.driver",
                "./src/test/resources/drivers/chromedriver");
        driver = new ChromeDriver();
        driver.get("http://demo-store.seleniumacademy.com");
    }

    @Test
    public void loadCookies() {
        try {
            File dataFile = new File("./target/browser.data");
            FileReader fr = new FileReader(dataFile);
            BufferedReader br = new BufferedReader(fr);
            String line;
            while ((line = br.readLine()) != null) {
                StringTokenizer str = new StringTokenizer(line, ";");
                while (str.hasMoreTokens()) {
                    String name = str.nextToken();
                    String value = str.nextToken();
                    String domain = str.nextToken();
                    String path = str.nextToken();
                    Date expiry = null;
                    String dt;
                    if (!(dt = str.nextToken()).equals("null")) {
                        SimpleDateFormat formatter =
                                new SimpleDateFormat("E MMM d HH:mm:ss z
yyyy");

                        expiry = formatter.parse(dt);
                    }

                    boolean isSecure = new Boolean(str.nextToken()).
                            booleanValue();
                    Cookie ck = new Cookie(name, value, domain, path,
expiry, isSecure);

                    driver.manage().addCookie(ck);
                }
            }

        driver.get("http://demo-
```

```
store.seleniumacademy.com/customer/account/index/");
            assertThat(driver.findElement(By.cssSelector("div.page-
title")).getText())
                    .isEqualTo("MY DASHBOARD");

        } catch (Exception ex) {
            ex.printStackTrace();
        }
    }

    @AfterMethod
    public void tearDown() {
        driver.quit();
    }
}
```

Hence, we can be directly taken to the home page without logging in again and again. As you can see, after creating the driver instance, we have the following line:

```
driver.get("http://demo-store.seleniumacademy.com");
```

Ideally, this line should be visible after we have set the cookies to the driver. But the reason it is at the top is that the WebDriver doesn't allow you to set the cookies directly to this session, because it treats those cookies as if they were from a different domain. Try removing the previous line of code and execute it, and you will see the error. So, initially, you will try to visit the home page to set the domain value of the driver to the application server domain and load all the cookies. When you execute this code, initially, you will see the home page of the application.

Hence, you can avoid entering the username and the password on the server, validating them again and again for each test, and thereby save a lot of time, by using the WebDriver's cookies feature.

Summary

In this chapter, we discussed various features of WebDriver, such as capturing screenshots and handling `Windows` and `Frames`. We also discussed implicit and explicit wait conditions for synchronization, and we used Navigation and the cookies API. Using these features will help you test your target web application more effectively, by designing more innovative test frameworks and test cases. In the next `chapter`, we will look at the **Actions** API to perform user interaction using keyboard and mouse events.

Questions

1. Which are the different formats we can use to output a screenshot?
2. How can we switch to another browser tab with Selenium?
3. True or false: The `defaultContent()` method will switch to the previously selected frame.
4. What navigation methods are available with Selenium?
5. How can we add a cookie using Selenium?
6. Explain the difference between an implicit wait and an explicit wait.

Further information

You can check the following links for more information about the topics covered in this chapter:

- You can find out more about how you can use a set of predefined expected conditions while using an explicit wait at `https://seleniumhq.github.io/selenium/docs/api/java/org/openqa/selenium/support/ui/ExpectedConditions.html`
- You can read more about WebDriver's features in Chapter 4, *Working with Selenium API* and Chapter 5 , *Synchronizing Tests,* in *Selenium Testing Tools Cookbook*, 2nd Edition, by Unmesh Gundecha, Packt Publications.

5
Exploring Advanced Interactions of WebDriver

In the previous chapter, we discussed the WebDriver interface and its features, including taking screenshots, working with Windows, frames, alerts, cookies, and synchronizing tests. In this chapter, we will go through some advanced ways of performing actions on WebElements. We will learn how to perform actions, using the actions API of Selenium WebDriver, including the following:

- Complex mouse actions, such as moving the mouse, double-clicking, and dragging and dropping
- Keyboard shortcuts

Understanding the build and perform actions

We know how to perform some basic actions, such as clicking on a button and typing text into a textbox; however, there are many scenarios where we have to perform multiple actions at the same time, for example, keeping the *Shift* button pressed and typing text for uppercase letters, and the dragging and dropping mouse actions.

Let's see a simple scenario here. Open the `http://guidebook.seleniumacademy.com/Selectable.html`. A box of tiles numbered 1 to 12 will appear, as seen in this screenshot:

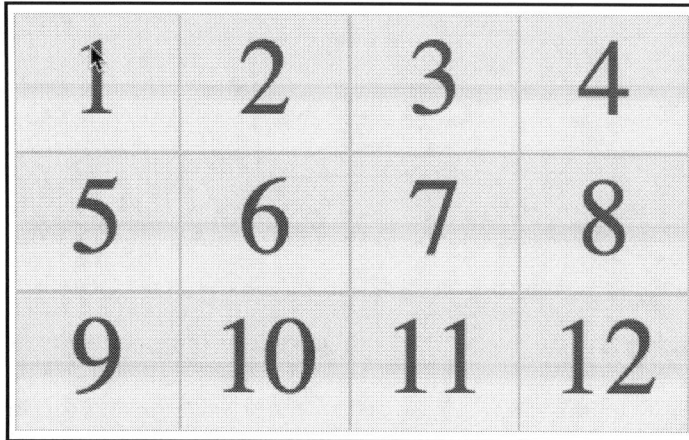

If you inspect the elements with browser developer tools, you will see an ordered list tag:

```
<ol id="selectable" class="ui-selectable">
    <li class="ui-state-default ui-selectee" name="one">1</li>
    <li class="ui-state-default ui-selectee" name="two">2</li>
    <li class="ui-state-default ui-selectee" name="three">3</li>
    <li class="ui-state-default ui-selectee" name="four">4</li>
    <li class="ui-state-default ui-selectee" name="five">5</li>
    <li class="ui-state-default ui-selectee" name="six">6</li>
    <li class="ui-state-default ui-selectee" name="seven">7</li>
    <li class="ui-state-default ui-selectee" name="eight">8</li>
    <li class="ui-state-default ui-selectee" name="nine">9</li>
    <li class="ui-state-default ui-selectee" name="ten">10</li>
    <li class="ui-state-default ui-selectee" name="eleven">11</li>
    <li class="ui-state-default ui-selectee" name="twelve">12</li>
</ol>
```

If you click a number, its background color changes to orange. Try selecting the tiles 1, 3, and 5. You do that by holding down *Ctrl* + tile 1 + tile 3 + tile 5. This involves performing multiple actions, that is, holding *Ctrl* continuously and clicking on tiles 1, 3, and 5. How do we perform these multiple actions using WebDriver? The following code demonstrates how:

```
@Test
public void shouldPerformCompositeAction() {

    driver.get("http://guidebook.seleniumacademy.com/Selectable.html");
```

```
WebElement one = driver.findElement(By.name("one"));
WebElement three = driver.findElement(By.name("three"));
WebElement five = driver.findElement(By.name("five"));

// Add all the actions into the Actions builder.
Actions actions = new Actions(driver);
actions.keyDown(Keys.CONTROL)
        .click(one)
        .click(three)
        .click(five)
        .keyUp(Keys.CONTROL);

// Generate the composite action.
Action compositeAction = actions.build();

// Perform the composite action.
compositeAction.perform();
}
```

Now, if you refer to the code, we are getting introduced to a new class named Actions. This Actions class is the one that is used to emulate all the complex user events. Using this, the developer of the test script could combine all the necessary user gestures into one composite action. We have declared all the actions that are to be executed to achieve the functionality of clicking on the numbers 1, 3, and 5. Once all the actions are grouped together, we build that into a composite action. Action is an interface that has only the perform() method, which executes the composite action. When we execute the test, tiles 1, 3, and 5 will be selected one by one. Finally, tile 5 will be selected, as shown in this screenshot:

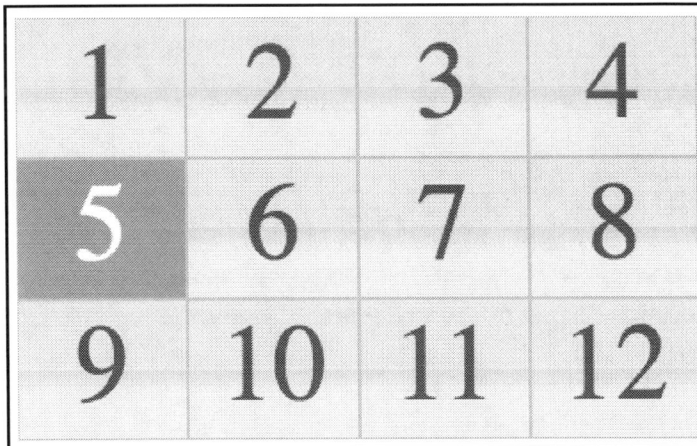

So, to make WebDriver perform multiple actions at the same time, you need to follow a three-step process of using the user-facing API of the actions class to group all the actions, then build the composite action, and perform the action. This process can be made into a two-step process, as the perform() method internally calls the build() method. So the previous code will look as follows:

```
@Test
public void shouldPerformAction() {

    driver.get("http://guidebook.seleniumacademy.com/Selectable.html");

    WebElement one = driver.findElement(By.name("one"));
    WebElement three = driver.findElement(By.name("three"));
    WebElement five = driver.findElement(By.name("five"));

    // Add all the actions into the Actions builder.
    Actions actions = new Actions(driver);
    actions.keyDown(Keys.CONTROL)
            .click(one)
            .click(three)
            .click(five)
            .keyUp(Keys.CONTROL);

    // Perform the action
    actions.perform();
}
```

In the preceding code, we have directly invoked the perform() method on the Actions instance, which internally calls the build() method to create a composite action before executing it. In the subsequent sections of this chapter, we will take a closer look at the Actions class. All the actions are basically divided into two categories: mouse-based actions and keyboard-based actions. In the following sections, we will discuss all the actions that are specific to the mouse and keyboard available in the Actions class.

Learning mouse based interactions

There are around eight different mouse actions that can be performed using the actions class. We will see each of their syntax and a working example.

The moveByOffset action

The `moveByOffset()` method is used to move the mouse from its current position to another point on the web page. Developers can specify the *x* distance and the *y* distance the mouse has to be moved. When the page is loaded, generally the initial position of the mouse would be (0, 0), unless there is an explicit focus declared by the page.

The API syntax for the `moveByOffset()` method is as follows:

```
public Actions moveByOffset(int xOffSet, int yOffSet)
```

In the preceding code, `xOffSet` is the input parameter providing the WebDriver the amount of offset to be moved along the *x* axis. A positive value is used to move the cursor to the right, and a negative value is used to move the cursor to the left.

`yOffSet` is the input parameter providing the WebDriver the amount of offset to be moved along the *y* axis. A positive value is used to move the cursor down along the *y* axis, and a negative value is used to move the cursor toward the top.

When the `xOffSet` and `yOffSet` values result in moving the cursor out of the document, a `MoveTargetOutOfBounds` exception is raised.

Let's see a working example of it. The objective of the following code is to move the cursor on to tile 3 on the web page:

```java
@Test
public void shouldMoveByOffSet() {

    driver.get("http://guidebook.seleniumacademy.com/Selectable.html");

    WebElement three = driver.findElement(By.name("three"));
    System.out.println("X coordinate: " + three.getLocation().getX()
            + ", Y coordinate: " + three.getLocation().getY());
    Actions actions = new Actions(driver);
    actions.moveByOffset(three.getLocation().getX() + 1, three.
            getLocation().getY() + 1);
    actions.perform();
}
```

The output will be as follows:

We have added +1 to the coordinates, because if you observe the element in Firebug, we have a style border of 1 px. The border is a CSS-style attribute, which when applied to an element will add a border of the specified color around the element, with the specified amount of thickness. Though the previous code does move your mouse over tile 3, we don't realize this, because we are not performing any action there. We will see this shortly, when we use the moveByOffset() method in combination with the click() method.

The click at current location action

The click() method is used to simulate the left-click of your mouse at its current point of location. This method doesn't really realize where or on which element it is clicking. It just clicks wherever it is at that point in time. Hence, this method is used in combination with some other action, rather than independently, to create a composite action.

The API syntax for the click() method is as follows:

```
public Actions click().
```

The `click()` method doesn't really have any context about where it is performing its action; hence, it doesn't take any input parameter. Let's see a code example of the `click()` method:

```
@Test
public void shouldMoveByOffSetAndClick() {

    driver.get("http://guidebook.seleniumacademy.com/Selectable.html");

    WebElement seven = driver.findElement(By.name("seven"));
    System.out.println("X coordinate: " + seven.getLocation().getX() +
            ", Y coordinate: " + seven.getLocation().getY());
    Actions actions = new Actions(driver);
    actions.moveByOffset(seven.getLocation().getX() + 1, seven.
            getLocation().getY() + 1).click();
    actions.perform();
}
```

In the above example we have used a combination of the `moveByOffset()` and `click()` methods to move the cursor from point (0, 0) to the point of tile **7**. Because the initial position of the mouse is (0, 0), the *x*, *y* offset provided for the `moveByOffset()` method is nothing but the location of the tile 7 element. Now let's try to move the cursor from tile 1 to tile 11, and from there to tile 5, and see how the code looks. Before we get into the code, let's inspect the `Selectable.html` page using Firebug. The following is the style of each tile:

```
#selectable li {
    float: left;
    font-size: 4em;
    height: 80px;
    text-align: center;
    width: 100px;
}
.ui-state-default, .ui-widget-content .ui-state-default, .ui-widgetheader
.ui-state-default {
    background: url("images/ui-bg_glass_75_e6e6e6_1x400.png") repeat-x
    scroll 50% 50% #E6E6E6;
    border: 1px solid #D3D3D3;
    color: #555555;
    font-weight: normal;
}
```

The three elements with which we are concerned for our offset movement in the preceding style code are: height, width, and the border thickness. Here, the height value is 80px, the width value is 100px, and the border value is 1px. Use these three factors to calculate the offset to navigate from one tile to the other. Note that the border thickness between any two tiles will result in 2 px, that is, 1 px from each tile. The following is the code that uses the moveByOffset and click() methods to navigate from tile 1 to tile 11, and from there to tile 5:

```
@Test
public void shouldMoveByOffSetAndClickMultiple() {

    driver.get("http://guidebook.seleniumacademy.com/Selectable.html");

    WebElement one = driver.findElement(By.name("one"));
    WebElement eleven = driver.findElement(By.name("eleven"));
    WebElement five = driver.findElement(By.name("five"));
    int border = 1;
    int tileWidth = 100;
    int tileHeight = 80;
    Actions actions = new Actions(driver);

    //Click on One
    actions.moveByOffset(one.getLocation().getX() + border,
one.getLocation().getY() + border).click();
    actions.build().perform();

    // Click on Eleven
    actions.moveByOffset(2 * tileWidth + 4 * border, 2 * tileHeight + 4 *
border).click();
    actions.build().perform();

    //Click on Five
    actions.moveByOffset(-2 * tileWidth - 4 * border, -tileHeight - 2 *
border).
            click();
    actions.build().perform();
}
```

The click on a WebElement action

We have seen how to click a WebElement by calculating the offset to it. This process may not be needed every time, especially when the WebElement has its own identifiers, such as a name or an ID. We can use another overloaded version of the `click()` method to click directly on the WebElement.

The API syntax for clicking on a WebElement is as follows:

```
public Actions click(WebElement onElement)
```

The input parameter for this method is an instance of the WebElement on which the `click` action should be performed. This method, like all the other methods in the `Actions` class, will return an `Actions` instance.

Now let's try to modify the previous code example to use the `click(WebElement)` method, instead of using the `moveByOffset()` method, to move to the location of the WebElement and click on it using the `click()` method:

```
@Test
public void shouldClickOnElement() {

    driver.get("http://guidebook.seleniumacademy.com/Selectable.html");

    WebElement one = driver.findElement(By.name("one"));
    WebElement eleven = driver.findElement(By.name("eleven"));
    WebElement five = driver.findElement(By.name("five"));
    Actions actions = new Actions(driver);

    //Click on One
    actions.click(one);
    actions.build().perform();

    // Click on Eleven
    actions.click(eleven);
    actions.build().perform();

    //Click on Five
    actions.click(five);
    actions.build().perform();
}
```

Now the `moveByOffset()` method has been replaced by the `click(WebElement)` method, and, all of a sudden, the complex coordinate geometry has been removed from the code. If you're a tester, this is one more good reason to push your developers to provide identifiers for the WebElements.

If you observe the previous examples for the `moveByOffset` and `click` methods, all the operations of moving the mouse and clicking on tiles 1, 11, and 5 are built separately and performed separately. This is not how we use our `Actions` class. You can actually build all these actions together and then perform them. So, the preceding code will turn out to be as follows:

```
@Test
public void shouldClickOnElement() {

    driver.get("http://guidebook.seleniumacademy.com/Selectable.html");

    WebElement one = driver.findElement(By.name("one"));
    WebElement eleven = driver.findElement(By.name("eleven"));
    WebElement five = driver.findElement(By.name("five"));
    Actions actions = new Actions(driver);

    actions.click(one)
            .click(eleven)
            .click(five)
            .build().perform();
}
```

The click and hold at current location action

The `clickAndHold()` method is another method of the actions class that left-clicks on an element and holds it without releasing the left button of the mouse. This method will be useful when executing operations such as drag and drop. This method is one of the variants of the `clickAndHold()` method that the actions class provides. We will discuss the other variant in the next section.

Now open the `Sortable.html` file that came with the book. You can see that the tiles can be moved from one position to the other. Now let's try to move tile 3 to the position of tile 2. The sequence of steps that are involved to do this are the following:

1. Move the cursor to the position of tile 3.
2. Click and hold tile 3.
3. Move the cursor in this position to tile 2's location.

Now let's see how this can be accomplished, using the WebDriver's `clickAndHold()` method:

```
@Test
public void shouldClickAndHold() {

    driver.get("http://guidebook.seleniumacademy.com/Sortable.html");

    Actions actions = new Actions(driver);

    //Move tile3 to the position of tile2
    actions.moveByOffset(200, 20)
            .clickAndHold()
            .moveByOffset(120, 0)
            .perform();
}
```

Let's analyze the following line of code:

```
actions.moveByOffset(200, 20)
        .clickAndHold()
        .moveByOffset(120, 0)
        .perform();
```

The tile movement will be similar to the following screenshot:

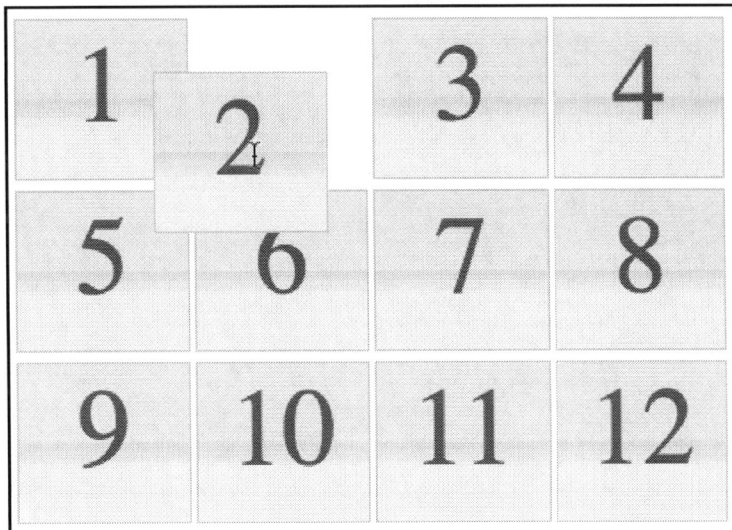

First, we move the cursor to the location of tile 3. Then, we click and hold tile 3. Then, we move the cursor by `120px` horizontally to the position of tile 2. The last line performs all the preceding actions. Now execute this in your eclipse and see what happens. If you observe closely, tile 3 doesn't properly go into the position of tile 2. This is because we are yet to release the left button. We just commanded the WebDriver to click and hold, but not to release.

The click and hold a WebElement action

In the previous section, we have seen the `clickAndHold()` method, which will click and hold a WebElement at the current position of the cursor. It doesn't care about which element it is dealing with. So, if we want to deal with a particular WebElement on the web page, we have to first move the cursor to the appropriate position and then perform the `clickAndHold()` action. To avoid the hassle of moving the cursor geometrically, WebDriver provides the developers with another variant or overloaded method of the `clickAndHold()` method that takes the WebElement as input.

The API syntax is this:

```
public Actions clickAndHold(WebElement onElement)
```

The input parameter for this method is the WebElement that has to be clicked and held. The return type, as in all the other methods of the `Actions` class, is the `Actions` instance. Now let's refactor the example in the previous section to use this method, as follows:

```
@Test
public void shouldClickAndHoldElement() {

    driver.get("http://guidebook.seleniumacademy.com/Sortable.html");

    Actions actions = new Actions(driver);
    WebElement three = driver.findElement(By.name("three"));

    //Move tile3 to the position of tile2
    actions.clickAndHold(three)
            .moveByOffset(120, 0)
            .perform();
}
```

The only change is that we have removed the action of moving the cursor to the (200, 20) position and provided the WebElement to the `clickAndHold()` method that will take care of identifying the WebElement.

The release at current location action

Now, in the previous example, we have seen how to click and hold an element. The ultimate action that has to be taken on a held WebElement is to release it so that the element can be dropped or released from the mouse. The `release()` method is the one that can release the left mouse button on a WebElement.

The API syntax for the `release()` method is as follows: `public Actions release()`.

The preceding method doesn't take any input parameter and returns the `Actions` class instance.

Now, let's modify the previous code to include the `release` action in it:

```
@Test
public void shouldClickAndHoldAndRelease() {

    driver.get("http://guidebook.seleniumacademy.com/Sortable.html");

    WebElement three = driver.findElement(By.name("three"));
    Actions actions = new Actions(driver);

    //Move tile3 to the position of tile2
    actions.clickAndHold(three)
            .moveByOffset(120, 0)
            .release()
            .perform();
}
```

The preceding code will make sure that the mouse is released at the specified location.

The release on another WebElement action

This is an overloaded version of the `release()` method. Using this, you can actually release the currently held WebElement in the middle of another WebElement. In this way, we don't have to calculate the offset of the target WebElement from the held WebElement.

The API syntax is as follows:

```
public Actions release(WebElement onElement)
```

The input parameter for the preceding method is obviously the target WebElement, where the held WebElement should be dropped. The return type is the instance of the `Actions` class.

Let's modify the preceding code example to use this method:

```
@Test
public void shouldClickAndHoldAndReleaseOnElement() {

    driver.get("http://guidebook.seleniumacademy.com/Sortable.html");

    WebElement three = driver.findElement(By.name("three"));
    WebElement two = driver.findElement(By.name("two"));
    Actions actions = new Actions(driver);

    //Move tile3 to the position of tile2
    actions.clickAndHold(three)
            .release(two)
            .perform();
}
```

Look at how simple the preceding code is. We have removed all the `moveByOffset` code and added the `release()` method that takes the WebElement with the name `two` as the input parameter.

> Invoking the `release()` or `release(WebElement)` methods without calling the `clickAndHold()` method will result in an undefined behavior.

The moveToElement action

The `moveToElement()` method is another method of WebDriver that helps us to move the mouse cursor to a WebElement on the web page.

The API syntax for the `moveToElement()` method is as follows:

```
public Actions moveToElement(WebElement toElement)
```

The input parameter for the preceding method is the target WebElement, where the mouse should be moved. Now go back to the `clickAndHold` at *current location action* section of this chapter and try to modify the code to use this method. The following is the code we have written in *The click-and-hold-at-current-location action* section:

```
@Test
public void shouldClickAndHold() {

    driver.get("http://guidebook.seleniumacademy.com/Sortable.html");

    Actions actions = new Actions(driver);

    //Move tile3 to the position of tile2
    actions.moveByOffset(200, 20)
            .clickAndHold()
            .moveByOffset(120, 0)
            .perform();
}
```

In the preceding code, we will replace the `moveByOffset(x, y)` method with the `moveToElement(WebElement)` method:

```
@Test
public void shouldClickAndHoldAndMove() {

    driver.get("http://guidebook.seleniumacademy.com/Sortable.html");

    WebElement three = driver.findElement(By.name("three"));
    Actions actions = new Actions(driver);

    //Move tile3 to the position of tile2
    actions.moveToElement(three)
            .clickAndHold()
            .moveByOffset(120, 0)
            .perform();
}
```

In the preceding code, we have moved to tile 3, clicked and held it, and then moved to the location of tile 2, by specifying its offset. If you want, you can add the `release()` method before the `perform()` method.

There might be a number of ways to achieve the same task. It is up to the user to choose the appropriate ones that best suit the given circumstances.

The dragAndDropBy action

There might be many instances where we may have to drag and drop components or WebElements of a web page. We can accomplish that by using many of the actions seen until now. But WebDriver has given us a convenient out-of-the-box method to use. Let's see its API syntax.

The API syntax for the dragAndDropBy() method is as follows:

```
public Actions dragAndDropBy(WebElement source, int xOffset,int yOffset)
```

The WebElement input parameter is the target WebElement to be dragged, the xOffset parameter is the horizontal offset to be moved, and the yOffset parameter is the vertical offset to be moved.

Let's see a code example for it. Open the HTML file, DragMe.html, provided with this book. It has a square box, as shown in the following screenshot:

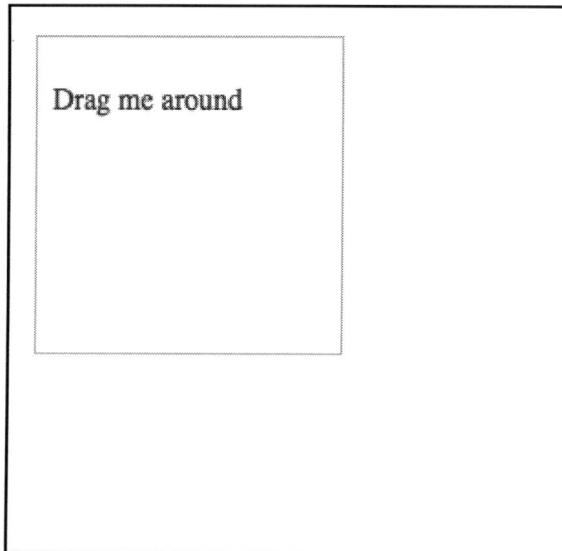

Drag me around

You can actually drag that rectangle to any location on the web page. Let's see how we can do that, using WebDriver. The following is the code example for that:

```
@Test
public void shouldDrag() {

    driver.get("http://guidebook.seleniumacademy.com/DragMe.html");

    WebElement dragMe = driver.findElement(By.id("draggable"));
    Actions actions = new Actions(driver);
    actions.dragAndDropBy(dragMe, 300, 200).perform();
}
```

In the preceding code, dragMe is the WebElement that is identified by its id, and that is dragged 300px horizontally and 200px vertically. The following screenshot shows how an element is dragged from this position:

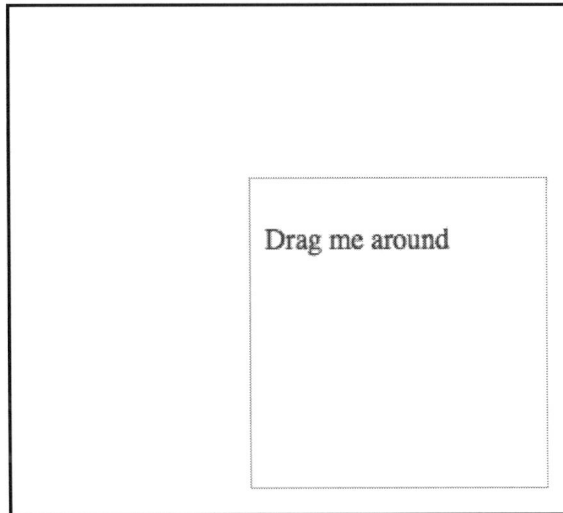

The dragAndDrop action

The dragAndDrop() method is similar to the dragAndDropBy() method. The only difference being that, instead of moving the WebElement by an offset, we move it on to a target element.

The API syntax for the `dragAndDrop()` method is as follows:

```
public Actions dragAndDrop(WebElement source, WebElement target)
```

The input parameters for the preceding method are the WebElement source and the WebElement target, while the return type is the `Actions` class.

Let's see a working code example for it. Open the `DragAndDrop.html` file, which is provided with the book, with two square boxes, as shown in this screenshot:

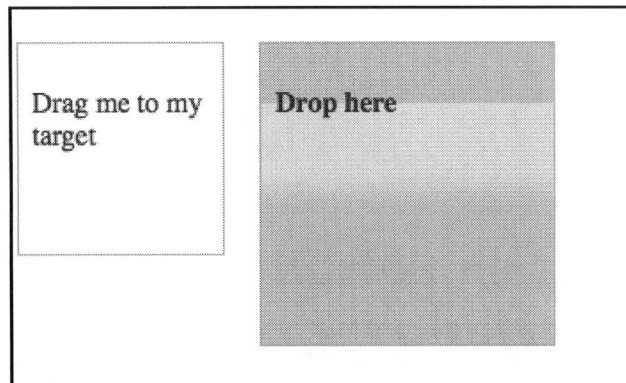

Here, we can actually drag the **Drag me to my target** rectangle to the **Drop here** rectangle. Try that. Let's see how that can be achieved, using WebDriver:

```
@Test
public void shouldDragAndDrop() {

    driver.get("http://guidebook.seleniumacademy.com/DragAndDrop.html");

    WebElement src = driver.findElement(By.id("draggable"));
    WebElement trgt = driver.findElement(By.id("droppable"));
    Actions actions = new Actions(driver);
    actions.dragAndDrop(src, trgt).perform();
}
```

In the preceding code, the source and target WebElements are identified by their IDs, and the dragAndDrop() method is used to drag one to the other. Here, out of the script with first square box dropped on the second box shown in the following screenshot:

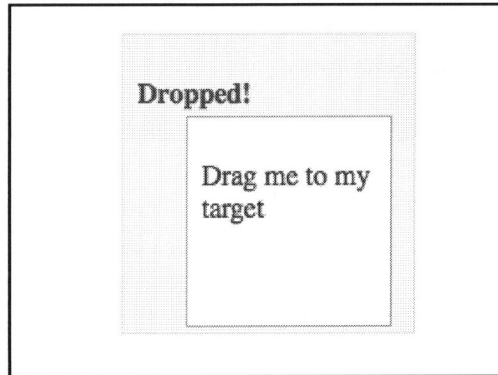

The double click at current location action

Moving on to another action that can be performed using a mouse, doubleClick() is another out- of-the-box method that WebDriver provides to emulate the double-clicking of the mouse. This method, like the click() method, comes in two flavors. One is double-clicking a WebElement, which we will discuss in next section; the second is clicking at the current location of the cursor, which will be discussed here.

The API syntax is as follows:

```
public Actions doubleClick()
```

Obviously, the preceding method doesn't take any input parameters, as it just clicks on the current cursor location and returns an actions class instance. Let's see how the previous code can be converted to use this method:

```
@Test
public void shouldDoubleClick() {

    driver.get("http://guidebook.seleniumacademy.com/DoubleClick.html");

    WebElement dblClick= driver.findElement(By.name("dblClick"));
    Actions actions = new Actions(driver);
    actions.moveToElement(dblClick).doubleClick().perform();
}
```

In the preceding code, we have used the `moveToElement(WebElement)` method to move the mouse to the location of the button element and just double-clicked at the current location. Here is the output after performing the double-click on the element on the sample page:

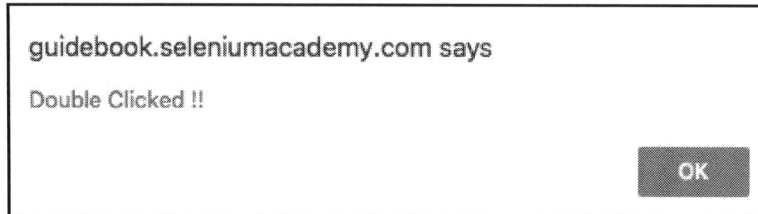

```
guidebook.seleniumacademy.com says

Double Clicked !!

                                                    OK
```

The double click on WebElement action

Now that we have seen a method that double-clicks at the current location, we will discuss another method that WebDriver provides to emulate the double-clicking of a WebElement.

The API syntax for the `doubleClick()` method is as follows:

```
public Actions doubleClick(WebElement onElement)
```

The input parameter for the preceding method is the target WebElement that has to be double-clicked, and the return type is the `Actions` class.

Let's see a code example for this. Open the `DoubleClick.html` file and *single*-click on the **Click Me** button. You shouldn't see anything happening. Now double-click on the button; you should see an alert saying **Double Clicked !!**. Now we will try to do the same thing using WebDriver. The following is the code to do that:

```
@Test
public void shouldDoubleClickElement() {
driver.get("http://guidebook.seleniumacademy.com/DoubleClick.html");

    WebElement dblClick = driver.findElement(By.name("dblClick"));
    Actions actions = new Actions(driver);
    actions.doubleClick(dblClick).perform();
}
```

After executing the preceding code, you should see an alert dialog saying that the button has been double-clicked.

The context click on WebElement action

The `contextClick()` method, also known as *right-click*, is quite common on many web pages these days. It displays a menu similar to this screenshot:

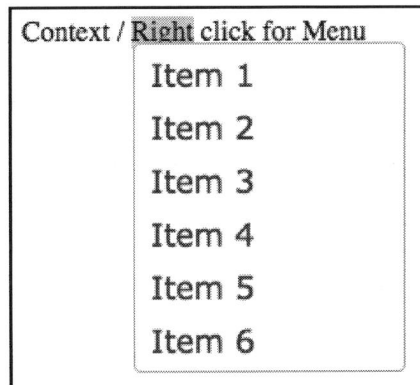

This context menu can be accessed by a right-click of the mouse on the WebElement. WebDriver provides the developer with an option of emulating that action, using the `contextClick()` method. Like many other methods, this method has two variants as well. One is clicking on the current location and the other overloaded method is clicking on the WebElement. Let's discuss the context of clicking on WebElement here.

The API syntax for the `contextClick()` method is as follows:

```
public Actions contextClick(WebElement onElement)
```

The input parameter is obviously the WebElement that has to be right-clicked, and the return type is the `Actions` instance. As we do normally, its time to see a code example. If you open the `ContextClick.html` file, you can right-click on the text visible on the page, and it will display the context menu. Now clicking any item pops up an alert dialog stating which item has been clicked. Now let's see how to implement this in WebDriver, using the following code:

```
@Test
public void shouldContextClick() {

    driver.get("http://guidebook.seleniumacademy.com/ContextClick.html");

    WebElement contextMenu = driver.findElement(By.id("div-context"));
    Actions actions = new Actions(driver);
    actions.contextClick(contextMenu)
        .click(driver.findElement(By.name("Item 4")))
```

```
        .perform();
}
```

In the preceding code, first we have right-clicked using the `contextClick()` method on the WebElement contextMenu, and then left-clicked on **Item 4** from the context menu. This should pop up an alert dialog saying **Item 4 Clicked**.

The context click at current location action

Now that we have seen context click on a WebElement, it's time to explore the `contextClick()` method at the current mouse location. The API syntax for the `contextClick()` method is as follows:

```
public Actions contextClick()
```

As expected, the preceding method doesn't expect any input parameter and returns the `Actions` instance. Let's see the necessary modifications needed for the previous example to use this method. The following is the code refactored to achieve this:

```
@Test
public void shouldContextClickAtCurrentLocation() {

    driver.get("http://guidebook.seleniumacademy.com/ContextClick.html");

    WebElement contextMenu = driver.findElement(By.id("div-context"));
    Actions actions = new Actions(driver);
    actions.moveToElement(contextMenu)
            .contextClick()
            .click(driver.findElement(By.name("Item 4")))
            .perform();
}
```

The preceding code first moves the cursor to the `div-context` WebElement and then context-clicks it.

.ı explains what has to be done to capture all of the events raised ver during the execution of test cases:

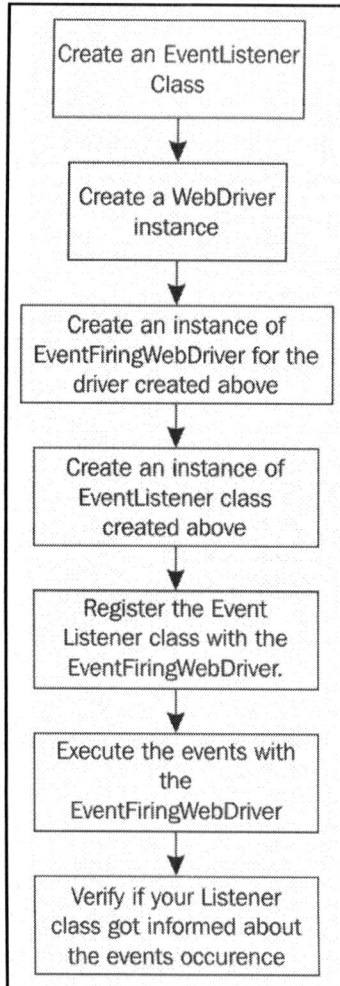

```
┌─────────────────────────────┐
│  ┌───────────────────────┐  │
│  │ Create an EventListener│  │
│  │        Class          │  │
│  └───────────────────────┘  │
│              │              │
│              ▼              │
│  ┌───────────────────────┐  │
│  │ Create a WebDriver    │  │
│  │      instance         │  │
│  └───────────────────────┘  │
│              │              │
│              ▼              │
│  ┌───────────────────────┐  │
│  │ Create an instance of │  │
│  │ EventFiringWebDriver  │  │
│  │ for the driver created│  │
│  │        above          │  │
│  └───────────────────────┘  │
│              │              │
│              ▼              │
│  ┌───────────────────────┐  │
│  │ Create an instance of │  │
│  │ EventListener class   │  │
│  │    created above      │  │
│  └───────────────────────┘  │
│              │              │
│              ▼              │
│  ┌───────────────────────┐  │
│  │ Register the Event    │  │
│  │ Listener class with   │  │
│  │ the EventFiringWebDriver.│
│  └───────────────────────┘  │
│              │              │
│              ▼              │
│  ┌───────────────────────┐  │
│  │ Execute the events    │  │
│  │ with the              │  │
│  │ EventFiringWebDriver  │  │
│  └───────────────────────┘  │
│              │              │
│              ▼              │
│  ┌───────────────────────┐  │
│  │ Verify if your Listener│ │
│  │ class got informed    │  │
│  │ about the events      │  │
│  │    occurence          │  │
│  └───────────────────────┘  │
└─────────────────────────────┘
```

Creating an instance of EventListener

The `EventListener` class handles all of the events that are dispatched by the `EventFiringWebDriver` class. There are two ways to create an `EventListener` class:

- By implementing the `WebDriverEventListener` interface.
- By extending the `AbstractWebDriverEventListener` class provided in the WebDriver library.

It is up to you, as a test-script developer, to choose which way to go.

Implementing WebDriverEventListener

The `WebDriverEventListener` interface has all the event methods declared. The `EventFiringWebDriver` class, as soon as it realizes an event has occurred, invokes the registered method of `WebDriverEventListener`. Here, we have created an `IAmTheEventListener` named class and have implemented `WebDriverEventListener`. Now we need to provide implementation for all the methods declared in it. Currently, in `WebDriverEventListener`, there are 15 methods. We will discuss each one of them shortly. Make sure the IDE provides us with the dummy implementation of these methods. The class that we have created with all 15 overridden methods is as follows (we have provided implementations for a couple of methods as an example):

```
public class IAmTheEventListener implements WebDriverEventListener {
    @Override
    public void beforeAlertAccept(WebDriver webDriver) {
    }

    @Override
    public void afterAlertAccept(WebDriver webDriver) {

    }

    @Override
    public void afterAlertDismiss(WebDriver webDriver) {

    }

    @Override
    public void beforeAlertDismiss(WebDriver webDriver) {
    }

    @Override
```

```java
    public void beforeNavigateTo(String url, WebDriver webDriver) {
        System.out.println("Before Navigate To " + url);
    }

    @Override
    public void afterNavigateTo(String s, WebDriver webDriver) {
        System.out.println("Before Navigate Back. Right now I'm at "
                + webDriver.getCurrentUrl());
    }

    @Override
    public void beforeNavigateBack(WebDriver webDriver) {
    }

    @Override
    public void afterNavigateBack(WebDriver webDriver) {
    }

    @Override
    public void beforeNavigateForward(WebDriver webDriver) {
    }

    @Override
    public void afterNavigateForward(WebDriver webDriver) {
    }

    @Override
    public void beforeNavigateRefresh(WebDriver webDriver)      {
    }

    @Override
    public void afterNavigateRefresh(WebDriver webDriver) {
    }

    @Override
    public void beforeFindBy(By by, WebElement webElement, WebDriver
webDriver) {
    }

    @Override
    public void afterFindBy(By by, WebElement webElement, WebDriver
webDriver) {
    }

    @Override
    public void beforeClickOn(WebElement webElement, WebDriver webDriver) {
    }
```

```
    @Override
    public void afterClickOn(WebElement webElement, WebDriver webDriver) {
    }

    @Override
    public void beforeChangeValueOf(WebElement webElement, WebDriver
webDriver, CharSequence[] charSequences) {

    }

    @Override
    public void afterChangeValueOf(WebElement webElement, WebDriver
webDriver, CharSequence[] charSequences) {

    }

    @Override
    public void beforeScript(String s, WebDriver webDriver)        {
    }

    @Override
    public void afterScript(String s, WebDriver webDriver)        {
    }

    @Override
    public void onException(Throwable throwable, WebDriver webDriver) {
    }
}
```

Extending AbstractWebDriverEventListener

The second way to create a listener class is by extending the
`AbstractWebDriverEventListene r` class. `AbstractWebDriverEventListener` is an
abstract class that implements `WebDriverEventListener`. Though it doesn't really
provide any implementation for the methods in the `WebDriverEventListener` interface,
it creates a dummy implementation such that the listener class that you are creating doesn't
have to contain all the methods, only the ones that you, as a test-script developer, are
interested in. The following is a class we have created that extends
`AbstractWebDriverEventListener` and provides implementations for a couple of
methods in it. This way, we can override only the methods that we are interested in rather
than all of the methods in our class:

```
package com.example;

import org.openqa.selenium.WebDriver;
```

```
import
org.openqa.selenium.support.events.AbstractWebDriverEventListener;

public class IAmTheEventListener2 extends AbstractWebDriverEventListener {

    @Override
    public void beforeNavigateTo(String url, WebDriver driver) {
        System.out.println("Before Navigate To "+ url);
    }
    @Override
    public void beforeNavigateBack(WebDriver driver) {
        System.out.println("Before Navigate Back. Right now I'm at "
                + driver.getCurrentUrl());
    }
}
```

Creating a WebDriver instance

Now that we have created our listener class that listens for all of the events generated, it's time to create our test script class and let it call `IAmTheDriver.java`. After the class is created, we declare a ChromeDriver instance in it:

```
WebDriver driver = new ChromeDriver();
```

The `ChromeDriver` instance will be the underlying driver instance that drives all the driver events. This is nothing new. The step explained in the next section is where we make this driver an instance of `EventFiringWebDriver`.

Creating EventFiringWebDriver and EventListener instances

Now that we have the basic driver instance, pass it as an argument while constructing the `EventFiringWebDriver` instance. We will be using this instance of the driver to execute all of the further user actions.

Now, using the following code, instantiate the `EventListener`, `IAmTheEventListener.java`, or `IAmTheEventListener2.java` class that we created previously. This will be the class to which all of the events are dispatched:

```
EventFiringWebDriver eventFiringDriver =
        new EventFiringWebDriver(driver);
IAmTheEventListener eventListener =
        new IAmTheEventListener();
```

Registering EventListener with EventFiringWebDriver

For the event executions to be notified by `EventListener`, we have registered `EventListener` to the `EventFiringWebDriver` class. Now the `EventFiringWebDriver` class will know where to send the notifications. This is done by the following line of code:
`eventFiringDriver.register(eventListener);`

Executing and verifying the events

Now it's time for our test script to execute events, such as navigation events. Let's first navigate to Google and then Facebook. We will use the browser back-navigation to go back to Google. The full code of the test script is as follows:

```
public class IAmTheDriver {
    public static void main(String... args){

        System.setProperty("webdriver.chrome.driver",
                "./src/test/resources/drivers/chromedriver");

        WebDriver driver = new ChromeDriver();

        try {
            EventFiringWebDriver eventFiringDriver = new
                    EventFiringWebDriver(driver);
            IAmTheEventListener eventListener = new IAmTheEventListener();
            eventFiringDriver.register(eventListener);
            eventFiringDriver.get("http://www.google.com");
            eventFiringDriver.get("http://www.facebook.com");
            eventFiringDriver.navigate().back();
        } finally {
            driver.close();
            driver.quit();
```

```
            }
        }
    }
```

In the preceding code, we modify our listener class to record navigateTo and navigateBack before and after events inherited from the AbstractWebDriverEventListener class. The modified methods are as follows:

```
@Override
public void beforeNavigateTo(String url, WebDriver driver) {
    System.out.println("Before Navigate To: " + url
            + " and Current url is: " + driver.getCurrentUrl());
}

@Override
public void afterNavigateTo(String url, WebDriver driver) {
    System.out.println("After Navigate To: " + url
            + " and Current url is: " + driver.getCurrentUrl());
}

@Override
public void beforeNavigateBack(WebDriver driver) {
    System.out.println("Before Navigate Back. Right now I'm at " +
driver.getCurrentUrl());
}

@Override
public void afterNavigateBack(WebDriver driver) {
    System.out.println("After Navigate Back. Right now I'm at " +
driver.getCurrentUrl());
}
```

Now if you execute your test script, the output will be as follows:

```
Before Navigate To: http://www.google.com and Current url is: data:,
 After Navigate To: http://www.google.com and Current url is:
https://www.google.com/?gws_rd=ssl
 Before Navigate To: http://www.facebook.com and Current url is:
https://www.google.com/?gws_rd=ssl
 After Navigate To: http://www.facebook.com and Current url is:
https://www.facebook.com/
 Before Navigate Back. Right now I'm at https://www.facebook.com/
 After Navigate Back. Right now I'm at https://www.google.com/?gws_rd=ssl
```

Registering multiple EventListeners

We can register more than one listener with `EventFiringWebDriver`. Once the event occurs, all of the registered listeners are notified about it. Let's modify our test script to register both our `IAmTheListener.java` and `IAmTheListener2.java` files:

```
public class RegisteringMultipleListeners {
    public static void main(String... args){

        System.setProperty("webdriver.chrome.driver",
                "./src/test/resources/drivers/chromedriver");

        WebDriver driver = new ChromeDriver();

        try {
            EventFiringWebDriver eventFiringDriver = new
                    EventFiringWebDriver(driver);
            IAmTheEventListener eventListener = new IAmTheEventListener();
            IAmTheEventListener2 eventListener2 = new
                    IAmTheEventListener2();
            eventFiringDriver.register(eventListener);
            eventFiringDriver.register(eventListener2);
            eventFiringDriver.get("http://www.google.com");
            eventFiringDriver.get("http://www.facebook.com");
            eventFiringDriver.navigate().back();
        } finally {
            driver.close();
            driver.quit();
        }
    }
}
```

Modify the listeners slightly to differentiate the log statements. Now if you execute the preceding code, you will see the following output:

```
Before Navigate To: http://www.google.com and Current url is: data:,
 Before Navigate To http://www.google.com
 After Navigate To: http://www.google.com and Current url is:
https://www.google.com/?gws_rd=ssl
 Before Navigate To: http://www.facebook.com and Current url is:
https://www.google.com/?gws_rd=ssl
 Before Navigate To http://www.facebook.com
 After Navigate To: http://www.facebook.com and Current url is:
https://www.facebook.com/
 Before Navigate Back. Right now I'm at https://www.facebook.com/
 Before Navigate Back. Right now I'm at https://www.facebook.com/
 After Navigate Back. Right now I'm at https://www.google.com/?gws_rd=ssl
```

Exploring different WebDriver event listeners

We have seen some of the methods in our `EventListeners` that get invoked when their corresponding events are executed, for example, before and after navigation methods are invoked when the `navigateTo` event is triggered. Here, we'll see all the methods that `WebDriverEventListener` provides us.

Listening for WebElement value changes

This event occurs when the value of a WebElement changes when the `sendKeys()` or `clear()` methods are executed on them. There are two methods associated with this event:

```
public void beforeChangeValueOf(WebElement element, WebDriver driver)
```

The preceding method is invoked before the WebDriver attempts to change the value of the WebElement. As a parameter, the WebElement itself is passed to the method so that you can log the value of the element before the change:

```
public void afterChangeValueOf(WebElement element, WebDriver driver)
```

The preceding method is the second method associated with the value-change event that is invoked after the driver changes the value of the WebElement. Again, the WebElement and the WebDriver are sent as parameters to the method. If an exception occurs when changing the value, this method is not invoked.

Listening for the clicked WebElement

This event occurs when a WebElement is clicked, that is, by executing `webElement.click()`. There are two methods to listen for this event in the `WebDriverEventListener` implementation:

```
public void beforeClickOn(WebElement element, WebDriver driver)
```

The preceding method is invoked when the WebDriver is about to click on a particular WebElement. The WebElement that is going to be clicked on and the WebDriver that is clicking on it are sent as parameters to this method so that the test-script developer can interpret which driver performed the click action, and on which element the action was performed:

```
public void afterClickOn(WebElement element, WebDriver driver)
```

The `EventFiringWebDriver` class notifies the preceding method after the click action is taken on a WebElement. Similar to the `beforeClickOn()` method, this method is also sent the WebElement and WebDriver instances. If an exception occurs during a click event, this method is not called.

Listening for a WebElement search event

This event is triggered when the WebDriver searches for a WebElement on the web page using `findElement()` or `findElements()`. There are, again, two methods associated with this event:

```
public void beforeFindBy(By by, WebElement element, WebDriver driver)
```

The preceding method is invoked just before WebDriver begins searching for a particular WebElement on the page. For parameters, it sends the locating mechanism, that is, the WebElement that is searched for, and the WebDriver instance that is performing the search:

```
public void afterFindBy(By by, WebElement element, WebDriver driver)
```

Similarly, the `EventFiringWebDriver` class calls the preceding method after the search for an element is over and the element is found. If there are any exceptions during the search, this method is not called, and an exception is raised.

Listening for browser back-navigation

The browser back-navigation event, as we have already seen, gets invoked when we use the `driver.navigation().back()` method. The browser goes back one level in its history. Just like all the other events, this event is associated with two methods:

```
public void beforeNavigateBack(WebDriver driver)
```

The preceding method is invoked before the browser takes you back in its history. The WebDriver that invoked this event is passed as a parameter to this method:

```
public void afterNavigateBack(WebDriver driver)
```

Just as in all the after <<event>> methods, the preceding method is invoked when the navigate-back action is triggered. The preceding two methods will be invoked irrespective of the navigation of the browser; that is, if the browser doesn't have any history and you invoke this method, the browser doesn't take you to any of its history. But, even in that scenario, as the event is triggered, those two methods are invoked.

Listening for browser forward-navigation

This event is very similar to the browser back-navigation, except that this is browser forward-navigation, so it is using `driver.navigate().forward()`. The two methods associated with this event are:

- `public void afterNavigateForward(WebDriver driver)`
- `public void beforeNavigateForward(WebDriver driver)`

Just as in browser back-navigation, these methods are invoked irrespective of whether or not the browser takes you one level forward.

Listening for browser NavigateTo events

As we've seen earlier, this event occurs whenever the driver executes `driver. get(url)`. The related methods for this event are as follows:

- `public void beforeNavigateTo(java.lang.String url, WebDriver driver)`
- `public void afterNavigateTo(java.lang.String url, WebDriver driver)`

The URL that is used for the driver-navigation is passed as a parameter to the preceding methods, along with the driver that triggered the event.

Listening for script execution

This event is triggered whenever the driver executes a JavaScript. The associated methods for this event are as follows:

- `public void beforeScript(java.lang.String script, WebDriver driver)`
- `public void afterScript(java.lang.String script, WebDriver driver)`

The preceding methods get the JavaScript that was executed as a string, and the WebDriver that executed it as a parameter. If an exception occurs during script execution, the `afterScript()` method will not be invoked.

Listening for an exception

This event occurs when the WebDriver comes across an exception. For instance, if you try to search for a WebElement using `findElement()`, and that element doesn't exist on the page, the driver throws an exception (`NoSuchElementException`). At this point, this event is triggered, and the following method gets notified:

```
public void onException(java.lang.Throwable throwable, WebDriver driver)
```

In all the `after<<event>>` methods, we have seen that they will not be invoked if the driver comes across any exception. In that case, instead of those `after<<event>>` methods, the `onException()` method is invoked and the throwable object and the WebDriver object are sent to it as parameters.

Unregistering EventListener with EventFiringWebDriver

Now, we have seen the different kinds of events that get triggered, and the `EventFiringWebDriver` class that notifies all of the listeners registered to it. If, at any point, you want one of your event listeners to stop listening from `EventFiringWebDriver`, you can do that by unregistering from that driver. The following API unregisters an event listener from a driver:

```
public EventFiringWebDriver unregister(WebDriverEventListener eventListener)
```

The parameter of the method should be the event listener that wants to opt out of getting event notifications.

Performing accessibility testing

We can perform basic accessibility checks by using tools such as Google's Accessibility Developer Tools (https://github.com/GoogleChrome/accessibility-developer-tools). We can inject the Google Accessibility testing library in a web page and perform the Accessibility Audit. This can be done automatically every time afterNavigatTo() is called. In the following code example, we will inject the axe_testing.js file provided by the Google Accessibility Developer Tools and perform the audit, which will print a report on the console:

```
public class IAmTheEventListener2 extends AbstractWebDriverEventListener {

    @Override
    public void beforeNavigateTo(String url, WebDriver driver) {
        System.out.println("Before Navigate To "+ url);
    }

    @Override
    public void beforeNavigateBack(WebDriver driver) {
        System.out.println("Before Navigate Back. Right now I'm at "
                + driver.getCurrentUrl());
    }

    @Override
    public void afterNavigateTo(String to, WebDriver driver) {
        try {
            JavascriptExecutor jsExecutor = (JavascriptExecutor) driver;
            URL url = new
URL("https://raw.githubusercontent.com/GoogleChrome/" +
                    "accessibility-developer-
tools/stable/dist/js/axs_testing.js");
            String script = IOUtils.toString(url.openStream(),
StandardCharsets.UTF_8);
            jsExecutor.executeScript(script);
            String report = (String) jsExecutor.executeScript("var results
= axs.Audit.run();" +
                    "return axs.Audit.createReport(results);");
            System.out.println("### Accessibility Report for " +
driver.getTitle() + "####");
            System.out.println(report);
            System.out.println("### END ####");
```

```
        } catch (MalformedURLException e) {
            e.printStackTrace();
        } catch (IOException e) {
            e.printStackTrace();
        }
    }
}
```

The report is printed in the console, as shown here:

```
### Accessibility Report for Google####
 *** Begin accessibility audit results ***
 An accessibility audit found
 Warnings:
 Warning: AX_FOCUS_01 (These elements are focusable but either invisible or
obscured by another element) failed on the following element:
 #hplogo > DIV > .fOwUFe > A
 See
https://github.com/GoogleChrome/accessibility-developer-tools/wiki/Audit-Ru
les#-ax_focus_01--these-elements-are-focusable-but-either-invisible-or-
obscured-by-another-element for more information.
 Warning: AX_TEXT_02 (Images should have an alt attribute) failed on the
following element:
 #hplogo > DIV > .fOwUFe > A > .fJOQGe
 See
https://github.com/GoogleChrome/accessibility-developer-tools/wiki/Audit-Ru
les#-ax_text_02--images-should-have-an-alt-attribute-unless-they-have-an-
aria-role-of-presentation for more information.
 ...
 *** End accessibility audit results ***
 ### END ####
```

This report contains a collection of audit rules that check for common accessibility problems.

Capturing page-performance metrics

Measuring and optimizing the client-side performance is essential for a seamless user experience, and this is critical for Web 2.0 applications using AJAX.

Capturing vital information, such as the time taken for page load, rendering of the elements, and the JavaScript code execution, will help in identifying the areas where performance is slow and optimizes the overall client-side performance.

Navigation Timing is a W3C-Standard JavaScript API to measure performance on the web. The API provides a simple way to get accurate and detailed timing statistics natively for page navigation and load events. It is available on Internet Explorer 9, Google Chrome, Firefox, and WebKit-based browsers.

The API is accessed via the properties of the timing interface of the `window.performance` object using JavaScript. We will capture the page-load time every time we navigate to a page. This can be done by using `JavaScriptExecutor` to call `winodw.performance` in the `afterNavigateTo()` method in `IAmTheEventListener2.java`, as shown in the following code snippet:

```
@Override
public void afterNavigateTo(String to, WebDriver driver) {
    try {

        JavascriptExecutor jsExecutor = (JavascriptExecutor) driver;

        // Get the Load Event End
        long loadEventEnd = (Long) jsExecutor.executeScript("return
window.performance.timing.loadEventEnd;");
        // Get the Navigation Event Start
        long navigationStart = (Long) jsExecutor.executeScript("return
window.performance.timing.navigationStart;");
        // Difference between Load Event End and Navigation Event Start is
// Page Load Time
        System.out.println("Page Load Time is " + (loadEventEnd -
navigationStart)/1000 + " seconds.");

    } catch (MalformedURLException e) {
        e.printStackTrace();
    } catch (IOException e) {
        e.printStackTrace();
    }
```

As discussed in the previous code, the `window.performance` object provides us with the performance metric that is available within the `Browser Window object`. We need to use JavaScript to retrieve this metric. Here, we are collecting the `loadEventEnd` time and the `navigationEventStart` time, and calculating the difference between them, which will give us the page-load time.

Summary

In this chapter, you have learned about `EventFiringWebDriver` and `EventListeners`, and how they work together to make a developer's life easier by helping them to debug what is going on at each step while the test cases get executed. You also learned how to use WebDriver events to perform different types of testing on a page, such as accessibility and client-side performance checks. In the next `chapter`, you will learn more about RemoteWebDriver for running tests on remote machines in distributed and parallel mode for Cross-Browser Testing.

Questions

1. You can listen to WebDriver events using `WebDriverEventListener` interface— True or False?
2. How you can automatically clear an input field before calling the `sendKeys` method using `WebDriverEventListener`?
3. Selenium supports accessibility testing— True or False?

Further information

You can check out the following links for more information about the topics covered in this chapter:

- Find out more about the Navigation Timing API at `https://www.w3.org/TR/navigation-timing/`
- Find more details on Google's Accessibility Developer Tools at `https://github.com/GoogleChrome/accessibility-developer-tools`

7
Exploring RemoteWebDriver

So far, we have created our test cases and tried to execute them on various browsers. All of these tests were executed against the browsers that were installed on a local machine where the test cases reside. This may not be possible at all times. There is a high possibility that you may be working on Mac or Linux, but want to execute your tests on IE on a Windows machine. In this chapter, we will learn about the following topics:

- Executing test cases on a remote machine using RemoteWebDriver
- A detailed explanation of the JSON wire protocol

Introducing RemoteWebDriver

RemoteWebDriver is an implementation class of the WebDriver interface that a test-script developer can use to execute their test scripts via the Selenium Standalone server on a remote machine. There are two parts to RemoteWebDriver: a server and a client. Before we start working with them, let's rewind and see what we've been doing.

The following diagram explains what we've done so far:

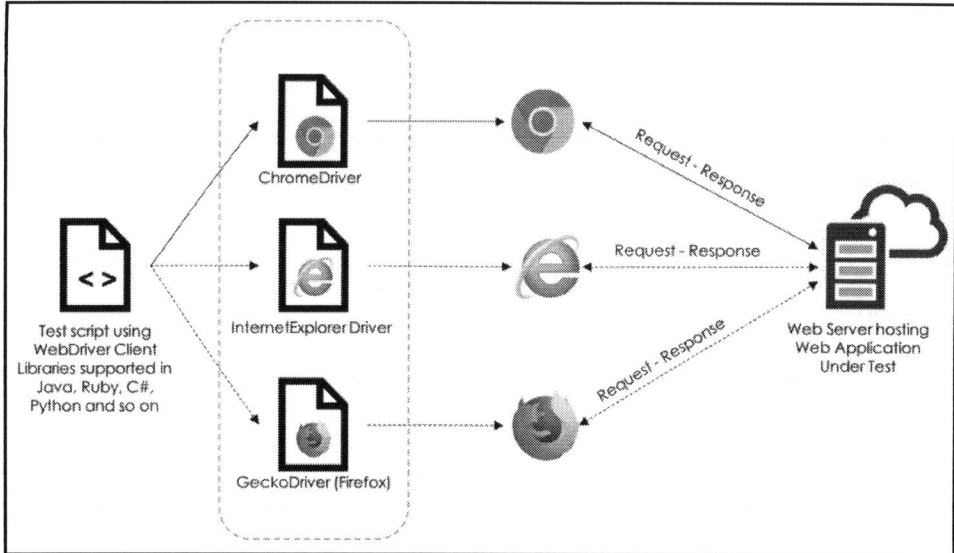

The test script using **WebDriver client** libraries, **Chrome Driver** (or IE Driver or Gecko Driver for Firefox), and Chrome browser (or IE browser or Firefox browser) is sitting on the same machine. The browser is loading the web application, which may or may not be hosted remotely; anyway, this is outside the scope of our discussion. We will discuss different scenarios of test-script execution, as follows:

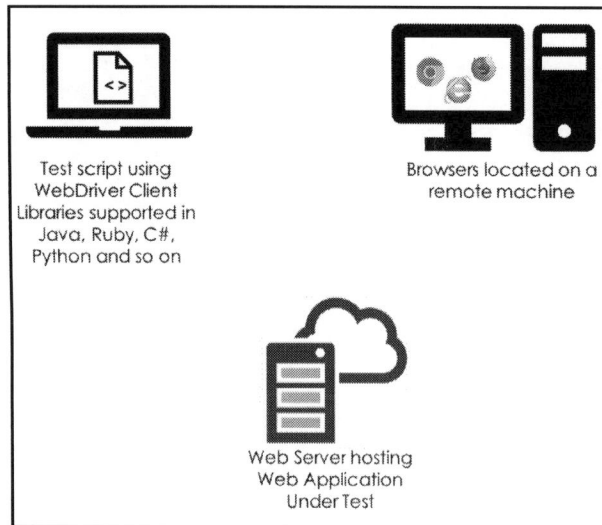

The test script is located on a local machine, while the browsers are installed on a remote machine. In this scenario, `RemoteWebDriver` comes into the picture. As mentioned earlier, there are two components associated with `RemoteWebDriver`: the server and the client. Let's start with the `Selenium Standalone server`.

Understanding Selenium Standalone Server

`Selenium Standalone Server` is a component that listens on a port for various requests from a `RemoteWebDriver` client. Once it receives the requests, it forwards them to any of the following: Chrome Driver, IE Driver, or Gecko Driver for Firefox, whichever is requested by the `RemoteWebDriver` client.

Downloading Selenium Standalone Server

Let's download `Selenium Standalone Server` and start running it. You can download it from `https://www.seleniumhq.org/download/`, but, for our purposes, let's download a specific version of it, as we are using WebDriver Version 3.12.0. This server JAR should be downloaded to the remote machine on which the browsers are located. Also, make sure the remote machine has Java Runtime installed on it.

Running the server

Open your command-line tool on the remote machine and navigate to the location where you have downloaded the JAR file. Now, to start Selenium Standalone Server, execute the following command:

```
java -jar selenium-server-standalone-3.12.0.jar
```

The following screenshot shows what you should see in your console:

Now the server has started and is listening on the `<remote-machine-ip>:4444` address for remote connections from the `RemoteWebDriver` client. The previously seen image (the second image in the *Introducing RemoteWebDriver* section) will appear as follows:

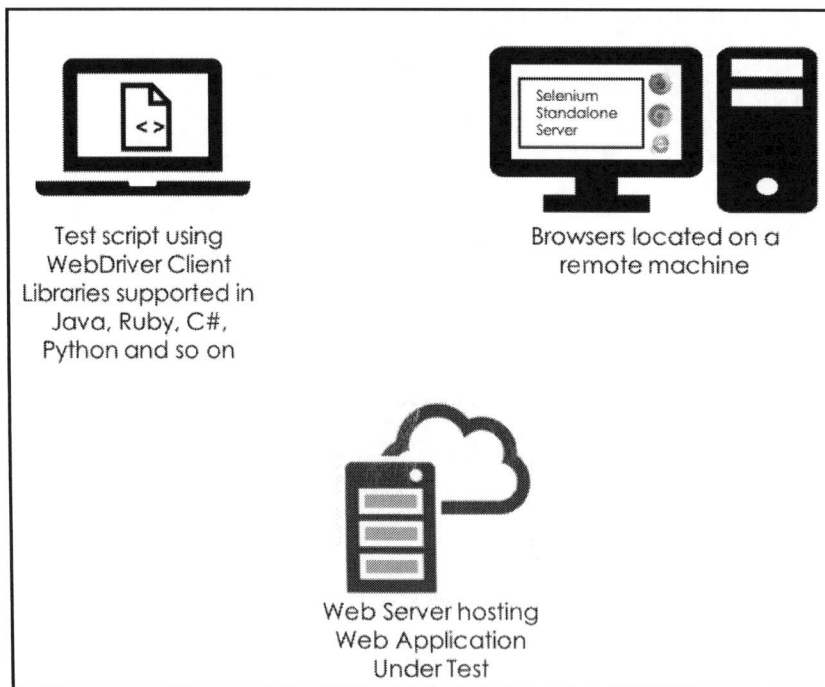

On the remote machine, Selenium Standalone Server will interface between the test script and the browsers, as shown in the preceding diagram. The test script will first establish a connection with Selenium Standalone Server that will forward the commands to the browser installed on the remote machine.

Understanding the RemoteWebDriver client

Now that we have our Selenium Standalone server up and running, it's time for us to create the RemoteWebDriver client. Fortunately, we don't have to do much to create a RemoteWebDriver client. It's nothing but the language-binding client libraries that serve as a RemoteWebDriver client. RemoteWebDriver will translate the test-script requests or commands to JSON payload and send them across to the RemoteWebDriver server using the JSON wire protocol.

When you execute your tests locally, the WebDriver client libraries talk to the Chrome Driver, IE Driver, or Gecko Driver directly. Now when you try to execute your tests remotely, the WebDriver client libraries talk to Selenium Standalone Server and the server talks to either the Chrome Driver, the IE Driver, or the Gecko Driver for Firefox requested by the test script, using the DesiredCapabilities class. We will explore the DesiredCapabilities class in the next section.

Converting an existing test script to use the RemoteWebDriver server

Let's take a test script that we have executed locally; that is, where the test scripts and the browser were on the same machine:

```
@BeforeClass
public void setup() {

    System.setProperty("webdriver.chrome.driver",
            "./src/test/resources/drivers/chromedriver");
    driver = new ChromeDriver();

}
```

The preceding test script creates an instance of Chrome Driver and launches the Chrome browser. Now, let's try to convert this test script to use `Selenium Standalone Server` that we started earlier. Before we do that, let's see the constructor of `RemoteWebDriver`, which is as follows:

```
RemoteWebDriver(java.net.URL remoteAddress, Capabilities
desiredCapabilities)
```

The input parameters for the constructor include the address (hostname or IP) of `Selenium Standalone Server` running on the remote machine and the desired capabilities required for running the test (for example name of the browser and/or operating system). We will see these desired capabilities shortly.

Now, let's modify the test script to use `RemoteWebDriver`. Replace `WebDriver driver = new ChromeDriver();` with the following code:

```
@BeforeMethod
public void setup() throws MalformedURLException {

    DesiredCapabilities caps = new DesiredCapabilities();
    caps.setBrowserName("chrome");

    driver = new RemoteWebDriver(new URL("http://10.172.10.1:4444/wd/hub"),
caps);
    driver.get("http://demo-store.seleniumacademy.com/");

}
```

We have created a RemoteWebDriver instance that tries to connect to `http://10.172.10.1:4444/wd/hub`, where `Selenium Standalone Server` is running and listening for requests. Having done that, we also need to specify which browser your test case should get executed on. This can be done using the `DesiredCapabilities` instance.

> For this example, the IP used is 10.172.10.1. However, in your case, it will be different. You need to obtain the IP of the machine where the Selenium Standalone Server is running and replace the example IP used in this book.

Before running tests, we need to restart the Selenium Standalone Server by specifying the path of ChromeDriver:

```
java -jar -Dwebdriver.chrome.driver=chromedriver selenium-server-
standalone-3.12.0.jar
```

Running the following test with `RemoteWebDriver` will launch the Chrome browser and execute your test case on it. So the modified test case will look as follows:

```
public class SearchTest {

    WebDriver driver;

    @BeforeMethod
    public void setup() throws MalformedURLException {

        DesiredCapabilities caps = new DesiredCapabilities();
        caps.setBrowserName("chrome");

        driver = new RemoteWebDriver(new
URL("http://10.172.10.1:4444/wd/hub"), caps);
        driver.get("http://demo-store.seleniumacademy.com/");

    }

    @Test
    public void searchProduct() {

        // find search box and enter search string
        WebElement searchBox = driver.findElement(By.name("q"));

        searchBox.sendKeys("Phones");

        WebElement searchButton =
                driver.findElement(By.className("search-button"));

        searchButton.click();

        assertThat(driver.getTitle())
                .isEqualTo("Search results for: 'Phones'");
    }

    @AfterMethod
    public void tearDown() {
        driver.quit();
    }
}
```

Now execute this test script from your local machine to establish a connection between the `RemoteWebDriver` client and `Selenium Standalone Server`. The Server will launch the Chrome browser. The following is the output you will see in the console where the Server is running:

```
18:25:32.155 INFO [ActiveSessionFactory.apply] - Capabilities are: Capabilities {
browserName: chrome}
18:25:32.157 INFO [ActiveSessionFactory.lambda$apply$11] - Matched factory org.op
enqa.selenium.remote.server.ServicedSession$Factory (provider: org.openqa.seleniu
m.chrome.ChromeDriverService)
Starting ChromeDriver 2.38.552518 (183d19265345f54ce39cbb94cf81ba5f15905011) on p
ort 3315
Only local connections are allowed.
18:25:52.564 INFO [ProtocolHandshake.createSession] - Detected dialect: OSS
18:25:58.340 INFO [RemoteSession$Factory.lambda$performHandshake$0] - Started new
 session 3cb5c118e1a5b2bdd7bc568bf147beed (org.openqa.selenium.chrome.ChromeDrive
rService)
```

It says that a new session with the desired capabilities is being created. Once the session is established, a session ID will be printed to the console. At any point in time, you can view all of the sessions that are established with `Selenium Standalone Server` by navigating to the host or IP of the machine where the Selenium server is running `http://<hostnameOrIP>:4444/wd/hub`.

> The Selenium Standalone Server, by default, listens to port number 4444. We can change the default port by passing the `-port` argument.

It will give the entire list of sessions that the server is currently handling. The screenshot of this is as follows:

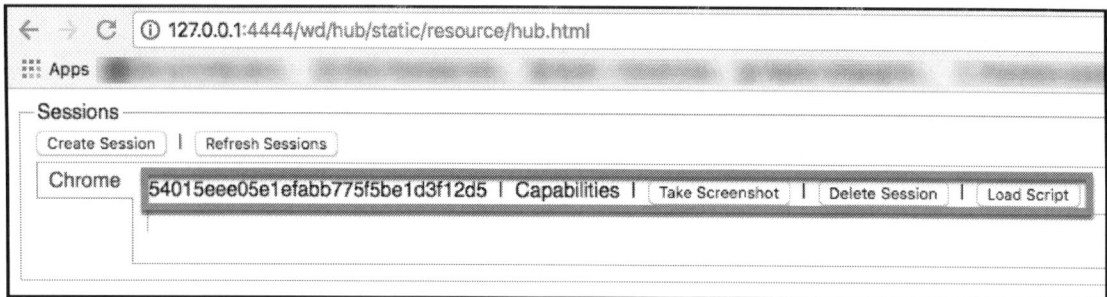

This is a very basic portal that lets the test-script developer see all of the sessions created by the server and perform some basic operations on it, such as terminating a session, taking a screenshot of a session, loading a script to a session, and seeing all of the desired capabilities of a session. The following screenshot shows all of the default desired capabilities of our current session.

You can see the popup by hovering over the **Capabilities** link, as shown in the following screenshot:

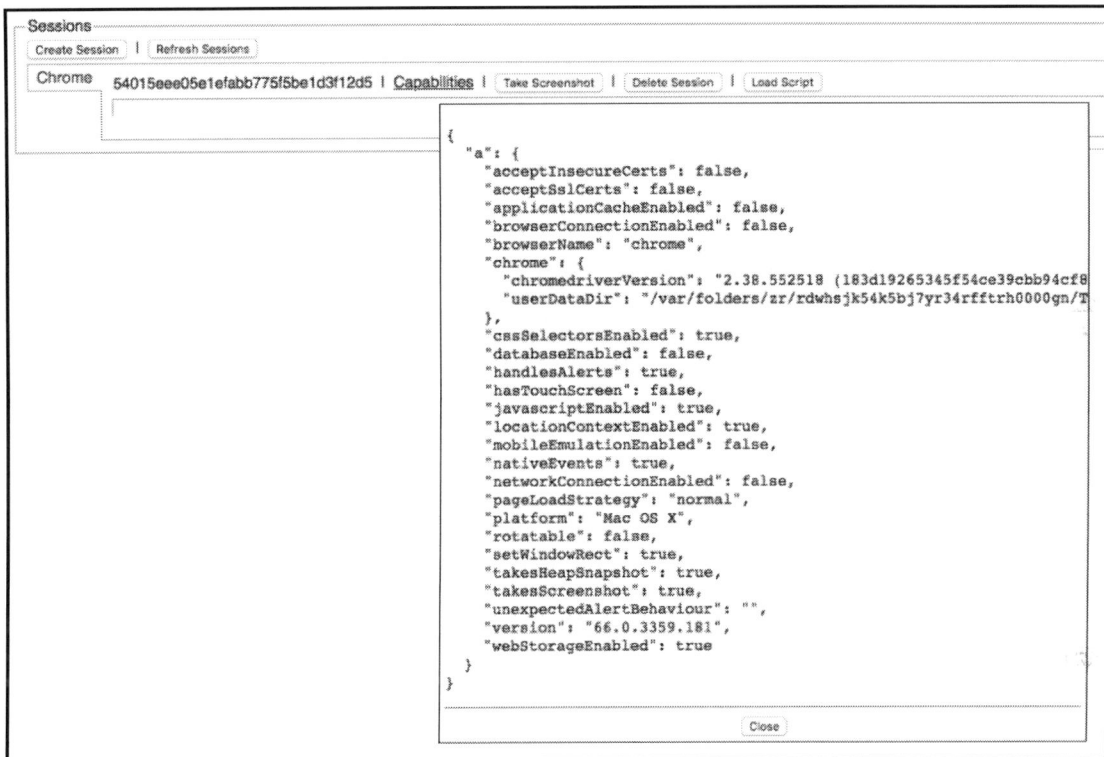

Those are the default desired capabilities that are set implicitly by the server for this session. Now we have successfully established a connection between our test script, which is using a RemoteWebDriver client on one machine, and the Selenium Standalone Server on another machine. The original diagram of running the test scripts remotely is as follows:

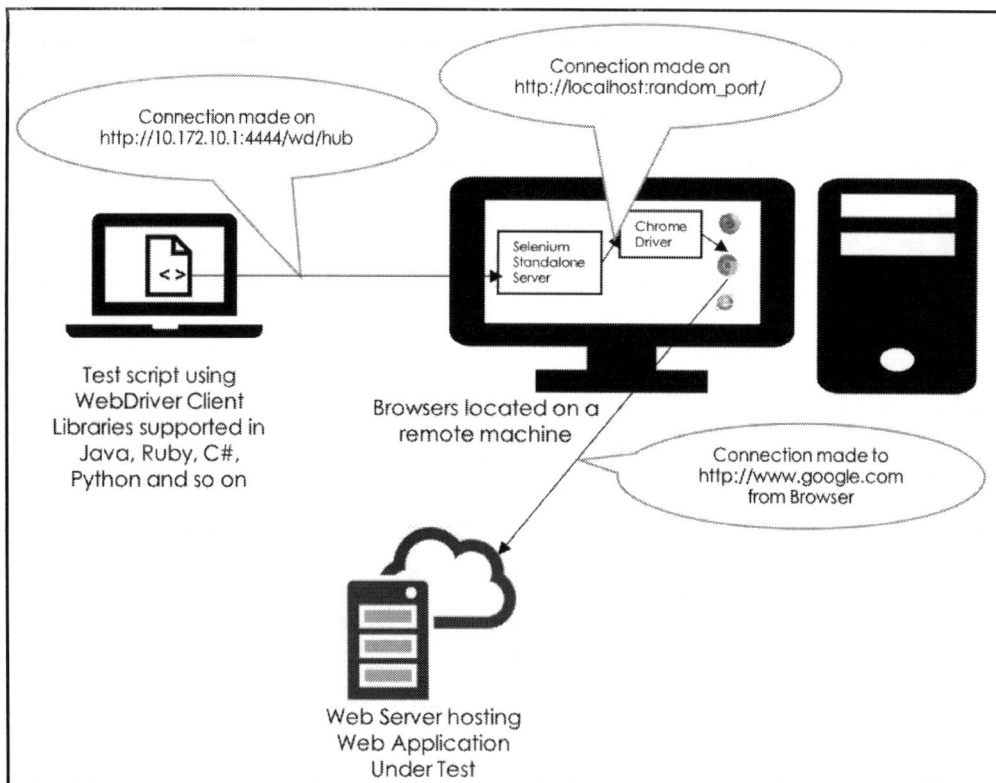

Using RemoteWebDriver for Firefox

Using the Firefox browser to execute our test scripts is similar to using the Chrome browser, except for a couple of variations in how GeckoDriver is launched.

Let's see this by changing the test script that we used for the Chrome browser to the following script, using "firefox":

```
@BeforeMethod
public void setup() throws MalformedURLException {

    DesiredCapabilities caps = new DesiredCapabilities();
```

```
caps.setBrowserName("firefox");
caps.setCapability("marionette", true);

driver = new RemoteWebDriver(new URL("http://10.172.10.1:4444/wd/hub"),
caps);
    driver.get("http://demo-store.seleniumacademy.com/");

}
```

Before you try to execute this code, restart `Selenium Standalone Server` to use `GeckoDriver`:

```
java -jar -Dwebdriver.gecko.driver=geckodriver selenium-server-
standalone-3.12.0.jar
```

Try executing the preceding test script now, and you should see the Firefox browser getting launched and executing your test commands. `Selenium Standalone Server` has started `GeckoDriver`, created a connection to it, and started executing the test-script commands.

Using RemoteWebDriver for Internet Explorer

For executing tests on the Internet Explorer driver, the steps are similar to what we did with the Chrome and Firefox browsers.

Let's see this by changing the test script that we used for the Chrome or Firefox browser to the following script, using `"internet explorer"`:

```
@BeforeMethod
public void setup() throws MalformedURLException {

    DesiredCapabilities caps = new DesiredCapabilities();
    caps.setBrowserName("internet explorer");

    driver = new RemoteWebDriver(new URL("http://127.0.0.1:4444/wd/hub"),
caps);
    driver.get("http://demo-store.seleniumacademy.com/");

}
```

Before you try to execute this code, restart `Selenium Standalone Server` to use `InternetExplorerDriver`:

```
java -jar -Dwebdriver.ie.driver=InternetExplorerDriver.exe selenium-server-standalone-3.12.0.jar
```

Try executing the preceding test script now, and you should see the Internet Explorer browser getting launched and executing your test commands. `Selenium Standalone Server` has started `InternetExplorerDriver`, created a connection with it, and started executing the test-script commands.

Understanding the JSON wire protocol

In many places, we have mentioned that WebDriver uses the JSON wire protocol to communicate between client libraries and different driver (that is, Chrome Driver, IE Driver, Gecko Driver, and so on) implementations. In this section, we will see exactly what it is and which different JSON APIs a client library should implement to talk to the drivers.

JavaScript Object Notation (JSON) is used to represent objects with complex data structures. It is used primarily to transfer data between a server and a client on the web. It has become an industry standard for various REST web services, offering a strong alternative to XML.

A sample JSON file, saved as a `.json` file, will look as follows:

```
{
    "firstname":"John",
    "lastname":"Doe",
    "address":{
        "streetnumber":"678",
        "street":"Victoria Street",
        "city":"Richmond",
        "state":"Victoria",
        "country":"Australia"
    } "phone":"+61470315430"
}
```

A client can send a person's details to a server in the preceding JSON format, which the server can parse, and then create an instance of the person object for use in its execution. Later, the response can be sent back by the server to the client in the JSON format, the data of which the client can use to create an object of a class. This process of converting an object's data into the JSON format and JSON-formatted data into an object is called **serialization** and **de-serialization**, respectively, which is quite common in REST-based web services.

WebDriver uses the same approach to communicate between client libraries (language bindings) and drivers, such as Firefox Driver, IE Driver, and Chrome Driver. Similarly, the `RemoteWebDriver` client and `Selenium Standalone Server` use the JSON wire protocol to communicate among themselves. But all of these drivers use it under the hood, hiding all the implementation details from us and making our lives simpler. The list of APIs for various actions that we can take on a web page is as follows:

```
/status /session /sessions /session/:sessionId /session/:sessionId/timeouts
/session/:sessionId/timeouts/async_script
/session/:sessionId/timeouts/implicit_wait
/session/:sessionId/window_handle /session/:sessionId/window_handles
/session/:sessionId/url /session/:sessionId/forward
/session/:sessionId/back /session/:sessionId/refresh
/session/:sessionId/execute /session/:sessionId/execute_async
/session/:sessionId/screenshot /session/:sessionId/ime/available_engines
/session/:sessionId/ime/active_engine
. . .
. . . /session/:sessionId/touch/flick /session/:sessionId/touch/flick
/session/:sessionId/location /session/:sessionId/local_storage
/session/:sessionId/local_storage/key/:key
/session/:sessionId/local_storage/size /session/:sessionId/session_storage
/session/:sessionId/session_storage/key/:key
/session/:sessionId/session_storage/size /session/:sessionId/log
/session/:sessionId/log/types /session/:sessionId/application_cache/status
```

The complete documentation is available at `https://code.google.com/p/selenium/wiki/ JsonWireProtocol`. The client libraries will translate your test-script commands into the JSON format and send the requests to the appropriate WebDriver API. The WebDriver will parse these requests and take necessary actions on the web page. Let's see that as an example. Suppose your test script has this code: `driver.get("http://www.google.com");`.

The client library will translate that into JSON by building a JSON payload (JSON document) and post the request to the appropriate API. In this case, the API that handles the `driver. get(URL)` method is `/session/:sessionId/url`.

The following code shows what happens in the client library layer behind the scenes before the request is sent to the driver; the request is sent to the RemoteWebDriver server running on 10.172.10.1:4444:

```
HttpClient httpClient = new DefaultHttpClient();
HttpPost postMethod = new
HttpPost("http://10.172.10.1:4444/wd/hub/session/"+sessionId+"/url");
JSONObject jo=new JSONObject();
jo.put("url","http://www.google.com");
StringEntity input = new StringEntity(jo.toString());
input.setContentEncoding("UTF-8");
input.setContentEncoding(new BasicHeader(HTTP.CONTENT_TYPE,
"application/json"));
postMethod.setEntity(input);
HttpResponse response = httpClient.execute(postMethod);
```

`Selenium Standalone Server` will forward that request to the driver; the driver will execute the test-script commands that arrive in the preceding format on the web application, under the test that is loaded in the browser.

The following diagram shows the dataflow at each stage:

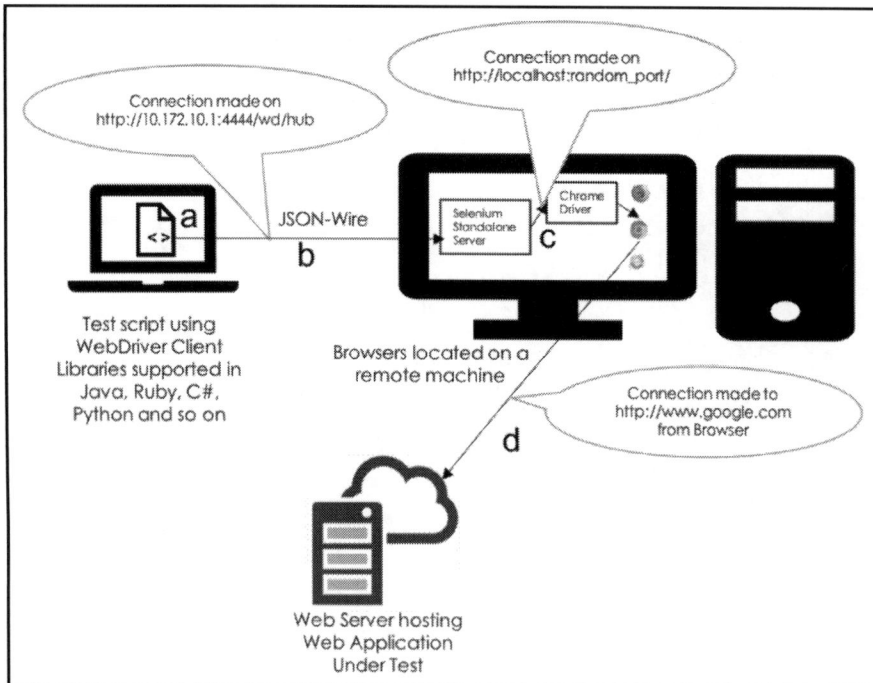

The preceding diagram shows the following:

- The first stage is communication between the test script and the client library. The data or command that flows between them is a call to the `get()` method of the driver: `driver.get("http://www.google.com");`.
- The client library, as soon as it receives the preceding command, will convert it into the JSON format and communicate with `Selenium Standalone Server`.
- Next, `Selenium Standalone Server` forwards the JSON payload request to the Chrome Driver.
- The Chrome Driver will communicate with the Chrome browser natively, and then the browser will send a request for the asked URL to load.

Summary

In this chapter, we learned about `RemoteWebDriver` and how to execute test scripts remotely on a different machine using `Selenium Standalone Server` and the `RemoteWebDriver` client. This enables Selenium WebDriver tests to be executed on remote machines with different browser and OS combinations. We also looked at the JSON wire protocol and how client libraries work behind the scenes to send and receive requests and responses to and from the drivers.

In the next `chapter`, we will extend the usage of Selenium Standalone Server and RemoteWebDriver to create a Selenium Grid for cross-browser and distributed testing.

Questions

1. With Selenium, we can execute tests on remote machine(s)— true or false
2. Which driver class is used to run tests on a remote machine?
3. Explain desired capabilities.
4. What protocol is used between the Selenium test and Selenium Standalone Server?
5. What is the default port used by Selenium Standalone Server?

Further information

You can check out the following link for more information about the topics covered in this chapter:

- Selenium WebDriver W3C specification explains the WebDriver Protocol and all the endpoints: `https://www.w3.org/TR/webdriver/`

Setting up Selenium Grid

8

Now that we know what RemoteWebDriver is and how it works, we are ready to learn about Selenium Grid. In this chapter, we will cover the following topics:

- Why we need Selenium Grid
- What Selenium Grid is
- How we can use Selenium Grid
- Test cases using Selenium Grid
- Configuring Selenium Grid

Exploring Selenium Grid

Let's try to understand why we need Selenium Grid by analyzing a scenario. You have a web application that needs to be tested on the following browser-machine combinations:

- Google Chrome on Windows 10
- Google Chrome on macOS
- Internet Explorer 11 on Windows 10
- Firefox on Linux

We can simply alter the test script we created in the previous chapter and point to the Selenium Standalone Server running on each of these combinations (that is, Windows 10, macOS, or Linux), as shown in the following code.

Windows 10:

```
DesiredCapabilities caps = new DesiredCapabilities();
caps.setBrowserName("chrome");
caps.setPlatform(Platform.WIN10);
WebDriver driver = new RemoteWebDriver(new
URL("http://<win_10_ip>:4444/wd/hub"), capabilities);
```

macOS:

```
DesiredCapabilities caps = new DesiredCapabilities();
caps.setBrowserName("chrome");
caps.setPlatform(Platform.MAC);
WebDriver driver = new RemoteWebDriver(new
URL("http://<mac_os_ip>:4444/wd/hub"), capabilities);
```

Linux:

```
DesiredCapabilities caps = new DesiredCapabilities();
caps.setBrowserName("chrome");
caps.setPlatform(Platform.LINUX);
WebDriver driver = new RemoteWebDriver(new
URL("http://<linux_ip>:4444/wd/hub"), capabilities);
```

In the preceding code, your test scripts are tightly coupled to the machines that host the target platform and the target browsers. If the Windows 10 host changes, you should refactor your test script to handle that. This is not an ideal way to design your tests. The focus of your test scripts should be on the functionality of your web application and not on the infrastructure that is used to execute these test scripts. There should be a central point to manage all the different environments. To solve this, we make use of **Selenium Grid**.

The **Selenium Grid** offers a cross-browser testing environment with several different platforms (such as Windows, Mac, and Linux) to execute tests. The Selenium Grid is managed from a central point, called the **hub.** The hub has the information of all the different testing platforms, known as **nodes** (the machines that have the desired operating systems and browser versions and connected to the hub). The hub assigns these nodes to execute tests whenever the test scripts request them, based on the capabilities requested by the test. The following diagram shows what a Selenium Grid looks like:

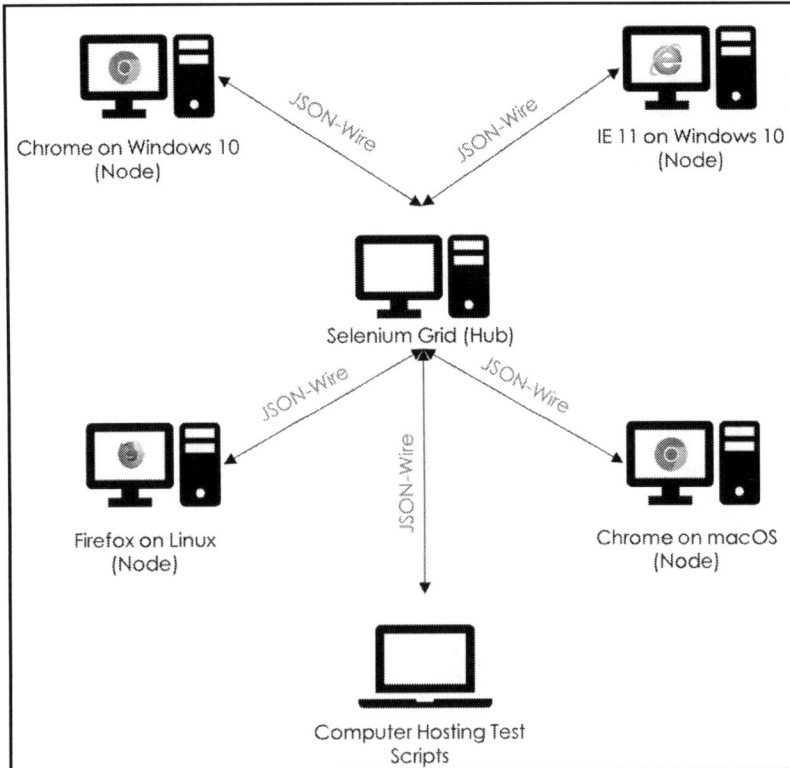

In the preceding diagram, there is one **hub**, four **nodes** of different platforms, and the machine where the test scripts are located. The test script will communicate with the hub and request a target platform to be executed. The hub assigns a node with the target platform to the test script. The node executes the test script and sends the result back to the hub, which in turn forwards the results to the test script. This is what Selenium Grid looks like and how it works at a high level.

Now that we have seen how Selenium Grid works theoretically, let's see what works as hubs and nodes in it. Fortunately, as we are dealing with Selenium Grid, we can use the same Remote WebDriver server that we used in the previous chapter to work as Selenium Grid as well. If you remember, we used `seleniumserver-standalone-3.12.0.jar` to start as a Selenium Standalone Server. We can use the same JAR file to be started in the hub mode on the hub machine, and a copy of the JAR file can be started in the node mode on the node machine. Try executing the following command on your JAR file:

```
java -jar selenium-server-standalone-3.12.0.jar -help
```

The following output shows how to use the server in a grid environment:

```
upgundecha@Unmeshs-iMac  ~/Downloads  java -jar selenium-server-standalone-3.12.0.
jar -help
Usage: <main class> [options]
  Options:
    --debug, -debug
      <Boolean> : enables LogLevel.FINE.
      Default: false
    --version, -version
      Displays the version and exits.
      Default: false
    -browserTimeout
      <Integer> in seconds : number of seconds a browser session is allowed to
      hang while a WebDriver command is running (example: driver.get(url)). If
      the timeout is reached while a WebDriver command is still processing,
      the session will quit. Minimum value is 60. An unspecified, zero, or
      negative value means wait indefinitely.
    -config
      <String> filename : JSON configuration file for the standalone server.
      Overrides default values
    -host
      <String> IP or hostname : usually determined automatically. Most
      commonly useful in exotic network configurations (e.g. network with VPN)
    -jettyThreads, -jettyMaxThreads
      <Integer> : max number of threads for Jetty. An unspecified, zero, or
      negative value means the Jetty default value (200) will be used.
    -log
      <String> filename : the filename to use for logging. If omitted, will
      log to STDOUT
    -port
      <Integer> : the port number the server will use.
    -role
      <String> options are [hub], [node], or [standalone].
    -timeout, -sessionTimeout
      <Integer> in seconds : Specifies the timeout before the server
      automatically kills a session that hasn't had any activity in the last X
      seconds. The test slot will then be released for another test to use.
      This is typically used to take care of client crashes. For grid hub/node
      roles. cleanUpCycle must also be set.
```

You will see two options: to use it as a Standalone Server, which acts as a Remote WebDriver, and to use it in a grid environment, which describes Selenium Grid. In this chapter, we will use this JAR file as a Selenium Grid.

Understanding the hub

The hub is the central point of a Selenium Grid. It has a registry of all the available nodes that are connected and part of a particular grid. The hub is a Selenium Standalone server running in the hub mode, listening on port 4444 of a machine by default. The test scripts will try to connect to the hub on this port, just as any Remote WebDriver. The hub will take care of rerouting the test-script traffic to the appropriate test-platform node. Let's see how we can start a hub node. Navigate to the location where you have your Selenium server JAR file and execute the following command:

```
java -jar selenium-server-standalone-3.12.0.jar -role hub
```

Doing this will start your server in the hub mode. By default, the server starts listening on port 4444; however, you can start your server on the port of your choice. Suppose you want to start the server on port 1111; it can be done as follows:

```
java -jar selenium-server-standalone-3.12.0.jar -role hub -port 1111
```

The following screenshot shows the console output of the Grid Hub being started on port 1111:

All the test scripts should connect to the hub on this port. Now launch your browser and connect to the machine that is hosting your hub on port 1111. Here, the machine that is hosting my hub has the IP address 192.168.0.101.

What you should see on your browser is shown in the following screenshot:

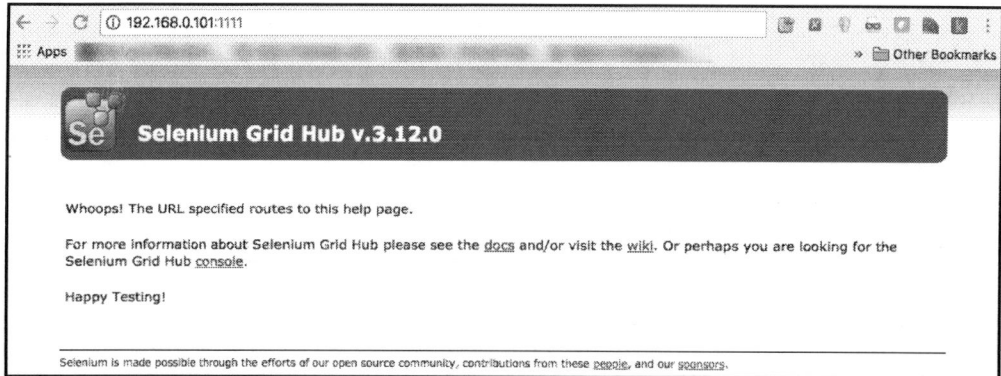

It shows the version of the server that is being used as the Grid Hub. Now click the **Console** link to navigate to the Grid Console:

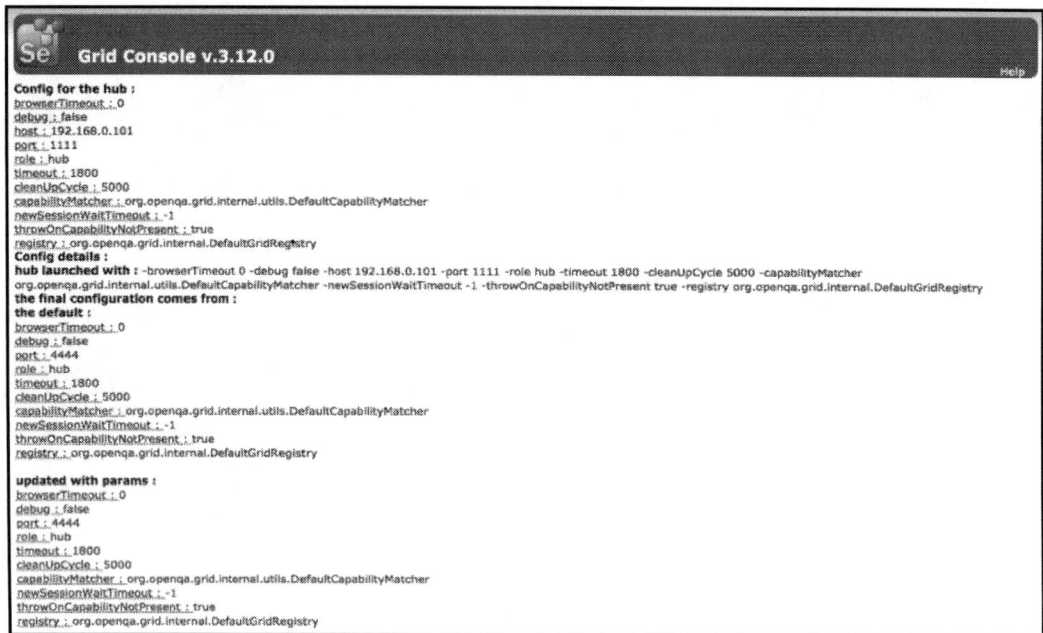

As you can see, the page talks about many configuration parameters. We will discuss these configuration parameters in the *Configuring Selenium Grid* section. So, you've now learned how to start a grid on a port and listen for connections.

Understanding the node

As our hub is up and running, it's now time to start a node and connect it to the hub. In this example, we will configure a macOS machine that has Chrome installed on it. So, if any test script requests the hub for a macOS platform and Chrome browser, the hub will choose this node. Let's see how we can start the node. The command to start the node and register with the hub is as follows:

```
java -jar selenium-server-standalone-3.12.0.jar -role node -hub
http://192.168.0.101:1111/grid/register
```

This will start the Selenium server in the node mode and register this node with the already-started hub:

```
upgundecha@Unmeshs-iMac   ~/Downloads   java -jar -Dwebdriver.chrome.driver=chromedriver selenium-server-standalo
ne-3.12.0.jar -role node -hub http://192.168.0.101:1111/grid/register
12:06:59.722 INFO [GridLauncherV3.launch] - Selenium build info: version: '3.12.0'; revision: '7c6e0b3'
12:06:59.748 INFO [GridLauncherV3$3.launch] - Launching a Selenium Grid node on port 16784
2018-06-10 12:06:59.890:INFO::main: Logging initialized @621ms to org.seleniumhq.jetty9.util.log.StdErrLog
12:07:00.086 INFO [SeleniumServer.boot] - Selenium Server is up and running on port 16784
12:07:00.086 INFO [GridLauncherV3$3.launch] - Selenium Grid node is up and ready to register to the hub
12:07:00.096 INFO [SelfRegisteringRemote$1.run] - Starting auto registration thread. Will try to register every 50
00 ms.
12:07:00.096 INFO [SelfRegisteringRemote.registerToHub] - Registering the node to the hub: http://192.168.0.101:11
11/grid/register
12:07:00.449 INFO [SelfRegisteringRemote.registerToHub] - Updating the node configuration from the hub
12:07:00.498 INFO [SelfRegisteringRemote.registerToHub] - The node is registered to the hub and ready to use
```

If you go back to the Grid Console on the browser, you will see the following:

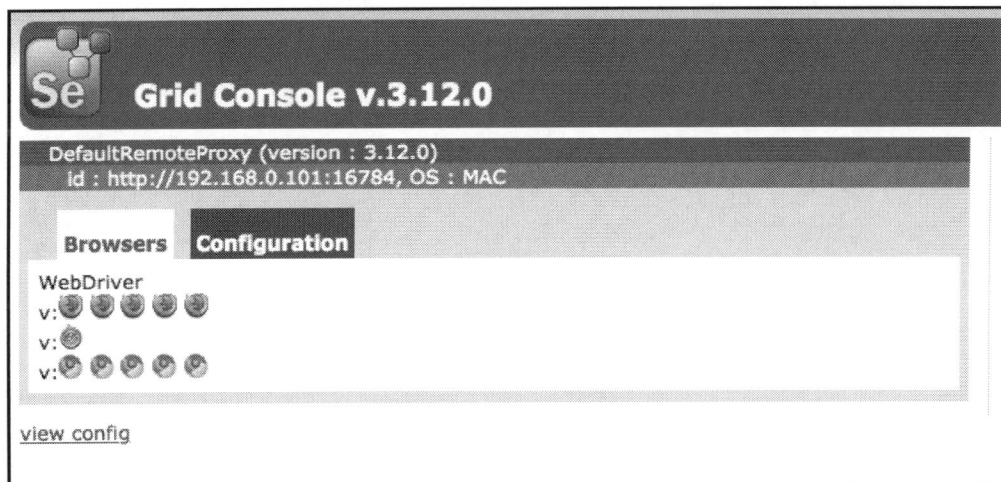

The preceding screenshot shows the **http://192.168.0.101:16784** node URL, which, in this case, is running on the Mac platform. By default, the number of browsers listed for every node is 11: 5 for Firefox, five for Chrome, and one for IE. This can be overridden by specifying the browser option, which we will see in the *Configuring Selenium Grid* section.

Similarly, start another node on Windows and register to the hub using the same command used to start the node on macOS.

Modifying the existing test script to use Selenium Grid

So far, we have seen test scripts that run on our local machines or on Selenium Standalone servers. Executing test scripts on Selenium Grid is very similar to executing tests on Remote WebDriver, except that you will also mention the platform details for Grid.

Let's look at a test script that uses the Remote WebDriver server:

```
public class SearchTest {

    WebDriver driver;

    @BeforeMethod
    public void setup() throws MalformedURLException {

        DesiredCapabilities caps = new DesiredCapabilities();

        caps.setBrowserName("chrome");
        caps.setPlatform(Platform.MAC);

        driver = new RemoteWebDriver(new
URL("http://192.168.0.101:1111/wd/hub"), caps);
        driver.get("http://demo-store.seleniumacademy.com/");

    }

    @Test
    public void searchProduct() {

        // find search box and enter search string
        WebElement searchBox = driver.findElement(By.name("q"));

        searchBox.sendKeys("Phones");

        WebElement searchButton =
```

```
        driver.findElement(By.className("search-button"));

    searchButton.click();

    assertThat(driver.getTitle())
            .isEqualTo("Search results for: 'Phones'");
    }

    @AfterMethod
    public void tearDown() {
        driver.quit();
    }
}
```

Now try executing the preceding test script and observe the log output of the hub and the node. The output log of the hub is as follows:

```
12:21:19.197 INFO [ActiveSessionFactory.apply] - Capabilities are: Capabilities {browserName: chrome, platform: MA
C}
12:21:19.197 INFO [ActiveSessionFactory.lambda$apply$11] - Matched factory org.openqa.selenium.remote.server.Servi
cedSession$Factory (provider: org.openqa.selenium.chrome.ChromeDriverService)
Starting ChromeDriver 2.38.552518 (183d19265345f54ce39cbb94cf81ba5f15905011) on port 39474
Only local connections are allowed.
12:21:20.034 INFO [ProtocolHandshake.createSession] - Detected dialect: OSS
12:21:20.102 INFO [RemoteSession$Factory.lambda$performHandshake$0] - Started new session c9b6c5f5cf8f97312faadbed
f56bbb73 (org.openqa.selenium.chrome.ChromeDriverService)
12:21:25.202 INFO [ActiveSessions$1.onStop] - Removing session c9b6c5f5cf8f97312faadbedf56bbb73 (org.openqa.seleni
um.chrome.ChromeDriverService)
```

The sequence of steps that happens at the hub end is as follows:

1. The hub gets a request to create a new session for platform=MAC, browserName=chrome.
2. It verifies the available nodes that match the capabilities request.
3. If available, it creates a new session with the node host; if not, it rejects the request from the test script, saying that the desired capabilities don't match any of the registered nodes.
4. If a session is created with the node host in the preceding step, create a new test-slot session and hand over the test script to the node. Similarly, the output you should see in the console log of the hub is as follows:

```
12:21:19.181 INFO [RequestHandler.process] - Got a request to create a new session: Capabilities {browserName: chr
ome, platform: MAC}
12:21:19.182 INFO [TestSlot.getNewSession] - Trying to create a new session on test slot {server:CONFIG_UUID=4a2db
c4a-ae28-4398-897c-27ff56f71b99, seleniumProtocol=WebDriver, browserName=chrome, maxInstances=5, platformName=MAC,
platform=MAC}
```

The sequence of steps performed on the node is as follows:

1. The node host creates a new session with the requested desired capabilities. This will launch the browser.
2. It executes the test script's steps on the launched browser.
3. It ends the session and forwards the result to the hub, which in turn sends it to the test script.

Requesting for non-registered capabilities

The hub will reject the request from the test script when the test script asks for a capability that is not registered with the hub. Let's modify the preceding test script to request the Opera browser instead of Chrome. The test script should look as follows:

```
@BeforeMethod
public void setup() throws MalformedURLException {

    DesiredCapabilities caps = new DesiredCapabilities();

    caps.setBrowserName("opera");
    caps.setPlatform(Platform.MAC);

    driver = new RemoteWebDriver(new
URL("http://192.168.0.101:1111/wd/hub"), caps);
    driver.get("http://demo-store.seleniumacademy.com/");

}
```

The hub checks whether there is any node that matches the desired capabilities. If it doesn't find one (as in this case), it will reject the request from the test script by throwing a `CapabilityNotPresentOnTheGridException` exception, as shown in the following screenshot:

```
12:28:59.965 INFO [RequestHandler.process] - Got a request to create a new session: Capabilities {browserName: ope
ra, platform: MAC}
12:28:59.966 INFO [RequestHandler.process] - Error forwarding the new session cannot find : Capabilities {browserN
ame: opera, platform: MAC}
org.openqa.grid.common.exception.CapabilityNotPresentOnTheGridException: cannot find : Capabilities {browserName:
opera, platform: MAC}
        at org.openqa.grid.internal.ProxySet.verifyAbilityToHandleDesiredCapabilities(ProxySet.java:153)
        at org.openqa.grid.internal.DefaultGridRegistry.addNewSessionRequest(DefaultGridRegistry.java:217)
        at org.openqa.grid.web.servlet.handler.RequestHandler.process(RequestHandler.java:111)
        at org.openqa.grid.web.servlet.DriverServlet.process(DriverServlet.java:86)
        at org.openqa.grid.web.servlet.DriverServlet.doPost(DriverServlet.java:70)
        at javax.servlet.http.HttpServlet.service(HttpServlet.java:707)
```

Queuing up the request if the node is busy

By default, you can send five test-script requests to any node. Although it is possible to change that configuration, let's see what happens when a node is already serving five requests, and you fire up another request for that node via the hub. The hub will keep polling the node until it gets a free test slot from the node. The test scripts are made to wait during this time. The hub says there are no free slots for the sixth session to be established with the same node. Meanwhile, on the node host, the node tries to create sessions for the five requests and starts executing the test scripts.

Upon creating the sessions, five Chrome windows are launched and the test scripts are executed on them. After serving the first five test-script requests, the hub will establish the waiting sixth session with the node, and the sixth request will be served.

Dealing with two nodes with matching capabilities

There are many configuration options that Selenium Grid provides to control the behavior of a node and a hub while you execute your test scripts. We will discuss them here.

Configuring Selenium Grid

There are many configuration options that Selenium Grid provides to control the behavior of a node and a hub while you execute your test scripts. We will discuss them here.

Specifying node-configuration parameters

In this section, we will go through the configuration parameters for a node.

Setting supported browsers by a node

As we saw earlier, when we register a node with a hub, by default, the node is shown as supporting five instances of the Firefox browser, five instances of the Chrome browser, and one instance of Internet Explorer, irrespective of whether the node actually supports them. But to register your node with the browsers of your choice, Selenium Grid provides a browser option, using which we can achieve this. Let's say we want our node to be registered to support Firefox, Chrome, and Safari; we can do that using the following command:

```
java -jar selenium-server-standalone-3.12.0.jar -role node -hub
http://192.168.0.1:1111/grid/register -browser browserName=firefox -browser
browserName=chrome -browser browserName=safari
```

The **Grid Console** looks like this:

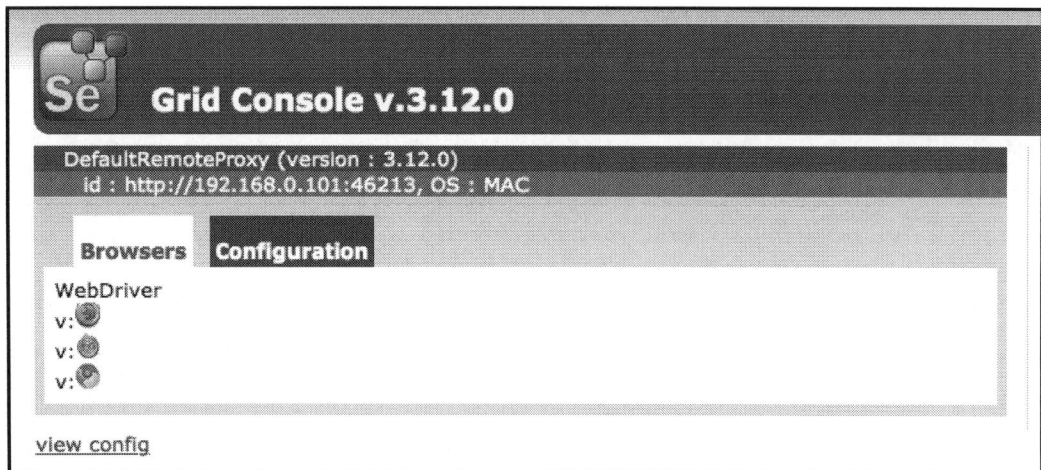

Setting node timeouts

This parameter is set when registering a node with a hub. The value provided to these parameters is the time in seconds that a hub can actually wait before it terminates a test script execution on a node if the test script doesn't perform any kind of activity on the node.

The command to configure your node with a node timeout is as follows:

```
java -jar selenium-server-standalone-3.12.0.jar -role node -hub
http://192.168.0.1:1111/grid/register -nodeTimeout 300
```

Here, we have registered a node with a node timeout value of 300 seconds. So, the hub will terminate the test script if it doesn't perform any activity on the node for more than 300 seconds.

Setting the limit on browser instances

We have seen that, by default, there are 11 instances of browsers getting registered to a node. We have seen how to register our own browser. In this section, we will see how many instances of those browsers we can allow in our node. For this to be controlled, Selenium Grid comes out with a configuration parameter, called `maxInstances`, using which we can specify how many instances of a particular browser we want our node to provide. The command to do that is as follows:

```
java -jar selenium-server-standalone-3.12.0.jar -role node -hub
http://192.168.0.1:1111/grid/register -browser "browserName=firefox,max
Instances=3" -browser "browserName=chrome,maxInstances=3" -browser
"browserName=safari,maxInstances=1"
```

Here, we are registering a node that provides three instances of Firefox, three instances of Chrome, and one instance of Safari.

Reregistering the node automatically

If the hub crashes or restarts after a node registers to it, all the information of the nodes that are already registered is lost. Going back to each of the nodes and reregistering them manually would prove to be tedious. The impact will be even worse if we haven't realized that the hub has restarted, because all the test scripts would fail as a result. So, to handle this kind of situation, Selenium Grid provides a configuration parameter to a node, through which we can specify the node to reregister itself automatically to the hub after a specified amount of time. If not specified, the default time of reregistration is five seconds. This way, we really don't have to worry; even if the hub crashes or restarts, our node will try to reregister every five seconds.

If you want to modify this time interval, the configuration parameter to deal with is `registerCycle`. The command to specify is as follows:

```
java -jar selenium-server-standalone-3.12.0.jar -role node -hub
http://192.168.0.1:1111/grid/register -registerCycle 10000
```

The output you will see on the node log console during startup is as follows:

```
17:47:01.231 INFO - starting auto register thread. Will try to register
every 10000 ms.
 17:47:01.232 INFO - Registering the node to hub
:http://192.168.0.1:1111/grid/register
```

The node will try to register to the hub every 1,000 milliseconds.

Setting node health-check times

Using this configuration parameter, we can specify how frequently the hub can poll a node for its availability. The parameter that is used to achieve this is `nodePolling`. By specifying this to the hub at the node level, each node can specify its own frequency at which it can be health-checked. The command to configure your node is as follows:

```
java -jar selenium-server-standalone-3.12.0.jar -role node -hub
http://192.168.0.1:1111/grid/register -nodePolling 10
```

Now the hub will poll this node every 10 seconds, to check its availability.

Unregistering an unavailable node

Although the `nodePolling` configuration will make the hub poll the node often, the `unregisterIfStillDownAfter` configuration will let the hub unregister the node if the poll doesn't produce an expected result. Let's say a node is down, and the hub tries to poll the node and is unable to connect to it. At this point, how long the hub is going to poll for the availability of the node is determined by the `unregisterIfStillDownAfter` parameter. Beyond this time, the hub will unregister the node.

The command to do that is as follows:

```
java -jar selenium-server-standalone-3.12.0.jar -role node -hub
http://192.168.0.1:1111/grid/register -nodePolling 5 -
unregistIfStillDownAfter 20000
```

Here, the hub will poll the node every five seconds; if the node is down, the polling will continue for 20 seconds, that is, the hub will poll four times and then unregister the node from the grid.

Setting the browser timeout

This configuration is to let the node know how long it should wait before it ends a test script session when the browser seems to hang. After this time, the node will abort the browser session and start with the next waiting test script. The configuration parameter for this is `browserTimeout`. The command to specify that is as follows:

```
java -jar selenium-server-standalone-3.12.0.jar -role node -hub
http://192.168.0.1:1111/grid/register -browserTimeout 60
```

So, these are the some of the configuration parameters that you can specify at the node's end to have better control over the Selenium Grid environment.

Hub-configuration parameters

This section talks about some of the configuration parameters on the hub side.

Waiting for a match of the desired capability

As we saw earlier, when the test script asks for a test platform with a desired capability, the hub will reject the request if it doesn't find a suitable node with the desired capability.

Altering the value for the `throwOnCapabilityNotPresent` parameter can alter this behavior. By default, it is set to `true`, which means the hub will reject the request if it doesn't find a suitable node with that capability. But setting this parameter to `false` will queue the request, and the hub will wait until a node with that capability is added to the grid. The command that has to be invoked is as follows:

```
java -jar selenium-server-standalone-3.12.0.jar -role hub -port 1111 -
throwOnCapabilityNotPresent false
```

Now the hub will not reject the request, but will place the request in a queue and wait until the requested platform is available.

Customized CapabilityMatcher

By default, the hub will use the `org.openqa.grid.internal.utils.DefaultCapabilityMatcher` class to match the requested node. If you do not like the implementation logic of the `DefaultCapabilityMatcher` class, you can extend the class, implement your own `CapabilityMatcher` class, and provide your own logic in it.

Once developed, you can ask the hub to use that class to match the capabilities with the nodes, using a configuration parameter named `capabilityMatcher`. The command to achieve this is as follows:

```
java -jar selenium-server-standalone-3.12.0.jar -role hub -port 1111 -
capabilityMatcher com.yourcomp.CustomCapabilityMatcher
```

The hub will use the logic defined in your `CustomCapabilityMatcher` class to identify the nodes to be assigned to the test-script requests.

WaitTimeout for a new session

When a capability-matched node is busy executing other test scripts, the latest test script will wait for the node to be available. By default, there is no wait timeout; that is, the test script will wait for the node to be available indefinitely. To alter that behavior and to let the test script throw an exception if it doesn't get the node within a limited time, Selenium Grid opens a configuration that enables the test script to do so. The configuration parameter controlling that behavior is `newSessionWaitTimeout`. The command for that is as follows:

```
java -jar selenium-server-standalone-3.12.0.jar -role hub -port 1111 -
newSessionWaitTimeout 120000
```

Here, the test script will wait for two minutes before it throws an exception saying it couldn't obtain a node to execute itself.

Different ways to specify the configuration

There are two ways to specify the configuration parameter to the Selenium Grid's hub and node. The first one is what we have seen all this time; that is, specifying the configuration parameters over the command line. The second way of doing it is by providing a JSON file that contains all these configuration parameters.

A node configuration file (say, `nodeConfig.json`) — a typical JSON file having all the configuration parameters — looks similar to the following:

```
{
  "class": "org.openqa.grid.common.RegistrationRequest",
  "capabilities": [
    {
    "seleniumProtocol": "WebDriver",
    "browserName": "internet explorer",
    "version": "10",
    "maxInstances": 1,
```

```
    "platform" : "WINDOWS"
  }
],
"configuration": {
  "port": 5555,
  "register": true,
  "host": "192.168.1.102",
  "proxy": "org.openqa.grid.selenium.proxy.
  DefaultRemoteProxy",
  "maxSession": 2,
  "hubHost": "192.168.1.100",
  "role": "webdriver",
  "registerCycle": 5000,
  "hub": "http://192.168.1.101:111/grid/register",
  "hubPort": 1111,
  "remoteHost": "http://192.168.1.102:5555"
  }
}
```

Once these files are configured, they can be provided to the node and the hub, using the following command:

```
java -jar selenium-server-standalone-3.12.0.jar -role node -nodeConfig
nodeconfig.json
```

This way, you can specify the configuration of your hub and node using JSON files.

Using cloud-based grids for cross-browser testing

To set up a Selenium Grid for cross-browser testing, you need to set up physical or virtual machines with different browsers and operating systems. This requires an investment in the required hardware, software, and support to run the test lab. You also need to put in effort to keep this infrastructure updated with the latest versions and patches. Not everybody can afford these costs and the effort.

Instead of investing and setting up a cross-browser test lab, you can easily outsource a virtual test lab to a third-party cloud provider for cross-browser testing. The Sauce Labs and BrowserStack are leading cloud-based cross-browser testing cloud providers. Both of these have support for over 400 different browser and operating system configurations, including mobile and tablet devices, and support running Selenium WebDriver tests in their cloud.

Here, we will set up and run a test in the Sauce Labs cloud. The steps are similar if you want to run tests with BrowserStack.

Let's set up and run a test with Sauce Labs. You need a free Sauce Labs account, to begin with. Register for a free account on Sauce Labs at `https://saucelabs.com/`, and get the username and access key. Sauce Labs provides all the needed hardware and software infrastructure to run your tests in the cloud. You can get the access key from the Sauce Labs dashboard after you log in from the **My Account** page:

Access Key

c6e7132c-ae27-4217-b6fa-

Generate a new access key

Let's create a new test to execute on the Sauce Labs cloud. We need to add the Sauce username and access key to the test, and change the Grid address to the Sauce Labs Grid address instead of the local Selenium Grid, as shown in the following code example:

```
public class BmiCalculatorTest {

    WebDriver driver;

    @BeforeMethod
    public void setUp() throws Exception {

        String SAUCE_USER = "upgundecha";
        String SAUCE_KEY = "5768f2a9-33be-4ebd-9a5f-3826d7c38ec9";

        DesiredCapabilities caps = new DesiredCapabilities();
        caps.setCapability("platform", "OS X 10.9");
        caps.setCapability("browserName", "Safari");
        caps.setCapability("name", "BMI Calculator Test");
        driver = new RemoteWebDriver(
                new
    URL(MessageFormat.format("http://{0}:{1}@ondemand.saucelabs.com:80/wd/hub'"
    ,
                SAUCE_USER, SAUCE_KEY)), caps);
        driver.get("http://bit.ly/1zdNrFZ");

    }

    @Test
    public void testBmiCalc() {
```

```
        WebElement height = driver.findElement(By.name("heightCMS"));
        height.sendKeys("181");

        WebElement weight = driver.findElement(By.name("weightKg"));
        weight.sendKeys("80");

        WebElement calculateButton =
    driver.findElement(By.id("Calculate"));
        calculateButton.click();

        WebElement bmi = driver.findElement(By.name("bmi"));
        assertEquals(bmi.getAttribute("value"), "24.4");

        WebElement bmi_category =
    driver.findElement(By.name("bmi_category"));
        assertEquals(bmi_category.getAttribute("value"), "Normal");
    }

    @AfterMethod
    public void tearDown() throws Exception {
        driver.quit();
    }
}
```

When you execute the test, it will connect to Sauce Lab's hub and request the desired operating system and browser configuration. The sauce Labs cloud-management software automatically assigns a virtual machine for our test to run on a given configuration. We can monitor this run on a dashboard, as shown in the following screenshot:

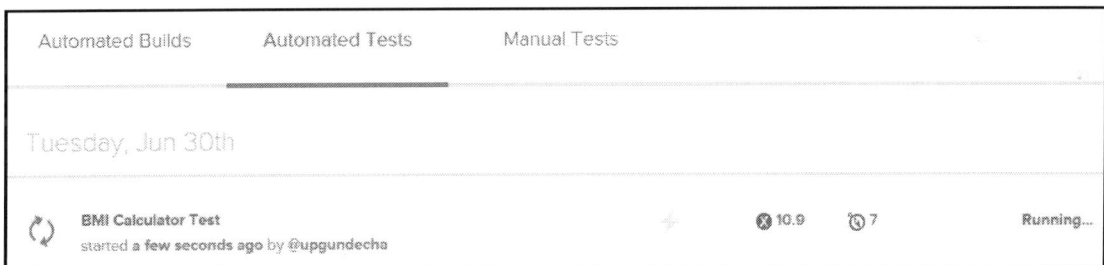

We can further drill down into the session and see exactly what happened during the run. It provides details of the Selenium commands, screenshots, logs, and a video of the execution on multiple tabs, as shown in the following screenshot:

Selenium details window

> **TIP**
>
> You can also test applications that are securely hosted on internal servers, by using the Sauce Connect utility. sauce connect creates a secure tunnel between your machine and the Sauce cloud.

Summary

In this chapter, we learned about Selenium Grid, how a hub and node will work, and, more importantly, how to configure your Selenium Grid to have better control over the environment and infrastructure. The Selenium Grid will enable cross-browser testing for the application by covering combinations of operating systems and browsers. We also saw how to use cloud services, such as Sauce Labs, to execute tests in a remote cloud environment.

In the next `chapter`, we will learn how to create reusable and modular tests using the Page Object pattern.

Questions

1. Which argument can be used to specify how many browser instances can be supported by the node?
2. Explain how Selenium Grid can be used to support Cross Browser Testing.
3. What is the URL you need to specify with RemoteWebDriver to run tests on Selenium Grid?
4. Selenium Grid Hub acts as a load balancer— true or false?

Further information

You can check out the following link for more information about the topics covered in this chapter:

- Read more about Selenium Grid
  at `https://www.seleniumhq.org/docs/07_selenium_grid.jsp`

The PageObject Pattern

9

So far, we have seen various APIs of WebDriver and learned how to use them to accomplish various actions on the web application we have been testing. We created a number of tests that use these APIs and are executed continuously to validate the application. However, as your test suite grows, the complexity of your tests and code will also grow. This becomes a challenge, with respect to the maintainability of your scripts and code. You will need to design a maintainable, modular, and reusable test code that will scale as you add more test coverage. In this chapter, we will explore the PageObject pattern to build a highly maintainable test suite. We will cover the following topics:

- What is the PageObject pattern design?
- Good practices for designing PageObjects
- Extensions to the PageObject pattern
- An end-to-end example

A decently written test script would work just fine, as long as the target web application doesn't change. But once one or more pages in your web application change, as a test-script developer, you shouldn't be in a position where you have to refactor your test scripts in a hundred different places. Let's understand this statement better with the help of an example. We will try to go through this chapter by working on a WordPress blog. Before we start, I would like you to create a WordPress blog (`http://wordpress.com/about`) or use one of your existing ones.

Creating test cases for our WordPress blog

Here, we are using a WordPress blog: `http://demo-blog.seleniumacademy.com/wp/`. Let's create three test cases for it before we start talking about the PageObject pattern.

Test case 1 – adding a new post to our WordPress blog

The following test script will log into the Admin portal of our WordPress blog and add a new blog post:

```
@Test
public void testAddNewPost() {
    WebElement email = driver.findElement(By.id("user_login"));
    WebElement pwd = driver.findElement(By.id("user_pass"));
    WebElement submit = driver.findElement(By.id("wp-submit"));
    email.sendKeys("admin");
    pwd.sendKeys("$$SUU3$$N#");
    submit.click();

    // Go to AllPosts page
  driver.get("http://demo-blog.seleniumacademy.com/wp/wp-admin/edit.php");

  // Add New Post
  WebElement addNewPost = driver.findElement(By.linkText("Add New"));
  addNewPost.click();

    // Add New Post's Content
    WebElement title = driver.findElement(By.id("title"));
    title.click();
    title.sendKeys("My First Post");

    driver.switchTo().frame("content_ifr");
    WebElement postBody = driver.findElement(By.id("tinymce"));
    postBody.sendKeys("This is description");
    driver.switchTo().defaultContent();

    // Publish the Post
    WebElement publish = driver.findElement(By.id("publish"));
    publish.click();
}
```

The following is the sequence of steps that the preceding code performs:

1. Log into the WordPress Admin portal.
2. Go to the **All Posts** page.
3. Click on the **Add New** post button.
4. Add a new post by providing the title and description.
5. Publish the post.

Test case 2 – deleting a post from our WordPress blog

The following test script will log into our WordPress blog and delete an existing post:

```
@Test
public void testDeleteAPost() {
    WebElement email = driver.findElement(By.id("user_login"));
    WebElement pwd = driver.findElement(By.id("user_pass"));
    WebElement submit = driver.findElement(By.id("wp-submit"));
    email.sendKeys("admin");
    pwd.sendKeys("$$SUU3$$N#");
    submit.click();

    // Go to AllPosts page
    driver.get("http://demo-blog.seleniumacademy.com/wp/wp-
admin/edit.php");

    // Click on the post to be deleted
    WebElement post = driver.findElement(By.linkText("My First Post"));
    post.click();

    // Delete Post
    WebElement publish = driver.findElement(By.linkText("Move to Trash"));
    publish.click();
}
```

The following is the sequence of steps that the preceding test script follows to delete a post:

1. Log into the WordPress Admin portal.
2. Go to the **All Posts** page.
3. Click on the post to be deleted.
4. Delete the post.

Test case 3 – counting the number of posts on our WordPress blog

The following test script will count all the posts currently available on our WordPress blog:

```
@Test
public void testPostCount() {
    WebElement email = driver.findElement(By.id("user_login"));
    WebElement pwd = driver.findElement(By.id("user_pass"));
    WebElement submit = driver.findElement(By.id("wp-submit"));
    email.sendKeys("admin");
    pwd.sendKeys("$$SUU3$$N#");
    submit.click();

    // Count the number of posts
    driver.get("http://demo-blog.seleniumacademy.com/wp/wp-
admin/edit.php");
    WebElement postsContainer = driver.findElement(By.id("the-list"));
    List postsList = postsContainer.findElements(By.
            tagName("tr"));

    Assert.assertEquals(postsList.size(), 1);
}
```

The following is the sequence of steps that the preceding test script follows to count the number of posts currently available on our blog:

1. Log into the Admin portal.
2. Go to the **All Posts** page.
3. Count the number of posts available.

In the previous three test scripts, we log into WordPress and perform an action, such as creating a post, deleting a post, or counting the number of existing posts. Imagine that the ID of an element on the login page has changed, and we have to modify that in all three different test cases; or, if the **All Posts** page has changed, that we have to edit all three test cases to reflect the new changes. If you have 50 test cases, changing each of them every time there is a change in the target application is very difficult. For this purpose, you need to design a test framework that keeps the changes that you need to make in the test cases to a minimum. The PageObject pattern is a design pattern that can be used to design your test framework.

What is the PageObject pattern?

Whenever we are designing an automation framework for testing web applications, we have to accept the fact that the target application and its elements are bound to change. An efficient framework is one that needs minimal refactoring to adapt to new changes in the target application. Let's try to build the preceding test scenarios into the PageObject design pattern model. Let's first start building a PageObject for the login page. This should look like the following:

```
public class AdminLoginPage {
    WebDriver driver;
    WebElement email;
    WebElement password;
    WebElement submit;

    public AdminLoginPage(WebDriver driver) {
        this.driver = driver;
        driver.get("http://demo-blog.seleniumacademy.com/wp/wp-admin");
        email = driver.findElement(By.id("user_login"));
        password = driver.findElement(By.id("user_pass"));
        submit = driver.findElement(By.id("wp-submit"));
    }

    public void login() {
        email.sendKeys("admin");
        password.sendKeys("$$SUU3$$N#");
        submit.click();
    }
}
```

So, all the elements that are part of the process of signing in are listed in the `AdminLoginPage` class and there is a method named `login()`, which manages the populating of these elements and submits the login form. Thus, this `AdminLoginPageobject` class, will represent WordPress's administration login page, constituting all the elements that are listed on the page as member variables and all the actions that can be taken on the page as methods. Now, let's see how we need to refactor the test case to use our newly created PageObject. Let's consider the following `testAddNewPost` test case:

```
@Test
public void testAddNewPost() {
    AdminLoginPage admLoginPage = new AdminLoginPage(driver);
    admLoginPage.login();
    // Go to New Posts page
    driver.get("http://demo-blog.seleniumacademy.com/wp/wp-admin/edit.php");
```

```
    WebElement addNewPost = driver.findElement(By.linkText("Add New"));
            addNewPost.click();
    // Add New Post
    driver.switchTo().frame("content_ifr");
    WebElement postBody = driver.findElement(By.id("tinymce"));
    postBody.sendKeys("This is description");
    driver.switchTo().defaultContent();
    WebElement title = driver.findElement(By.id("title"));
    title.click();
    title.sendKeys("My First Post");
    WebElement publish = driver.findElement(By.id("publish"));
    publish.click();
}
```

In the preceding test case, the entire code for logging into the admin page is contained in just two lines:

```
AdminLoginPage admLoginPage = new AdminLoginPage(driver);
admLoginPage.login();
```

Navigating to the admin login page, identifying the elements, providing values for the elements, and submitting the form —everything is taken care of by the PageObject. Thus, from now on, the test case doesn't need to be refactored for any changes to the admin page. You just have to change the PageObject, and all the test cases using this PageObject will start using the new changes without even knowing they occurred.

Now that you have seen what a PageObject looks like, the Selenium library provides even more convenient ways to implement your PageObjects. Let's take a look at them.

Using the @FindBy annotation

An element in the PageObject is marked with the @FindBy annotation. It is used to direct the WebDriver to locate that element on a page. It takes the locating mechanism (that is, by Id, Name, or Class Name) and the value of the element for that locating mechanism as input.

There are two ways of using the @FindBy annotation:

Usage 1 is shown as follows:

```
@FindBy(id="user_login")
WebElement userId;
```

Usage 2 is shown as follows:

```
@FindBy(how=How.ID, using="user_login")
WebElement userId;
```

The preceding two usages direct the WebDriver to locate the element using the locating mechanism ID with the `user_login` value and assign that element to the `userId` WebElement. In usage 2, we have used the How enumeration. This enumeration supports all the different locating mechanisms that our `By` class supports. The enumeration constants supported in the How enumeration are as follows:

- CLASS_NAME
- CSS
- ID
- ID_OR_NAME
- LINK_TEXT
- NAME
- PARTIAL_LINK_TEXT
- TAG_NAME
- XPATH

Using the `@FindBy` annotation, we will see how our `AdminLoginPage` class changes:

```
public class AdminLoginPage {

    WebDriver driver;
    @FindBy(id="user_login")
    WebElement email;
    @FindBy(id="user_pass")
    WebElement password;
    @FindBy(id="wp-submit")
    WebElement submit;
    public AdminLoginPage(WebDriver driver){
        this.driver = driver;
        driver.get("http://demo-blog.seleniumacademy.com/wp/wp-admin");
    }
    public void login(){
        email.sendKeys("pageobjectpattern@gmail.com");
        password.sendKeys("webdriver123");
        submit.click();
    }
}
```

When the test case instantiates the preceding class in the constructor, we navigate to the WordPress login page using the following code specified in the constructor:

```
driver.get("http://demo-blog.seleniumacademy.com/wp/wp-admin");
```

Once the driver state is set to this page, all the FindBy declared elements, that is, email, password, and submit, are initialized by the WebDriver using the locating mechanisms specified in the FindBy annotation.

Understanding PageFactory

Another important class that the WebDriver library provides to support the PageObject pattern is the PageFactory class. Once the PageObject class declares elements using the FindBy annotation, you can instantiate that PageObject class and its elements using the PageFactory class. This class supports a static method named initElements. The API syntax for this method is as follows:

```
initElements(WebDriver driver, java.lang.Class PageObjectClass)
```

Now, let's see how this can be used in our test case to create AdminLoginPage:

```
public class TestAddNewPostUsingPageObjects { public static void
main(String... args){
AdminLoginPage loginPage= PageFactory
.initElements(driver, AdminLoginPage.class);
loginPage.login();
```

The PageFactory class instantiates the AdminLoginPage class and gives it the driver instance. The AdminLoginPage PageObject navigates the driver instance to a URL (http:// demo-blog.seleniumacademy.com/wp/wp-admin, in this case) and then populates all its elements annotated with the FindBy annotation.

Good practices for the PageObjects design

So, now that you have seen what a simple implementation of PageObject looks like, it's time to consider some good practices in designing PageObjects for your test framework.

Think of a web page as a services provider

At a high level, when you look at a page in a web application, you will find it is an aggregation of various User Services. For example, if you take a look at the **All Posts** page in our WordPress Admin console, there are many sections in it:

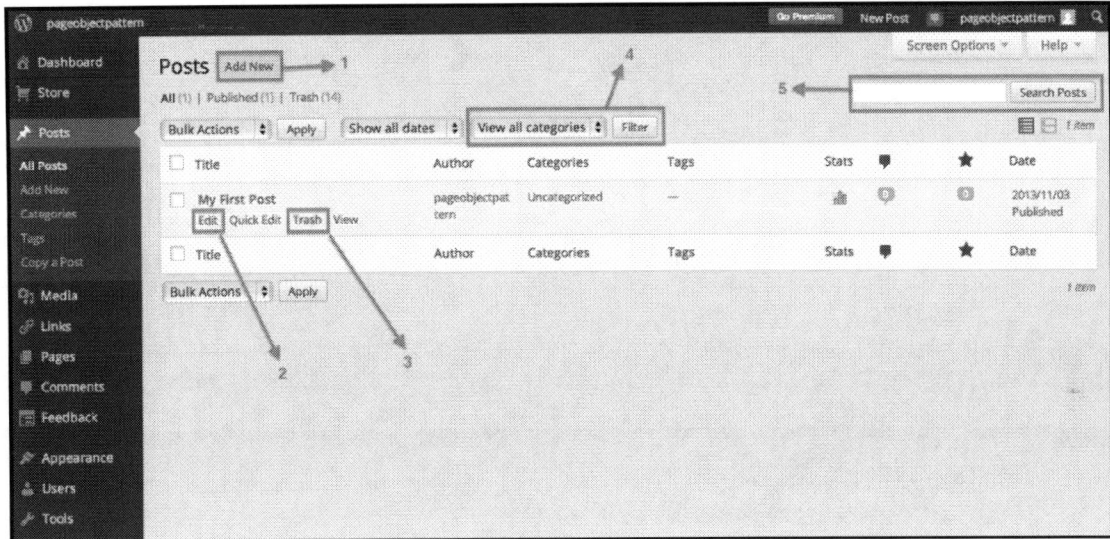

In the preceding screenshot, in the `All Posts` page, a user can perform the following five activities:

- Add a new post.
- Edit a selected post.
- Delete a selected post.
- Filter the posts by category.
- Search for text in all the posts.

The preceding activities are the services that the **All Posts** page provides to its users. So, your PageObject should also provide these services for the test case, which is the user of this PageObject. The code for the **All Posts** PageObject should look as follows:

```
public class AllPostsPage {

    WebDriver driver;
    @FindBy(id = "the-list")
    WebElement postsContainer;

    @FindBy(id = "post-search-input")
    WebElement searchPosts;

    @FindBy(id = "cat")
    WebElement viewByCategories;

    public AllPostsPage(WebDriver driver) {
        this.driver = driver;
driver.get("http://demo-blog.seleniumacademy.com/wp/wp-admin/edit.php");
    }

    public void createANewPost(String title, String description) {
    }

    public void editAPost(String title) {
    }

    public void deleteAPost(String postTitle) {
    }

    public void filterPostsByCategory(String category) {
    }

    public void searchInPosts(String searchText) {
    }
}
```

Now, we have mapped the identified services on the page to the methods in our PageObject. When a test case wants to execute a service, it will get assistance from the PageObject to accomplish that.

Always look for implied services

Some of a page's services can be identified very clearly on it. And there are some services that are not visible on the page but that are implied. For example, in the **All Posts** page, we have identified five services just by looking at the page. But let's say your test case wants to know the count of existing posts; this information is available on the **All Posts** page, and we have to make sure that your PageObject provides that as an implied service. Now you extend your PageObject for the **All Posts** page with this implied service, which looks as follows:

```java
public class AllPostsPage {

    WebDriver driver;
    @FindBy(id = "the-list")
    WebElement postsContainer;

    @FindBy(id = "post-search-input")
    WebElement searchPosts;

    @FindBy(id = "cat")
    WebElement viewByCategories;

    public AllPostsPage(WebDriver driver) {
        this.driver = driver;
        driver.get("http://demo-blog.seleniumacademy.com/wp/wp-admin/edit.php");
    }

    public void createANewPost(String title, String description) {
    }

    public void editAPost(String title) {
    }

    public void deleteAPost(String postTitle) {
    }

    public void filterPostsByCategory(String category) {
    }

    public void searchInPosts(String searchText) {
    }

    public int getAllPostsCount(){
    }
}
```

Now your test cases can employ the same PageObject to use the implied services relevant to the **All Posts** page.

Using PageObjects within a PageObject

There will be many situations where you need to use PageObjects within a PageObject. Let's analyze that using a scenario on the **All Posts** page. When you click on **Add New** to add a new post, the browser actually navigates to a different page. So, you have to create two PageObjects, one for the **All Posts** page and another for the **Add New** page. Designing your PageObjects to simulate the exact behavior of our target application will keep things very clear and independent of each other. You may be able to navigate to the **Add New** page in several different ways. Creating a PageObject of its own for the **Add New** page and using it wherever needed will make your test framework adhere to good object-oriented fundamentals, and make the maintenance of your test framework easy. Let us see what using PageObjects within a PageObject will look like.

The AddNewPost PageObject

The `AddNewPost` PageObject adds new posts, as shown in the following code:

```
public class AddNewPostPage {

    WebDriver driver;

    @FindBy(id = "content_ifr")
    WebElement newPostContentFrame;

    @FindBy(id = "tinymce")
    WebElement newPostContentBody;

    @FindBy(id = "title")
    WebElement newPostTitle;

    @FindBy(id = "publish")
    WebElement newPostPublish;

    public AddNewPostPage(WebDriver driver) {
        this.driver = driver;
    }

    public void addNewPost(String title, String descContent) {
        newPostTitle.click();
        newPostTitle.sendKeys(title);
```

```
        driver.switchTo().frame(newPostContentFrame);
        newPostContentBody.sendKeys(descContent);
        driver.switchTo().defaultContent();
        newPostPublish.click();
    }
}
```

The AllPostsPage PageObject

The `AllPostsPage` PageObject deals with the `All posts page`, as shown in the following code:

```
public class AllPostsPage {

    WebDriver driver;

    @FindBy(id = "the-list")
    WebElement postsContainer;

    @FindBy(id = "post-search-input")
    WebElement searchPosts;

    @FindBy(id = "cat")
    WebElement viewByCategories;

    @FindBy(linkText = "Add New")
    WebElement addNewPost;

    public AllPostsPage(WebDriver driver) {
        this.driver = driver;
driver.get("http://demo-blog.seleniumacademy.com/wp/wp-admin/edit.php");
    }

    public void createANewPost(String title, String description) {
        addNewPost.click();
        AddNewPostPage newPost = PageFactory.initElements(driver,
                AddNewPostPage.class);
        newPost.addNewPost(title, description);
    }

    public void editAPost(String title) {
    }

    public void deleteAPost(String title) {
    }

    public void filterPostsByCategory(String category) {
```

```
        }

    public void searchInPosts(String searchText) {
    }

    public int getAllPostsCount() {
    }
  }
}
```

Now, as you can see in the `AllPostsPage` PageObject, we have instantiated the `AddNewPage` PageObject in the `createNewPost()` method. Thus, we are using one PageObject with another and keeping the behavior as close as possible to the target application.

Think of methods in PageObjects as services and not as user actions

There might sometimes be confusion surrounding what methods make a PageObject. We saw earlier that each PageObject should contain **User Services** as their methods. But quite often, we see some implementations of PageObjects in several test frameworks that constitute `User Actions` as their methods. So what is the difference between a `User Service` and a `User Action`? As we have already seen, some of the examples of User Services on the WordPress Admin console are as follows:

- Create a new post
- Delete a post
- Edit a post
- Search in posts
- Filter posts
- Count all existing posts

All the preceding services talk about the various functionalities of the target application. Now, let's see some examples of `User Actions`:

- Mouse-click
- Typing text in a textbox
- Navigating to a page
- Clicking on a checkbox
- Select an option from a dropdown

The previous list showed some examples of User Actions on a page. They are common across many applications. Your PageObject is not meant to provide your test case with User Actions, but with User Services. So, each method in your PageObject should map to a service that the target page provides to the user. To accomplish a User Service, PageObject methods should contain many User Actions.

> Several User Actions come together to accomplish a User Service.

Here is an example of what your PageObject will look like if it provisions its methods with User Actions instead of User Services is as follows; let's see what the AddNewPage PageObject will look like:

```java
public class AddNewPost {

    WebDriver driver;

    @FindBy(id = "content_ifr")
    WebElement newPostContentFrame;

    @FindBy(id = "tinymce")
    WebElement newPostContentBody;

    @FindBy(id = "title")
    WebElement newPostTitle;

    @FindBy(id = "publish")
    WebElement newPostPublish;

    public AddNewPost(WebDriver driver) {
        this.driver = driver;
        System.out.println(driver.getCurrentUrl());
    }
    public void typeTextinTitle(String title) {
        newPostTitle.sendKeys(title);
    }

    public void clickPublishButton() {
        newPostPublish.click();
    }

    public void typeTextinContent(String descContent) {
        driver.switchTo().frame(newPostContentFrame);
        newPostContentBody.sendKeys(descContent);
```

```
        }
    }
```

So, in the code of the AddNewPage PageObject, we have three different methods to accomplish three different User Actions. The caller object, instead of just invoking the addNewPage(String title, String description) method, should now invoke the following:

```
typeTextinTitle(String title)
typeTextinContent(String description)
clickPublishButton()
```

The preceding User Actions are three different User Actions to accomplish adding a new post User Service. The caller of these methods should also keep in mind the order in which these User Actions need to be called; that is, the clickPublishButton() method should always come last. This introduces unnecessary complexity to your test cases and other PageObjects that try to add new posts to the system. Thus, User Services will hide most of the implementation details from the users of the PageObjects and reduce the cost of maintaining your test cases.

Identifying some WebElements on the fly

In all the PageObjects, we have initialized the elements that we are going to use during object instantiation, using the @FindBy annotation. It is always good to identify all the elements of a page that are required to accomplish a User Service and assign them to the member variables in your PageObject. However, it is not always possible to do that. For example, if you want to edit a particular post in the **All Posts** page, it is not mandatory, during PageObject initialization, to map each post on the page to a member variable in your PageObject. When you have a large number of posts, your PageObject initialization will be spending unnecessary time mapping the posts to your member variables, even though we don't use them. Besides, we don't even know how many member variables we need to map all the posts in the **All Posts** page. The HTML for the **All Posts** page looks as follows:

There is a root element identified by `the-list`, which contains all the posts in the WordPress blog. Within this element, we can see that there's Post1, Post2, and Post3. So having your PageObject initialized for all three posts is not an optimal solution. You can initialize your PageObject with a member variable mapped to the root element and the target post will be retrieved from it whenever required.

Let's take a look at the `AllPostsPage` PageObject that implements its `editPost()` method in the following way:

```
public void editAPost(String presentTitle,
                      String newTitle, String description){
    List<WebElement> allPosts
            = postsContainer.findElements(By.className("rowtitle"));
    for(WebElement ele : allPosts){
        if(ele.getText().equals(presentTitle)){
            Actions builder = new Actions(driver);
            builder.moveToElement(ele);
            builder.click(driver.findElement(
                    By.cssSelector(".edit>a")));
            // Generate the composite action.
            Action compositeAction = builder.build();
            // Perform the composite action.
            compositeAction.perform();
            break;
        }
    }
    EditPost editPost
            = PageFactory.initElements(driver, EditPost.class);
    editPost.editPost(newTitle, description);
}
```

Notice that in the previous code that only the root element is identified by `the-list`; the element that contains all the posts in the All Posts page is mapped to a member variable, named `pageContainer` in the `AllPostsPage` PageObject. The target post is extracted only when it is needed in the `editAPost()` method. This way, your PageObject initialization doesn't take much time and has all the necessary elements mapped.

Keeping the page-specific details off the test script

The ultimate aim of the PageObject pattern design is to maintain the page-specific details, such as the IDs of the elements on the page and the way we reach a particular page in the application, away from the test script. Building your test framework using the PageObject pattern should allow you to keep your test scripts very generic and not need a modification each time the page implementation details change. Finally, whenever there is a change done to a web page, such as a login page, the number of changes that need to be done for 50 test scripts that use this page should ideally be 0. Just changing the PageObject should handle adapting all the tests to the new changes.

Understanding loadable components

The loadable component is an extension of the PageObject pattern. The `LoadableComponent` class in the WebDriver library will help test-case developers make sure that the page or a component of the page is loaded successfully. It tremendously reduces the efforts to debug your test cases. The PageObject should extend this LoadableComponent abstract class and, as a result, it is bound to provide an implementation for the following two methods:

```
protected abstract void load()
protected abstract void isLoaded() throws java.lang.Error
```

The page or component that has to be loaded in the `load()` and `isLoaded()` methods determines whether the page or component is fully loaded. If it is not fully loaded, it throws an error.

Let's now modify the `AdminLoginPage` PageObject to extend the LoadableComponent class and see how it looks, using the following code:

```
public class AdminLoginPageUsingLoadableComponent extends
LoadableComponent<AdminLoginPageUsingLoadableComponent> {

    WebDriver driver;

    @FindBy(id = "user_login")
    WebElement email;

    @FindBy(id = "user_pass")
    WebElement password;

    @FindBy(id = "wp-submit")
```

```
        WebElement submit;

        public AdminLoginPageUsingLoadableComponent(WebDriver driver) {
            this.driver = driver;
            PageFactory.initElements(driver, this);
        }

        public AllPostsPage login(String username, String pwd) {
            email.sendKeys(username);
            password.sendKeys(pwd);
            submit.click();
            return PageFactory.initElements(driver, AllPostsPage.class);
        }

        @Override
        protected void load() {
            driver.get("http://demo-blog.seleniumacademy.com/wp/wp-admin");
        }

        @Override
        protected void isLoaded() throws Error {
            Assert.assertTrue(driver.getCurrentUrl().contains("wp-admin"));
        }
    }
```

The URL that has to be loaded is specified in the `load()` method and the `isLoaded()` method validates whether or not the correct page is loaded. Now, the changes that are to be done in your test case are as follows:

```
AdminLoginPageUsingLoadableComponent loginPage = new
AdminLoginPageUsingLoadableComponent(driver).get();
```

The `get()` method from the `LoadableComponent` class will make sure the component is loaded by invoking the `isLoaded()` method.

Working on an end-to-end example of WordPress

Now that we know what PageObjects are, it's time to take a look at an end-to-end example that interacts and tests the WordPress Admin console. First, we will see all the PageObjects and then the test cases that use them.

Looking at all the PageObjects

Let's first see all the PageObjects that are involved in testing the WordPress Admin console.

The AdminLoginPage PageObject

The AdminLoginPage PageObject deals with the login page. This object has to be refactored if any changes have been made to the page in the target application, using the following code:

```
package com.packt.webdriver.chapter9.pageObjects;
import org.openqa.selenium.WebDriver;
public class AdminLoginPage {

    WebDriver driver;

    @FindBy(id = "user_login")
    WebElement email;

    @FindBy(id = "user_pass")
    WebElement password;

    @FindBy(id = "wp-submit")
    WebElement submit;

    public AdminLoginPage(WebDriver driver) {
        this.driver = driver;
        driver.get("http://demo-blog.seleniumacademy.com/wp/wp-admin");
    }

    public AllPostsPage login(String username, String pwd) {
        email.sendKeys(username);
        password.sendKeys(pwd);
        submit.click();
        return PageFactory.initElements(driver,
                AllPostsPage.class);
    }
}
```

The constructor of the `AdminLoginPage` PageObject accepts the WebDriver instance. This will let the test framework use the same driver instance throughout the execution across test scripts as well as PageObjects; thus, the state of the browser and web application is preserved. You will see similar constructors for all the PageObjects. Apart from the constructor, the `AdminLoginPage` PageObject provides the `login(String username, String pwd)` service. This service lets the test scripts log into the WordPress blog and, in return, gets the `AllPostsPage` PageObject. Before returning the instance of the `AllPostsPage` PageObject, the PageFactory PageObject will initialize all the WebElements of the `AllPostsPage` PageObject. Thus, all of the implementation details of the login service are hidden from the test script, and it can work with the `AllPostsPage` PageObject.

The AllPostsPage PageObject

The `AllPostsPage` PageObject deals with the **All Posts** page, using the following code:

```
public class AllPostsPage {

    WebDriver driver;

    @FindBy(id = "the-list")
    WebElement postsContainer;

    @FindBy(id = "post-search-input")
    WebElement searchPosts;

    @FindBy(id = "cat")
    WebElement viewByCategories;

    @FindBy(linkText = "Add New")
    WebElement addNewPost;

    public AllPostsPage(WebDriver driver) {
        this.driver = driver;
driver.get("http://demo-blog.seleniumacademy.com/wp/wp-admin/edit.php");
    }

    public void createANewPost(String title, String description) {
        addNewPost.click();
        AddNewPostPage newPost = PageFactory.initElements(driver,
                AddNewPostPage.class);
        newPost.addNewPost(title, description);
    }

    public void editAPost(String presentTitle, String newTitle,
```

```
                            String description) {
        goToParticularPostPage(presentTitle);
        EditPostPage editPost = PageFactory.initElements(driver,
                EditPostPage.class);
        editPost.editPost(newTitle, description);
    }

    public void deleteAPost(String title) {
        goToParticularPostPage(title);
        DeletePostPage deletePost =
                PageFactory.initElements(driver, DeletePostPage.class);
        deletePost.delete();
    }

    public void filterPostsByCategory(String category) {
    }

    public void searchInPosts(String searchText) {
    }

    public int getAllPostsCount() {
        List<WebElement> postsList =
postsContainer.findElements(By.tagName("tr"));
        return postsList.size();
    }

    private void goToParticularPostPage(String title) {
        List<WebElement> allPosts
                = postsContainer.findElements(By.className("title"));
        for (WebElement ele : allPosts) {
            if (ele.getText().equals(title)) {
                Actions builder = new Actions(driver);
                builder.moveToElement(ele);
                builder.click(driver.findElement(
                        By.cssSelector(".edit>a")));
                // Generate the composite action.
                Action compositeAction = builder.build();
                // Perform the composite action.
                compositeAction.perform();
                break;
            }
        }
    }
}
```

The `AllPostsPage` PageObject provides six services:

- Create a post
- Edit a post
- Delete a post
- Filter posts by category
- Search for text in posts
- Count the number of posts available

Once the test scripts obtains an instance of this PageObject via the login service of the `AdminLoginPage` PageObject, it can use any of the six services of this PageObject and test it. If any of the implementation details change, such as the navigation to a particular post or the ID of a WebElement on this page, the test script doesn't really have to worry about it. Modifying this PageObject will apply the changes to the WordPress blog.

The AddNewPostPage PageObject

The `AddNewPostPage` PageObject deals with adding a new post to the blog, using the following code:

```
package com.example;

import org.openqa.selenium.WebDriver;
import org.openqa.selenium.WebElement;
import org.openqa.selenium.support.FindBy;

public class AddNewPostPage {

    WebDriver driver;

    @FindBy(id = "content_ifr")
    WebElement newPostContentFrame;

    @FindBy(id = "tinymce")
    WebElement newPostContentBody;

    @FindBy(id = "title")
    WebElement newPostTitle;

    @FindBy(id = "publish")
    WebElement newPostPublish;

    public AddNewPostPage(WebDriver driver) {
        this.driver = driver;
```

```
        }

    public void addNewPost(String title, String descContent) {
        newPostTitle.click();
        newPostTitle.sendKeys(title);
        driver.switchTo().frame(newPostContentFrame);
        newPostContentBody.sendKeys(descContent);
        driver.switchTo().defaultContent();
        newPostPublish.click();
    }
}
```

The `AddNewPostPage` PageObject is instantiated in the `createANewPost` service of the `AllPostsPage` PageObject. This PageObject provides a service named `addNewPost` that takes input for `title` and `description` for the post and publishes a new post in the blog with them.

The EditPostPage PageObject

The `EditPostPage` PageObject deals with editing an existing post, using the following code:

```
package com.example;

import org.openqa.selenium.WebDriver;
import org.openqa.selenium.WebElement;
import org.openqa.selenium.support.FindBy;

public class EditPostPage {

    WebDriver driver;

    @FindBy(id = "content_ifr")
    WebElement newPostContentFrame;

    @FindBy(id = "tinymce")
    WebElement newPostContentBody;

    @FindBy(id = "title")
    WebElement newPostTitle;

    @FindBy(id = "publish")
    WebElement newPostPublish;

    public EditPostPage(WebDriver driver) {
        this.driver = driver;
```

```
            System.out.println(driver.getCurrentUrl());
    }

    public void editPost(String title, String descContent) {
        newPostTitle.click();
        newPostTitle.clear();
        newPostTitle.sendKeys(title);
        driver.switchTo().frame(newPostContentFrame);
        newPostContentBody.clear();
        newPostContentBody.sendKeys(descContent);
        driver.switchTo().defaultContent();
        newPostPublish.click();
    }
}
```

The `EditPostPage` PageObject is similar to the `AddNewPostPage` PageObject and is instantiated at the `editAPost` service of the `AllPostsPage` PageObject. This provides a service named `editPost` to edit an existing post. The new `title` and `description` are passed as input parameters to this service.

The DeletePostPage PageObject

The `DeletePostPage` PageObject deals with deleting an existing post, using the following code:

```
package com.example;

import org.openqa.selenium.WebDriver;
import org.openqa.selenium.WebElement;
import org.openqa.selenium.support.FindBy;

public class DeletePostPage {

    WebDriver driver;

    @FindBy(linkText = "Move to Trash")
    WebElement moveToTrash;

    public DeletePostPage(WebDriver driver) {
        this.driver = driver;
        System.out.println(driver.getCurrentUrl());
    }

    public void delete() {
        moveToTrash.click();
    }
```

```
}
```

The `DeletePostPage` PageObject is similar to the `AddNewPostPage` and `EditPostPage` PageObjects and is instantiated at the `deleteAPost` service of the `AllPostsPage` PageObject. This provides a service, named `delete`, to delete an existing post. As you can see, the `AddNewPostPage`, `EditPostPage`, and `DeletePostPage` PageObjects take you to the same page. So, it makes sense to merge these three PageObjects into one that provides services for adding, editing, and deleting posts.

Looking at the test cases

Now it's time to see the test cases that use the PageObjects to interact with the WordPress Admin console.

Adding a new post

This test case deals with adding a new post to the blog, using the following code:

```java
package com.example;

import org.openqa.selenium.WebDriver;
import org.openqa.selenium.chrome.ChromeDriver;
import org.openqa.selenium.support.PageFactory;

import org.testng.annotations.AfterMethod;
import org.testng.annotations.BeforeMethod;
import org.testng.annotations.Test;

public class WordPressBlogTestsWithPageObject {

    WebDriver driver;
    String username = "admin";
    String password = "$$SUU3$$N#";

    @BeforeMethod
    public void setup() {

        System.setProperty("webdriver.chrome.driver",
                "./src/test/resources/drivers/chromedriver");
        driver = new ChromeDriver();
    }

    @Test
    public void testAddNewPost() {
```

```
        AdminLoginPage loginPage =
                PageFactory.initElements(driver, AdminLoginPage.class);
        AllPostsPage allPostsPage = loginPage.login(username, password);
        allPostsPage.createANewPost("Creating New Post using PageObjects",
                "Its good to use PageObjects");
    }

    @AfterMethod
    public void tearDown() {
        driver.quit();
    }

}
```

The following is the sequence of steps executed in the preceding test script to test how to add a new post to the WordPress blog:

1. The test script creates a ChromeDriver instance, because it intends to test the scenario of adding a new post to the blog on the Chrome browser.
2. It creates an instance of the `AdminLoginPage` PageObject that uses the same driver instance created in the previous step.
3. Once it gets the instance of the `AdminLoginPage` PageObject, it uses the `login` service to log into the WordPress admin console. The `login` service, in return, gives out an instance of the `AllPostsPage` PageObject instance to the test script.
4. The test script uses the instance of the `AllPostsPage` PageObject obtained in the previous step to use one of the many services provided by the `All Posts` page. In this case, it uses the `createANewPost` service.

Editing a post

This test case deals with the testing and editing of a post in the blog using the following code:

```
@Test
public void testEditPost() {
    AdminLoginPage loginPage =
            PageFactory.initElements(driver, AdminLoginPage.class);
    AllPostsPage allPostsPage = loginPage.login(username, password);
    allPostsPage.editAPost("Creating New Post using PageObjects",
            "Editing Post using PageObjects", "Test framework low
maintenance");
}
```

The following is the sequence of steps executed in the preceding test script to test how to add a new post to the WordPress blog:

1. It creates an instance of the `AdminLoginPage` PageObject that uses the same driver instance created in the previous step.
2. Once it gets the instance of the `AdminLoginPage` PageObject, it uses the `login` service to log into the WordPress admin console. The `login` service, in return, gives out an instance of the `AllPostsPage` PageObject instance to the test script.
3. The test script uses the instance of the `AllPostsPage` PageObject obtained in the previous step to use one of the many services provided by the **All Posts** page. In this case, it uses the `createANewPost` service.

Deleting a post

This test case deals with deleting a post, using the following code:

```
@Test (dependsOnMethods = "testEditPost")
public void testDeletePost() {
    AdminLoginPage loginPage =
            PageFactory.initElements(driver, AdminLoginPage.class);
    AllPostsPage allPostsPage = loginPage.login(username, password);
    allPostsPage.deleteAPost("Editing Post using PageObjects");
}
```

The following is the sequence of steps executed in the preceding test script to test the deleting of a post in the WordPress blog:

1. It creates an instance of the `AdminLoginPage` PageObject that uses the same driver instance created in the previous step.
2. Once it gets the instance of the `AdminLoginPage` PageObject, it uses the `login` service to log into the WordPress Admin console. The `login` service, in return, gives out an instance of the `AllPostsPage` PageObject instance to the test script.
3. The test script uses the instance of the `AllPostsPage` PageObject obtained in the previous step to use one of the many services provided by the **All Posts** page. In this case, it uses the `deleteAPost` service.

Counting posts

This test case deals with counting of the number of posts currently available in the blog, using the following code:

```
@Test
public void testCountPost() {
    AdminLoginPage loginPage =
            PageFactory.initElements(driver, AdminLoginPage.class);
    AllPostsPage allPostsPage = loginPage.login(username, password);
    Assert.assertEquals(allPostsPage.getAllPostsCount(), 1);
}
```

The following is the sequence of steps executed in the preceding test script to test counting the number of posts in the WordPress blog:

1. It creates an instance of the `AdminLoginPage` PageObject that uses the driver instance created in the previous step.
2. Once it gets the instance of the `AdminLoginPage` PageObject, it uses the `login` service to log into the WordPress Admin console. The `login` service, in return, gives out an instance of the `AllPostsPage` PageObject instance to the test script.
3. The test script uses the instance of the `AllPostsPage` PageObject obtained in the previous step to use one of the many services provided by the **All Posts** page. In this case, it uses the `getAllPostsCount` service.

Summary

In this chapter, we learned about the PageObject pattern and how we can implement a test framework using PageObjects. It has numerous advantages. The PageObject pattern and the `LoadableComponents` class provide a test framework that adapts easily to changes made to the target application, without changing any test cases. We should always remember that a well-designed test framework is always flexible to changes made to the target application. In the next chapter, we will look at testing iOS and Android mobile applications using, `Appium`.

Questions

1. How do you initialize a PageObject implemented with PageFactory?
2. Using which class can we implement methods to validate whether the page is loaded ?
3. Which `By class` methods are supported by @FindBy?
4. When using PageFactory, if you give the WebElement variable the name same ID or name attribute, then you don't need to use the @FindBy annotation— True or False?

Further information

You can check out the following links for more information about the topics covered in this chapter:

- **Test Design Considerations:** `https://www.seleniumhq.org/docs/06_test_design_considerations.jsp`
- **Automation in Selenium: PageObjectModel and PageFactory:** `https://www.toptal.com/selenium/test-automation-in-selenium-using-page-object-model-and-page-factory`

10
Mobile Testing on iOS and Android using Appium

In all the previous chapters, we have worked on web applications that are loaded in desktop browsers. But with the increasing number of mobile users, businesses today have to serve their users on mobile devices as well. In this chapter, you will learn about the following:

- The different types of mobile applications and testing tools
- How to test mobile application using Selenium WebDriver, more specifically, with Appium
- Testing mobile applications on Android and iOS
- Using cloud-based device labs for real device testing

`Appium` is an open source mobile-automation framework used to test mobile apps on iOS and Android platforms using the JSON wire protocol with Selenium WebDriver. Appium replaces the iPhoneDriver and AndroidDriver APIs in Selenium 2 that were used to test mobile web applications.

Different forms of mobile applications

There are three different forms in which an application can reach a user on the mobile platform:

- **Native apps**: Native apps are purely specific to the target mobile platform. They are developed in the platform-supported languages and are very much tied to underlying SDKs. For iOS, applications are developed in the Objective-C or Swift programming language and are dependent on iOS SDK; similarly, for the Android platform, they are developed in Java or Kotlin and are dependent on Android SDK.

- **m.site**: Also known as a mobile website, it is a mini version of your web application that loads on the browsers of your mobile devices. On iOS devices, it can be Safari or Chrome, and on Android devices, it can be the Android default browser or Chrome. For example, on your iOS or Android device, open your browser and type in `www.facebook.com`. Before the page loads, you will observe that a URL redirection happens from `www.facebook.com` to `m.facebook.com`. The Facebook application servers realize that the request has originated from a mobile device and start serving the mobile site rather than the desktop site. These m.sites use JavaScript and HTML5 to be developed like your normal web applications:

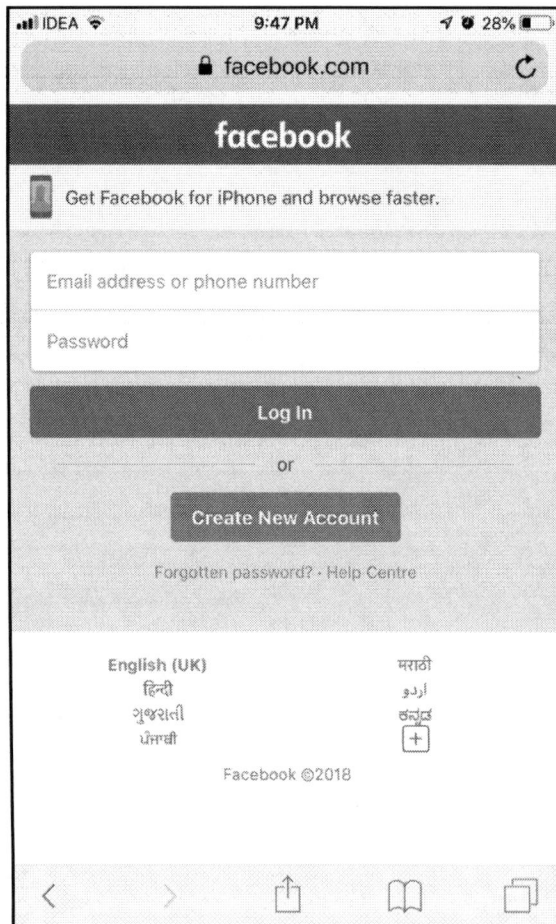

- **Hybrid apps**: The Hybrid app is a combination of the native app and the web app. When you develop a native app, some parts of it load HTML web pages into the app trying to make the user feel that they are using a native application. They generally use WebViews in native apps to load the web pages.

Now, as a test-scripts developer, you have to test all these different applications on various mobile devices.

Available software tools

To automate the testing of your applications on mobile devices, there are many software tools available. The following are some of the tools that are built based on Selenium WebDriver:

- **Appium**: A cross-platform and cross-technology mobile testing framework based on Selenium for native, hybrid, and mobile web applications. Appium enables the use and extension of the existing Selenium WebDriver framework to build mobile tests. As it uses Selenium WebDriver to drive the tests, we can use any language to create tests for which a Selenium client library exists. You can create and execute your test scripts against Android and iOS platforms without having to change the underlying driver. Appium can also work with Firefox OS platforms. In the rest of the chapter, we will see how we can work with Appium.
- **Selendroid**: This driver is similar to iOSDriver and can execute your native, hybrid, and m.site application test scripts on the Android platform. It uses the native UI Automator library provided by Google. The test scripts communicate with the Selendroid driver over the JSON wire protocol while using its favourite client-language bindings.

Automating iOS and Android tests using Appium

Appium is a popular and widely used tool that can be employed to automate mobile-app testing for both the Android and iOS platforms. It can be used to automate native, m.sites, and hybrid applications. It internally uses WebDriver's JSON wire protocol.

Automating iOS Application tests

For automating iOS app tests, Appium uses XCTest or UI Automation (for older iOS versions):

- **XCTest**: You can use XCTest to create and run unit tests, performance tests, and UI tests for your iOS applications built for iOS 9.3 and higher. It integrates with Xcode's testing workflow for testing the iOS application. Appium internally uses XCTest for automating the iOS applications.
- **UI Automation**: For testing apps developed for iOS 9.3 and lower, you need to use UI Automation. Appium receives the commands from test scripts over the JSON wire protocol. Appium sends these commands to Apple Instruments so that they can be executed on the app that is launched in a simulator or real device. While doing so, Appium translates the JSON commands into UI Automation JavaScript commands that can be understood by the instruments. The instruments take care of launching and closing the app in the simulator or device.

Appium works as a Remote WebDriver and receives the commands from your test scripts over the JSON wire protocol. These commands are passed to XCTest or Apple Instruments to be executed on the app launched on a simulator or a real device. This process is shown in the following diagram:

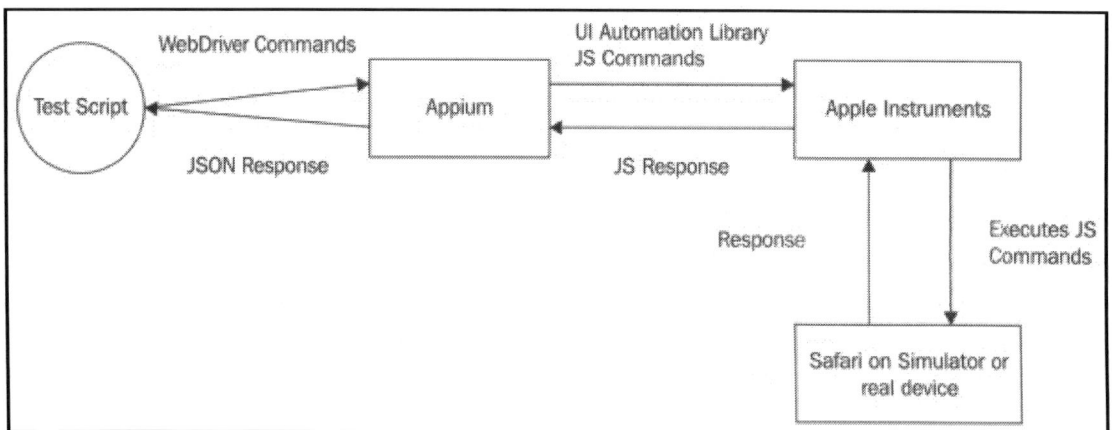

After the command is executed against your app on the simulator or device, the target app sends the response to XCTest or UI Automation Instrument, which is transferred to Appium in the JavaScript response format. Appium translates the responses into Selenium WebDriver JSON wire protocol responses and sends them back to your test script.

The main advantages of using Appium for your iOS automation testing are as follows:

- It uses the iOS platform-supported XCTest or the UI Automation library and instruments provided by Apple itself.
- Even though you are using the JavaScript library, you, and a test-script developer, and your tests are not really tied to it. You can use your own Selenium WebDriver client-language bindings, such as Java, Ruby, or Python, to develop your test scripts. Appium will take care of translating them into JavaScript for you.
- You don't have to modify your native or hybrid apps for the purpose of testing.

Automating Android application tests

Automating Android tests for your Android apps is similar to automating iOS apps tests. Except for the fact that your target platform is changing, your test scripts will not undergo any change. The following diagram that shows the workflow:

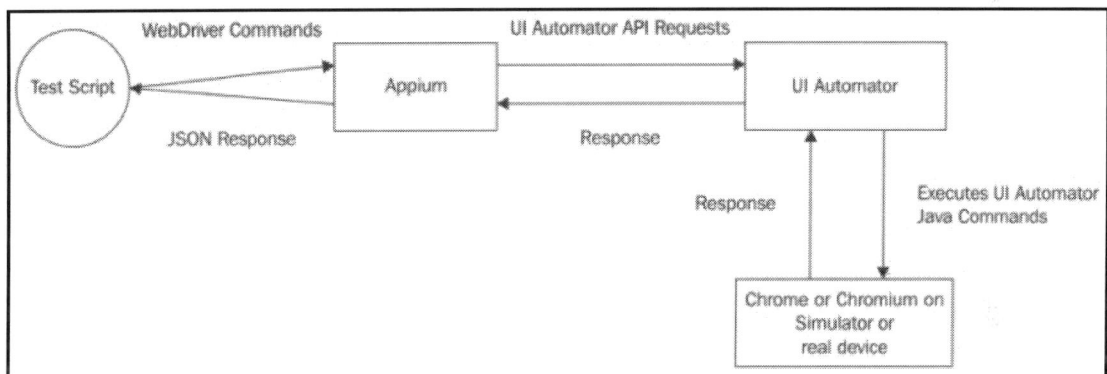

Again, Appium works as a Remote WebDriver and receives the commands from your test scripts over the JSON wire protocol. These commands are passed to Google UI Automator, which comes with Android SDK, to be executed on the native app launched on a simulator or a real device. Before the commands are passed on the UI Automator, Appium translates the JSON commands into UI Automator commands that can be understood by UI Automator. This UI Automator will launch your app on the simulator or real device and start executing your test-script commands on it. After the command is executed against your app on the simulator or device, the target app sends the response to the UI Automator, which is transferred to Appium in the UI Automator response format. Appium translates the UI Automator responses into Selenium WebDriver JSON wire protocol responses and sends them back to your test script.

This is the high-level architecture that helps you understand how Appium works with Android and iOS devices to execute your test commands.

Prerequisites for Appium

Before we start discussing some working examples for Appium, we need to install some prerequisite tools for the iOS and Android platforms. We need to set up Xcode and Android Studio for this purpose, for which I'll be showing the examples on macOS.

Setting up Xcode

To set up the Xcode, we will perform the following steps:

1. You can download the latest Xcode from `https://developer.apple.com/xcode/`.
2. After downloading it, install and open it.
3. Navigate to **Preferences | Components** to download and install command-line tools and iOS Simulators, as shown in the following screenshot:

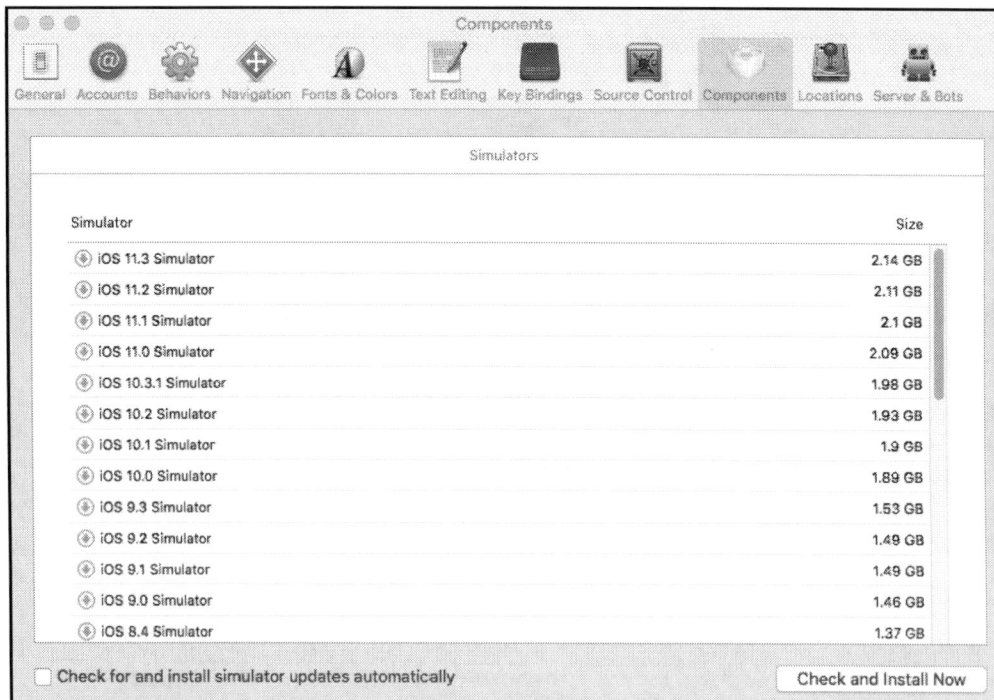

If you are using a real device, you need a provisioning profile installed on the device and USB-debugging enabled on it.

Try to launch the iPhone simulator and verify that it works. You can launch the simulator by navigating to **Xcode | Open Developer Tool | iOS Simulator**. The simulator should look similar to what is shown in the following screenshot:

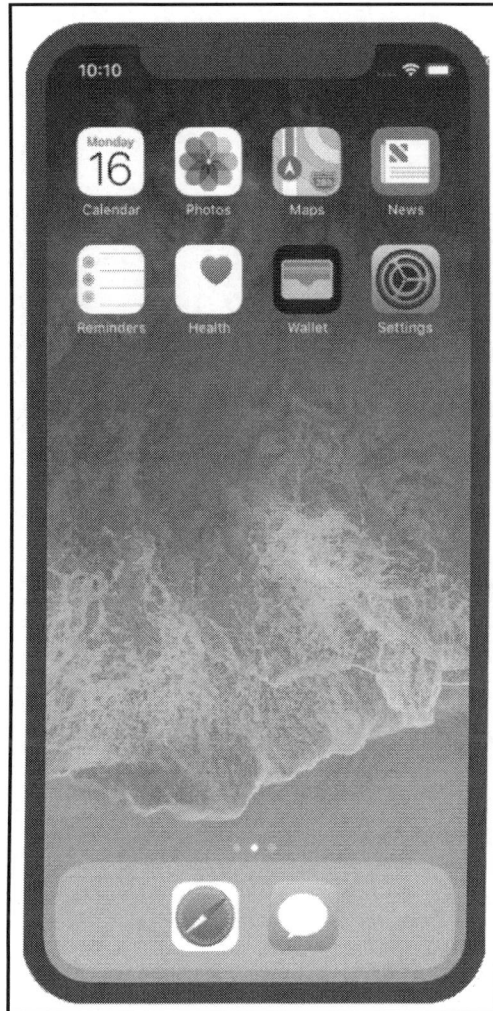

Setting up Android SDK

You need to install Android SDK from `https://developer.android.com/studio/`. Download and install Android Studio.

Launch the installed Android Studio. Now download any Android whose API level is 27, and install it. You can do that by navigating to **Tools | SDK Manager**. You should see something similar to what is shown in the following screenshot:

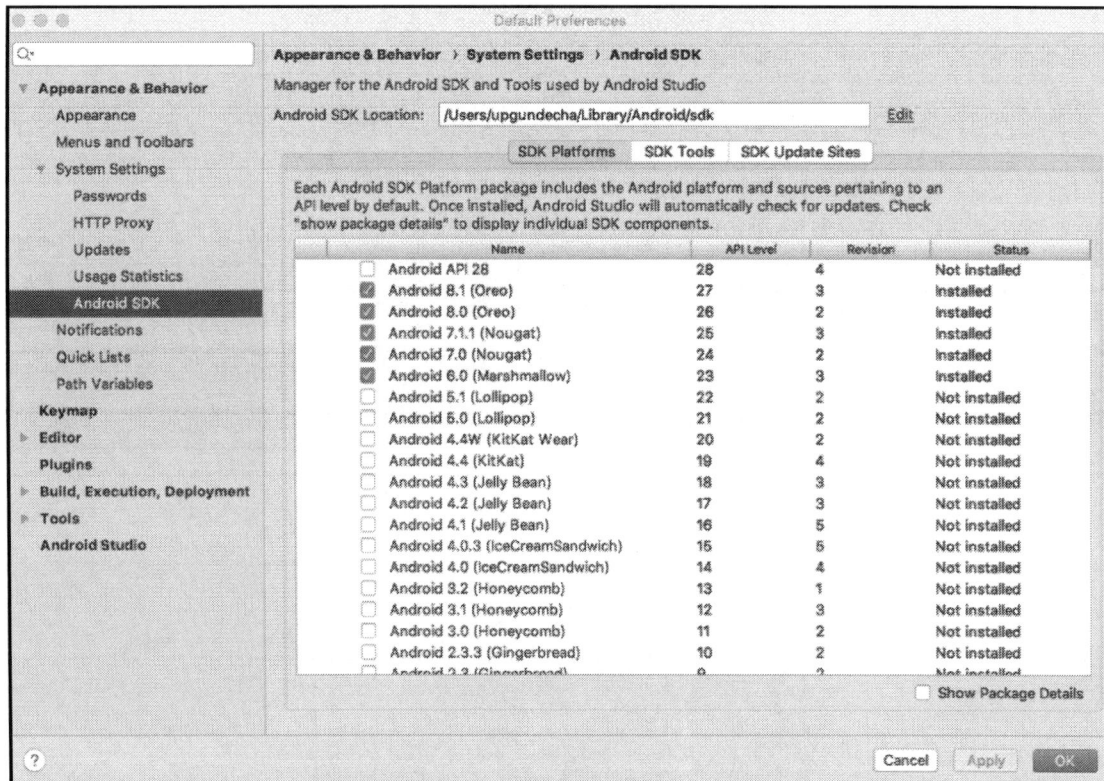

Here, we are installing Android 8.1, which has an API level of 27.

Creating the Android Emulator

If you want to execute your test scripts on an Android Emulator, you have to create one. To create one, we will perform the following steps:

1. In Android Studio, open the **AVD Manager** by navigating to **Tools | AVD Manager**. It launches the AVD Manager, as shown in the following screenshot:

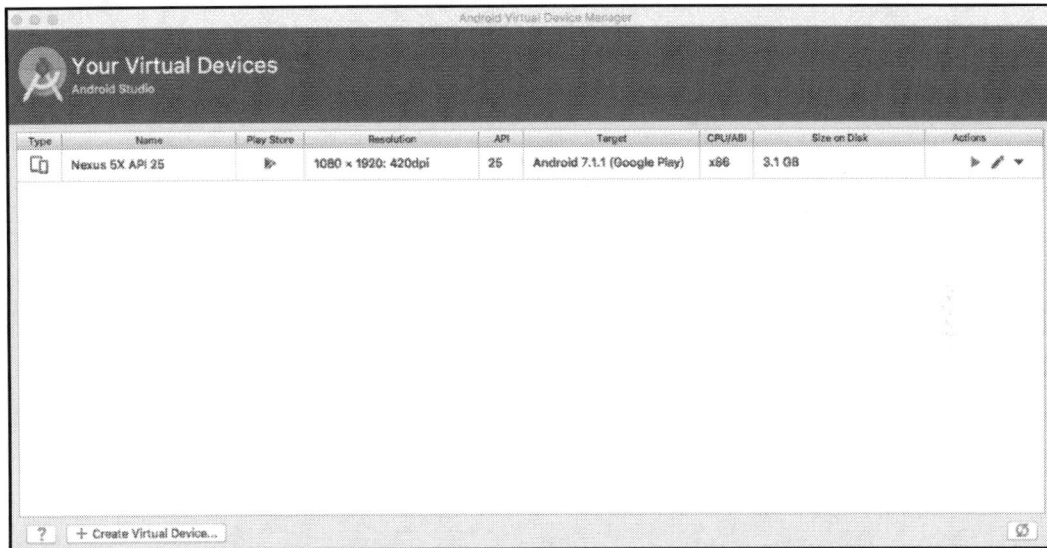

2. Create a new virtual device or emulator by clicking on the **Create Virtual Device...** button. You should see a window that will take all the necessary information from you, as shown in the following screenshot:

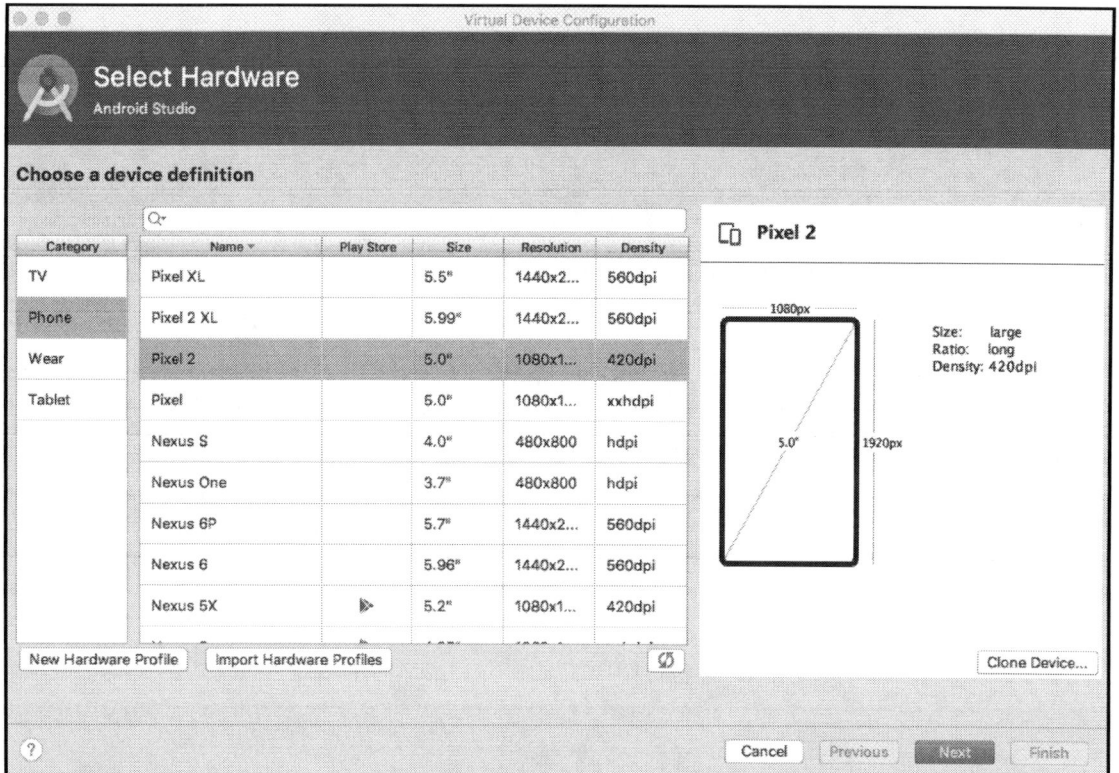

3. Launch the emulator to see whether it was created successfully. It might take several minutes for the Android Virtual Device to start. The following screenshot shows a started Android Emulator:

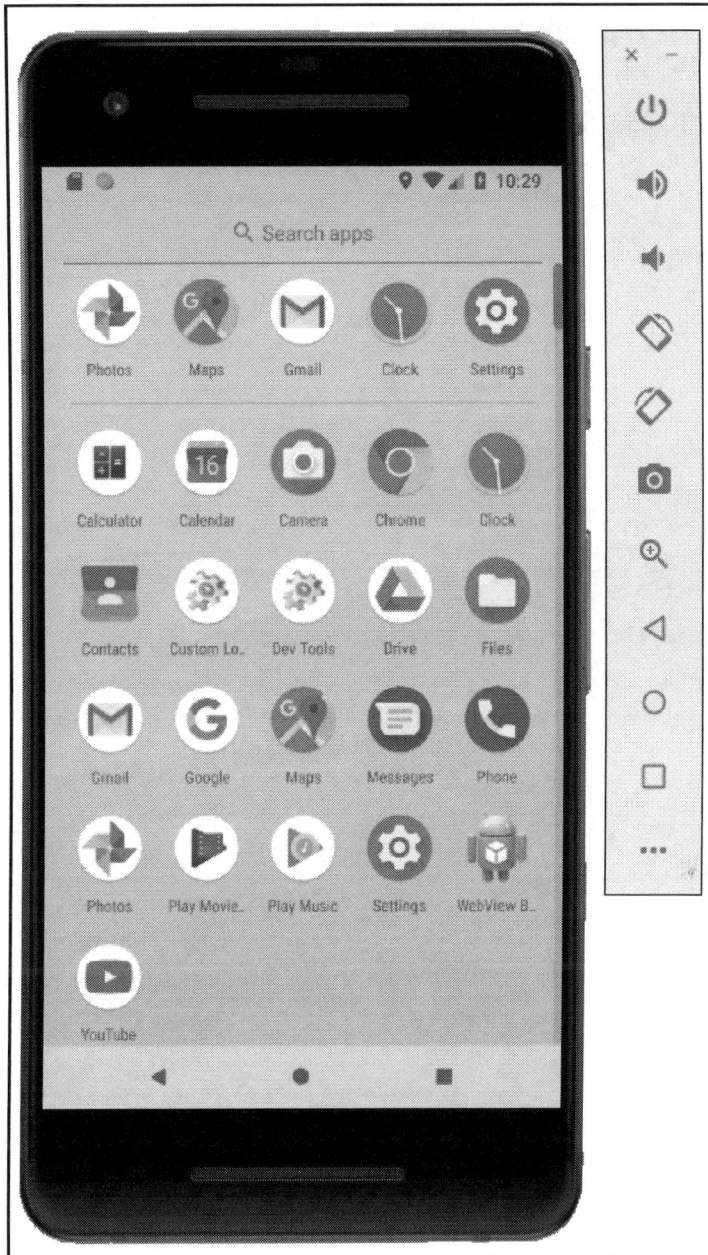

Installing Appium

You can download Appium from `http://appium.io/`. Click on the **Download Appium** button to download the Appium specific to your workstation platform. Here, I am using a Mac, so it will download the Appium DMG file.

Copy Appium to the `Applications` folder, and try to launch it. The first time it is launched, it asks for your authorization to run the iOS simulators, as shown in the following screenshot:

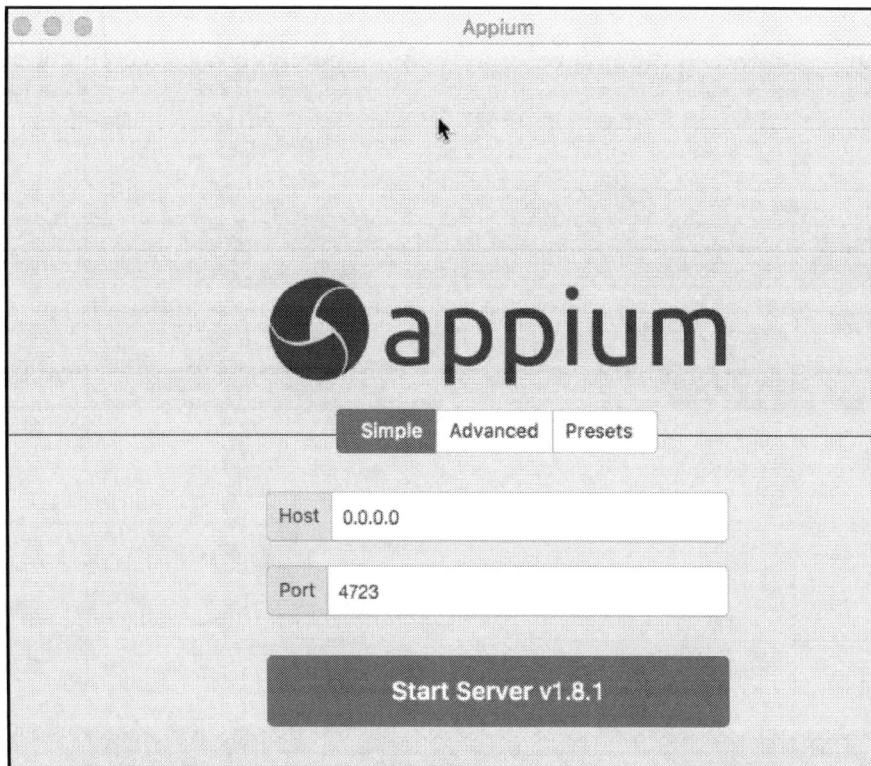

Click on Launch to **Start Server** button. By default, it starts at `http://localhost:4723`. This is the remote URL to which your test scripts should direct the test commands.

Automating for iOS

Now we have Appium running, so let's create a test that will check the search test on the iPhone Safari browser. Let's use the `DesiredCapabilities` class to provide capabilities to Appium for running tests on iPhone X and iOS 11.4, as shown in the following code:

```java
public class SearchTest {

    private WebDriver driver;

    @BeforeTest
    public void setUp() throws Exception {

        // Set the desired capabilities for iOS- iPhone X
        DesiredCapabilities caps = new DesiredCapabilities();
        caps.setCapability("platformName", "iOS");
        caps.setCapability("platformVersion", "11.4");
        caps.setCapability("deviceName", "iPhone X");
        caps.setCapability("browserName", "safari");

        // Create an instance of AndroidDriver for testing on Android
platform
        // connect to the local Appium server running on a different
machine
        // We will use WebElement type for testing the Web application
        driver = new IOSDriver<>(new URL(
                "http://192.168.0.101:4723/wd/hub"), caps);
        driver.get("http://demo-store.seleniumacademy.com/");
    }

    @Test
    public void searchProduct() {

        WebElement lookingGlassIcon =
                driver.findElement(By
                        .cssSelector("a.skip-search span.icon"));

        lookingGlassIcon.click();

        // find search box and enter search string
        WebElement searchBox = driver.findElement(By.name("q"));

        searchBox.sendKeys("Phones");

        WebElement searchButton =
                driver.findElement(By.className("search-button"));
```

```
        searchButton.click();

        List<WebElement> searchItems = new WebDriverWait(driver, 30)
                .until(ExpectedConditions
                        .presenceOfAllElementsLocatedBy(By
                                .cssSelector("h2.product-name a")));

        assertThat(searchItems.size())
                .isEqualTo(3);

    }

    @AfterTest
    public void tearDown() throws Exception {
        // Close the browser
        driver.quit();
    }
}
```

As you can see, the preceding code is similar to the test script for `RemoteWebDriver`. However, there are a few differences. The following code depicts that:

```
DesiredCapabilities caps = new DesiredCapabilities();
caps.setCapability("platformName", "iOS");
caps.setCapability("platformVersion", "11.4");
caps.setCapability("deviceName", "iPhone X");
caps.setCapability("browserName", "safari");
```

The Appium Java Client library provides the `IOSDriver` class that supports executed tests on the iOS platform to run the tests with Appium. However, for Appium to use the desired platform, we need to pass a set of desired The `platformName` capability is used by Appium to decide on which platform the test script should get executed. In this example, we used the iPhone X Simulator. To run the tests on an iPad, we can specify the iPad Simulator.

When running the tests on a real device, we need to specify the value of the iPhone or iPad for the device capability. Appium will pick the device that is connected to the Mac via USB. The last desired capability that we used is browserName, which is used by Appium to launch the Safari browser.

Automating for Android

Testing apps on Android is similar to testing on iOS. For Android, we will use a real device instead of an emulator (a simulator is called an emulator in the Android community). We will use the same application to test in Chrome for Android.

For this example, I am using the Samsung Galaxy S4 Android handset. We need to install the Google Chrome browser on the device. You can get Google Chrome at Google's Play store in case it is not pre-installed on your device. Next, we need to connect the device to the machine on which the Appium server is running. Let's run the following command to get a list of emulators or devices connected to the machine:

```
./adb devices
```

The Android Debug Bridge (ADB) is a command-line tool available in the Android SDK that lets you communicate with an emulator instance or an actual Android device connected to your computer. The ./adb devices command will display a list of all the Android devices that are connected to the host, as per the following output:

```
List of devices attached
4df1e76f39e54f43 device
```

Let's modify the script we created for iOS to use the Android capabilities and AndroidDriver class to execute tests on real Android devices, as shown in the following code:

```
public class MobileBmiCalculatorTest {
    private WebDriver driver;

@BeforeTest
public void setUp() throws Exception {

    // Set the desired capabilities for Android Device
    DesiredCapabilities caps = DesiredCapabilities.android();
    caps.setCapability("deviceOrientation", "portrait");
    caps.setCapability("platformVersion", "8.1");
    caps.setCapability("platformName", "Android");
    caps.setCapability("browserName", "Chrome");

    // Create an instance of AndroidDriver for testing on Android platform
    // connect to the local Appium server running on a different machine
    // We will use WebElement type for testing the Web application
    driver = new AndroidDriver<WebElement>(new URL(
            "http://192.168.0.101:4723/wd/hub"), caps);
    driver.get("http://demo-store.seleniumacademy.com/");
}
```

In the preceding example, we assigned the `platformName` capability value to `Android`, which will be used by Appium to run tests on Android. As we want to run the tests in Chrome for Android, we have mentioned Chrome in the browser capability section of the code. The other important change we made was using the `AndroidDriver` class from the Appium Java client libraries.

Appium will use the first device from the list of devices that `adb` returns, as shown in the following screenshot. It will use the desired capabilities that we mentioned, and will launch the Chrome browser on the device and start executing the test-script commands.

Using Device Cloud to run tests on Real Devices

Appium supports testing on mobile simulators, emulators, and real devices. To set up a mobile-testing lab with real devices requires capital investment as well as the maintenance of devices and infrastructure. Mobile phone manufacturers release new phone models and operating system updates almost every day and your application has to be compatible with the new launches.

To respond to these changes faster and keep the investment to a minimum, we can use Cloud-based mobile-testing labs. There are a number of vendors, such as Amazon Web Services, BrowserStack, and Sauce Labs, that provide cloud-based real-mobile-device labs to execute tests without requiring any upfront investment in real devices. You pay only for the amount of time used for testing. These vendors also allow you to run automated tests using Appium in their Device clouds.

In this section, we will explore BrowserStack to run tests on its real-device Cloud:

1. You need to have a BrowserStack account with a subscription to the **Automate** feature. You can sign up for a free trial account at `https://www.browserstack.com/`.

2. We need to get the desired capabilities from BrowserStack based on device combination. BrowserStack provides capability-suggestions based on the selected combination of devices and platforms. Go to `https://www.browserstack.com/automate/java` and select an OS and Device :

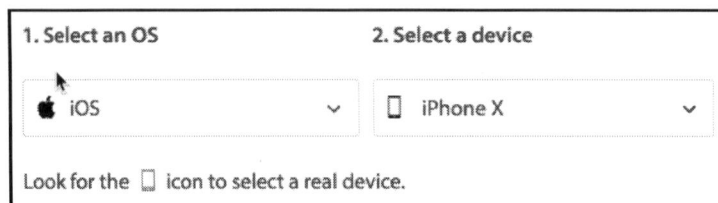

3. Based on your selection, BrowserStack will auto-generate code using your username and access key:

```java
import org.openqa.selenium.By;
import org.openqa.selenium.Platform;
import org.openqa.selenium.WebDriver;
import org.openqa.selenium.WebElement;
import org.openqa.selenium.remote.DesiredCapabilities;
import org.openqa.selenium.remote.RemoteWebDriver;

import java.net.URL;

public class JavaSample {

  public static final String USERNAME = "            ";
  public static final String AUTOMATE_KEY = "                    ";
  public static final String URL = "https://" + USERNAME + ":" + AUTOMATE_KEY + "@hub-cloud.browserstack.com/wd/hub";

  public static void main(String[] args) throws Exception {

    DesiredCapabilities caps = new DesiredCapabilities();
    caps.setCapability("browserName", "iPhone");
    caps.setCapability("device", "iPhone X");
    caps.setCapability("realMobile", "true");
    caps.setCapability("os_version", "11.0");

    WebDriver driver = new RemoteWebDriver(new URL(URL), caps);
    driver.get("http://www.google.com");
    WebElement element = driver.findElement(By.name("q"));

    element.sendKeys("BrowserStack");
    element.submit();

    System.out.println(driver.getTitle());
    driver.quit();

  }
}
```

We will not use the suggested code in step 3, and instead change our test as shown in the following code. Remember, you need to use the username and access key shown in the auto-generated code:

```java
public class SearchTest {

    private WebDriver driver;

    @BeforeTest
    public void setUp() throws Exception {

        String USERNAME = "username";
        String AUTOMATE_KEY = "access_key";
```

```
        String URL = "https://" + USERNAME + ":"
                + AUTOMATE_KEY + "@hub-cloud.browserstack.com/wd/hub";

        // Set the desired capabilities for iPhone X
        DesiredCapabilities caps = new DesiredCapabilities();
        caps.setCapability("browserName", "iPhone");
        caps.setCapability("device", "iPhone X");
        caps.setCapability("realMobile", "true");
        caps.setCapability("os_version", "11.0");

        driver = new RemoteWebDriver(new URL(URL), caps);
        driver.get("http://demo-store.seleniumacademy.com/");
    }

    @Test
    public void searchProduct() {

        WebElement lookingGlassIcon =
                driver.findElement(By
                        .cssSelector("a.skip-search span.icon"));
        lookingGlassIcon.click();

        // find search box and enter search string
        WebElement searchBox = driver.findElement(By.name("q"));
        searchBox.sendKeys("Phones");

        WebElement searchButton =
                driver.findElement(By.className("search-button"));

        searchButton.click();

        List<WebElement> searchItems = new WebDriverWait(driver, 30)
                .until(ExpectedConditions
                        .presenceOfAllElementsLocatedBy(By
                                .cssSelector("h2.product-name a")));

        assertThat(searchItems.size())
                .isEqualTo(3);
    }

    @AfterTest
    public void tearDown() throws Exception {
        // Close the browser
        driver.quit();
    }
}
```

Execute the test from your IDE, and it will run in the BrowserStack cloud. You can monitor the tests in the BrowserStack dashboard where it will show you capabilities used, the status of each step, console logs, network logs, Appium logs, and a video of the execution:

Summary

In this chapter, we discussed the different ways a business can reach out to its users on mobile platforms. We also learned about the various software tools that are created using Selenium WebDriver. Finally, we went through one of the upcoming software tools and modified our test script to work with iOS and Android platforms.

In the next `chapter`, we will see how to create parameterized and data-driven tests using `TestNG`. This will help us to reuse tests and increase test coverage.

Questions

1. What are the different types of mobile apps?
2. Which classes does the Appium Java Client library provide for testing iOS and Android applications?
3. What is the command to list the Android devices connected to a computer via USB ports?
4. What is the default port used by Appium Server?

Further information

You can check out the following link for more information about the topics covered in this chapter:

- For more examples of using Appium, please visit its website and GitHub forums at `http://appium.io/` and `https://github.com/appium/appium/tree/master/sample-code/java`

11
Data-Driven Testing with TestNG

In this chapter, we will see how to create data-driven tests using TestNG and Selenium WebDriver. We will look at the following topics:

- What is data-driven testing?
- Using TestNG suite parameters to parameterize tests.
- Using TestNG data providers for data-driven testing.
- Using the CSV and Excel file formats for storing and reading test data.

Overview of data-driven testing

By employing the data-driven testing approach, we can use a single test to verify different sets of test cases or test data by driving the test with input and expected values from an external data source instead of using the hardcoded values every time a test is run. This becomes useful when we have similar tests that consist of the same steps but differ in the input data and expected value or the application state. Here is an example of a set of login test cases with different combinations:

Description	Test data	Expected output
Test valid username and password	A pair of valid usernames and passwords	The user should log into the application with a success message
Test invalid username and password	An invalid username and password	The user should be displayed the login error
Valid username and invalid password	A valid username and an invalid password	The user should be displayed the login error

We can create a single script that can handle the test data and the conditions from the preceding table. By using the data-driven testing approach, we separate the test data from the test logic by replacing the hardcoded test data with variables using the data from external sources, such as CSV or a spreadsheet file. This also helps to create reusable tests that can run with different sets of data, which can be kept outside of the test. Data-driven testing also helps in increasing the test coverage, as we can handle multiple test conditions while minimizing the amount of test code we need to write and maintain.

The benefits of data-driven testing are as follows:

- We can get greater test coverage while minimizing the amount of test code we need to write and maintain
- It makes creating and running a lot of test conditions very easy
- Test data can be designed and created before the application is ready for testing
- Data tables can also be used in manual testing

Selenium WebDriver, being a pure browser-automation API, does not provide built-in features to support data-driven testing. However, we can add support for data-driven testing using testing frameworks such as JUnit or TestNG. In this book, we are using TestNG as our testing framework and we will use parameterization features of TestNG to create data-driven tests in the following sections.

Parameterizing Tests using suite parameters

In Chapter 1, *Introducing WebDriver and WebElements*, we created a search test that performs a simple search on the application under test. This test searches for a given product and validates the title. We used a hardcoded value, phones, for the search, as shown in the following code snippet:

```
@Test
public void searchProduct() {

        // find search box and enter search string
        WebElement searchBox = driver.findElement(By.name("q"));

        searchBox.sendKeys("Phones");

        WebElement searchButton =
                driver.findElement(By.className("search-button"));

        searchButton.click();
```

```
    assertThat(driver.getTitle())
         .isEqualTo("Search results for: 'Phones'");
  }
```

Instead of using hardcoded values, we can parameterize these values and provide them to the test method using the suite-parameter feature of TestNG. This will help to remove using hardcoded values in the test method and move them into TestNG suite files. The parameterized values can be used in multiple tests. When we need to change these values, we don't have to go to each test and make a change,the instead we can simply change these in suite file.

Now, let's look at steps for using the TestNG Parameters from the suite file. In Chapter 1, we created a testng.xml file, which is located in the src/test/resources/suites folder. Let's modify the file and add the parameter declaration, as highlighted in the following code snippet:

```
<!DOCTYPE suite SYSTEM "http://testng.org/testng-1.0.dtd" >

<suite name="Chapter 1" verbose="1">
    <listeners>
        <listener class-
name="com.vimalselvam.testng.listener.ExtentTestNgFormatter"/>
    </listeners>
    <test name="Search Test">
        <parameter name="searchWord" value="phones"/>
        <parameter name="items" value="3"/>
        <classes>
            <class name="com.example.SearchTest"/>
        </classes>
    </test>
</suite>
```

We can add parameters in the TestNG suite file using the <parameter> tag. We have to provide the name and value attributes for the parameter. In this example, we create two parameters: searchWord and items. These parameters store the search word and expected count of items returned by the application for that search word.

Now, let's modify the test to use parameters instead of hardcoded values. First, we need to use the `@Parameters` annotation before the `@Test` annotation for the test method. In the `@Parameters` annotation, we need to supply the exact names and order of the parameters declared in the suite file. In this case, we will supply `searchWord` and `items`. We also need to add arguments to the test method along with the required data type to map the XML parameters. In this case, the `String searchWord` and `int Items` arguments are added to the `searchProduct()` test method. Finally, we need to replace the hardcoded values with the arguments in the test method, as shown in the following code snippet:

```
@Parameters({"searchWord", "items"})
@Test
public void searchProduct(String searchWord, int items) {

    // find search box and enter search string
    WebElement searchBox = driver.findElement(By.name("q"));

    // use searchWord parameter value from XML suite file
    searchBox.sendKeys(searchWord);

    WebElement searchButton =
            driver.findElement(By.className("search-button"));

    searchButton.click();

    assertThat(driver.getTitle())
            .isEqualTo("Search results for: '" + searchWord  + "'");

    List<WebElement> searchItems = driver
            .findElements(By.xpath("//h2[@class='product-name']/a"));

    assertThat(searchItems.size())
            .isEqualTo(items);
}
```

We have to run the parameterized tests via the testng.xml file for TestNG to read the parameters defined in the suite file and pass the values to the test method.

During execution, TestNG will use the parameters defined in the XML suite file and map these in the same order to the Java parameters in test methods using the `@Parameters` annotation. It will pass the parameter values from the suite file using the arguments added in the test method. TestNG will throw an exception if the number of parameters between XML and the `@Parameters` annotation does not match.

In the next section, we will see a programmatic parameterization, which offers us the ability to run tests with multiple rows of test data.

Parameterizing Tests with a Data Provider

While suite parameters are useful for simple parameterization, they are not sufficient for creating data-driven tests with multiple test data values and reading data from external files, such as property files, CSV, Excel, or databases. In this case, we can use a Data Provider to supply the values need to test. A Data Provider is a method defined in the test class that returns an array of array of objects. This method is annotated with the @DataProvider annotation.

Let's modify the preceding test to use the Data Provider. Instead of using a single searchWord, we will now use three combinations of searchWords and expected items counts returned by the search. We will add a new method, named provider(), in the SearchTest class, as shown in following code, before the @BeforeMethod annotation:

```
public class SearchTest {

    WebDriver driver;

    @DataProvider(name = "searchWords")
    public Object[][] provider() {
        return new Object[][]{
                {"phones", 3},
                {"music", 5},
                {"iphone 5s", 0}
        };
    }

    @BeforeMethod
    public void setup() {
        ...
    }
    ...
}
```

When a method is annotated with @DataProvider, it becomes a data-feeder method by passing the test data to the test case. In addition to the @DataProvider annotation, we also need to provide a name for the data provider. In this example, we have given the name as searchWords.

Next, we need to update the `searchTest()` test method to link to the `data provider`. This is done with the following steps:

1. Provide the name of the `data provider` in the `@Test` annotation
2. Add two arguments `String searchWord` and `int items` to the `searchProduct` method
3. Use method parameters to substitute hardcoded values:

```
public class SearchTest {

    WebDriver driver;

    @DataProvider(name = "searchWords")
    public Object[][] provider() {
        ...
    }

    @BeforeMethod
    public void setup() {

        System.setProperty("webdriver.chrome.driver",
                "./src/test/resources/drivers/chromedriver");
        driver = new ChromeDriver();
        driver.get("http://demo-store.seleniumacademy.com/");

    }

    @Test(dataProvider = "searchWords")
    public void searchProduct(String searchWord, int items) {

        // find search box and enter search string
        WebElement searchBox = driver.findElement(By.name("q"));

        searchBox.sendKeys(searchWord);

        WebElement searchButton =
                driver.findElement(By.className("search-button"));

        searchButton.click();

        assertThat(driver.getTitle())
                .isEqualTo("Search results for: '" + searchWord + "'");

        List<WebElement> searchItems = driver
                .findElements(By.xpath("//h2[@class='product-name']/a"));

        assertThat(searchItems.size())
```

```
                    .isEqualTo(items);
    }

    @AfterMethod
    public void tearDown() {
        driver.quit();
    }
}
```

The `provider()` method will become the data-feeder method, which returns an array of objects that are combinations of `searchWords` and expected `items` counts, and TestNG will pass the array of data rows to the test method.

TestNG will execute the test four times with different test combinations. TestNG also generates a well-formatted report at the end of the test execution. Here is an example of the test results with TestNG using the defined values. The `searchProduct` test is executed three times, as shown in the following screenshot:

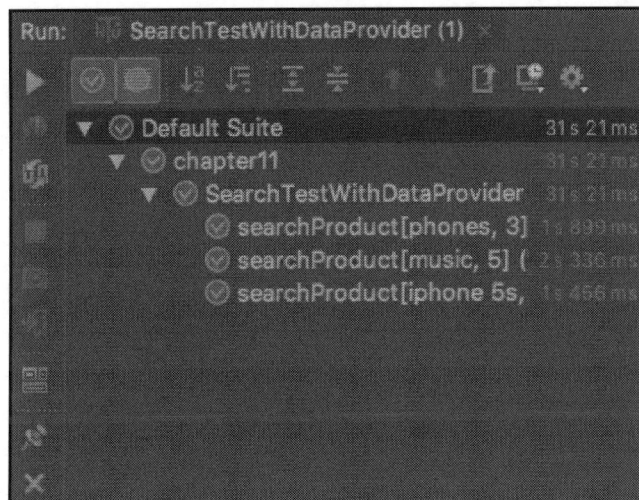

Reading data from a CSV file

We saw a simple data-driven test TestNG. The test data was hardcoded in the test-script code. This could become difficult to maintain. It is recommended that we store the test data separately from the test scripts. Often, we use data from the production environment for testing. This data can be exported in the CSV format. We can read these CSV files in data-provider methods and pass the data to the test instead of hardcoded object arrays.

In this example, we will use the OpenCSV library to read a CSV file. OpenCSV is a simple Java library for reading CSV files in Java. You can find more details on OpenCSV at `http:/ /opencsv.sourceforge.net/`.

Let's first create a CSV file, named `data.csv`, in the `src/test/resources/data` folder and copy the following combinations of `searchWords` and `items`:

```
searchWord,items
phones,3
music,5
iphone 5s,0
```

Next, we need to add the OpenCSV dependency to the Maven pom.xml file. For this example, we will use the latest version, 3.4, as shown in the following code snippet:

```
<dependency>
    <groupId>com.opencsv</groupId>
    <artifactId>opencsv</artifactId>
    <version>3.4</version>
</dependency>
```

Finally, we need to modify the `provider()` method in the test class to read the contents of the CSV file and return them as an array of objects, as shown in the following code:

```
public class SearchTest {

    WebDriver driver;

    @DataProvider(name = "searchWords")
    public Iterator<Object[]> provider() throws Exception {
        CSVReader reader = new CSVReader(
                new FileReader("./src/test/resources/data/data.csv")
                , ',', '\'', 1);
        List<Object[]> myEntries = new ArrayList<Object[]>();
        String[] nextLine;
        while ((nextLine = reader.readNext()) != null) {
            myEntries.add(nextLine);
        }
        reader.close();
        return myEntries.iterator();
    }

    @BeforeMethod
    public void setup() {

        System.setProperty("webdriver.chrome.driver",
                "./src/test/resources/drivers/chromedriver");
```

```
        driver = new ChromeDriver();
        driver.get("http://demo-store.seleniumacademy.com/");

    }

    @Test(dataProvider = "searchWords")
    public void searchProduct(String searchWord, String items) {

        // find search box and enter search string
        WebElement searchBox = driver.findElement(By.name("q"));

        searchBox.sendKeys(searchWord);

        WebElement searchButton =
                driver.findElement(By.className("search-button"));

        searchButton.click();

        assertThat(driver.getTitle())
                .isEqualTo("Search results for: '" + searchWord + "'");

        List<WebElement> searchItems = driver
                .findElements(By.xpath("//h2[@class='product-name']/a"));

        assertThat(searchItems.size())
                .isEqualTo(Integer.parseInt(items));
    }

    @AfterMethod
    public void tearDown() {
        driver.quit();
    }
}
```

In the provide method, the CSV file will be parsed using the CSVReader class of the OpenCSV library. We need to provide the path of the CSV file, the delimiter character, and the header row number (this will skip while fetching the data), as shown in the following code snippet:

```
@DataProvider(name = "searchWords")
public Iterator<Object[]> provider() throws Exception {

    CSVReader reader = new CSVReader(
            new FileReader("./src/test/resources/data/data.csv")
            , ',', '\'', 1);

    List<Object[]> myEntries = new ArrayList<Object[]>();
    String[] nextLine;
```

```
        while ((nextLine = reader.readNext()) != null) {
            myEntries.add(nextLine);
        }
        reader.close();
        return myEntries.iterator();
    }
```

In the preceding code, we will read each line of the CSV file ,copy it to an array of the object, and return it to the test method. The test method will be executed for each row in the CSV file.

Reading data from an Excel file

To maintain test cases and test data, Microsoft Excel is a favourite tool for testers. Compared to the CSV file format, Excel offers numerous features and a structured way to store data. A tester can create and maintain tables of test data in an Excel spreadsheet easily.

Let's create an Excel spreadsheet, named `data.xlsx`, in the `src/test/resources/data` folder with the following contents:

In this section, we will use an Excel spreadsheet as your data source. We will use the Apache POI API, developed by the Apache Foundation, to manipulate the Excel spreadsheet.

Let's modify the `provider()` method to use a helper class, called `SpreadsheetData`, to read the Excel file's contents:

```
@DataProvider(name = "searchWords")
public Object[][] provider() throws Exception {
    SpreadsheetData spreadsheetData = new SpreadsheetData();
    return
spreadsheetData.getCellData("./src/test/resources/data/data.xlsx");
}
```

The `SpreadsheetData` class This is available in the source code bundle for this book. This class supports both the old .xls and newer .xlsx formats:

```
public class SpreadsheetData {
    public String[][] getCellData(String path) throws
InvalidFormatException, IOException {
        FileInputStream stream = new FileInputStream(path);
        Workbook workbook = WorkbookFactory.create(stream);
        Sheet s = workbook.getSheetAt(0);
        int rowcount = s.getLastRowNum();
        int cellcount = s.getRow(0).getLastCellNum();
        String data[][] = new String[rowcount][cellcount];
        for (int rowCnt = 1; rowCnt <= rowcount; rowCnt++) {
            Row row = s.getRow(rowCnt);
            for (int colCnt = 0; colCnt < cellcount; colCnt++) {
                Cell cell = row.getCell(colCnt);
                try {
                    if (cell.getCellType() == cell.CELL_TYPE_STRING) {
                        data[rowCnt - 1][colCnt] =
cell.getStringCellValue();
                    } else {
                        data[rowCnt - 1][colCnt] =
String.valueOf(cell.getNumericCellValue());
                    }
                } catch (Exception e) {
                    e.printStackTrace();
                }
            }
        }
        return data;
    }
}
```

When the test is executed, the `provider()` method will create an instance of the `SpreadsheetData` class. The `SpreadsheetData` class reads the contents of the Excel spreadsheet row by row in a collection and returns this collection back to the `provider()` method:

```
InputStream spreadsheet = new
FileInputStream("./src/test/resources/data/data.xlsx");
return new SpreadsheetData(spreadsheet).getData();
```

For each row in the test data collection returned by the `provider()` method, the test runner will instantiate the test case class, passing the test data as parameters to the test-class constructor, and then execute all the tests in the test class.

Summary

In this chapter, we learned about an important technique to create parameterized and data-driven tests using TestNG features. This will help you to create highly-maintainable and robust tests with minimum coding effort and increased test coverage. We also looked at ways to read data from the CSV and Excel formats.

Questions

1. Explain what Data-driven Testing is.
2. Selenium supports data-driven testing— True or False?
3. What are two methods in TestNG to create data-driven tests?
4. Explain the `DataProvider` method in TestNG.

Further information

You can check out the following links for more information about the topics covered in this chapter:

- Read more about TestNG data-driven features at `https://testng.org/doc/documentation-main.html#parameters`
- Read more about the Apache POI library at `https://poi.apache.org/`

Assessments

Chapter 1

1. True or false: Selenium is a browser automation library.

   True.

2. What are the different types of locator mechanisms provided by Selenium?

   The different types of locator mechanisms are ID, Name, ClassName, TagName, Link, LinkText, CSS Selector, and XPATH.

3. True or false: With the `getAttribute()` method, we can read CSS attributes as well?

   False. The `getCssValue()` method is used to read CSS attributes.

4. What actions can be performed on a WebElement?

   The actions performed are click, type (**sendKeys**), and submit.

5. How can we determine whether the checkbox is checked or unchecked?

   By using the `isSelected()` method.

Chapter 2

1. What is the significance of WebDriver becoming a W3C specification?

   WebDriver is now a W3C specification. This means browsers have to be fully compliant with WebDriver spec set by the World Wide Web Consortium (W3C for short) and will be supported natively by the browser vendor the HTML5 and CSS are other prominent W3C specifications.

2. True or false: WebDriver is an interface.

   True.

3. Which browsers support headless testing?

   Google Chrome and Mozilla Firefox.

4. How can we test mobile websites with Chrome?

   By using the Mobile Emulation feature.

Chapter 3

1. Which version of Java Streams API is introduced?

   Java 8.

2. Explain the filter function of Streams API.

   Java Stream API provides a `filter()` method to filter stream elements on the basis of the given predicate. Suppose we want to get all the link elements that are visible on the page, we can use the `filter()` method to return the list in the following way:

   ```
   List<WebElement> visibleLinks = links.stream()
       .filter(item -> item.isDisplayed())
        .collect(Collectors.toList());
   ```

3. Which method of Streams API will return the number of matching elements from the `filter()` function?

   `count()`.

4. We can use the `map()` function to filter a list of WebElements by attribute values: True or false?

   False.

Chapter 4

1. Which are the different formats we can use to output a screenshot?

   The `OutputType` interface support screenshot types in `BASE64`, `BYTES`, and `FILE` formats.

2. How can we switch to another browser tab with Selenium?

> We can switch to another browser tab using the `driver.switchTo().window()` method.

3. True or false: The `defaultContent()` method will switch to the previously selected frame.

> False. The `defaultContent()` method will switch to the page.

4. What navigation methods are available with Selenium?

> The `Navigate` interface provides `to()`, `back()`, `forward()`, and `refresh()` methods.

5. How can we add a cookie using Selenium?

> We can add a cookie using the `driver.manage().addCookie(Cookie cookie)` method.

6. Explain the difference between an implicit wait and an explicit wait.

> An implicit wait once set will be available for the entire life of the WebDriver instance. It will wait for the element when `findElement` is called for the set duration. If the element doesn't appear in DOM in a set time, it will throw the `NoSuchElementFound` exception.
>
> An explicit wait, on the other hand, is used to wait for the specific condition to happen (for example, the visibility or invisibility of the element, a change in title, a change in attribute of the element, thee element becoming editable or for a custom condition). Unlike an implicit wait, the explicit wait will poll the DOM for the condition to fulfill instead of waiting for a fixed amount of time. It will come out if the condition is fulfilled before the defined timeout, else it will throw an exception. We can use various predefined conditions from the `ExpectedConditions` class with the explicit wait.

Chapter 5

1. True or false – the drag and drop action requires the source element and the target element.

> True.

2. List the keyboard methods that we can perform using the actions API.

    `sendKeys()`, `keyUp()`, and `keyDown()`.

3. Which method of the actions API will help in performing a double-click operation?

    `doubleClick(WebElement target)`.

4. Using the actions API, how can we perform a save option (that is to say, *Ctrl + S*)?

    `new Actions(driver) .sendKeys(Keys.chord(Keys.CONTROL, "s")) .perform();`.

5. How can we open a context menu using the actions API?

    By calling the `contextClick()` method.

Chapter 6

1. You can listen to WebDriver events using WebDriverEventListener interface: True or False?

    True.

2. How you can automatically clear an input field before calling the `sendKeys` method using WebDriverEventListener?

    We can call the `WebElement.clear()` method in the `beforeChangeValueOf()` event handler.

3. Selenium supports Accessibility Testing: True or false?

    False. Selenium does not support Accessibility testing

Chapter 7

1. True or false: with Selenium, we can execute tests on the remote machine(s)-

    True.

2. Which driver class is used to run tests on a remote machine?

   The RemoteWebDriver class.

3. Explain the DesiredCapabilities class.

   The DesiredCapabilities class is used to specify browser capabilities needed by the test script from the RemoteWebDriver. For example, we can specify the name of the browser, operating system, and version in DesiredCapabilities and pass it to RemoteWebDriver. The Selenium Standalone Server will match the configured capabilities with the available nodes and run the test on the matching node.

4. What protocol is used between the Selenium test and Selenium Standalone Server?

   JSON-Wire.

5. What is the default port used by the Selenium Standalone Server?

   Port 4444.

Chapter 8

1. Which argument can be used to specify how many browser instances can be supported by the node?

   maxInstances.

2. Explain how Selenium Grid can be used to support Cross Browser Testing.

   With Selenium Grid, we can set up nodes for various Browser and Operating System combinations and run tests in a distributed architecture. Based on capabilities provided by the test, Selenium Grid selects the appropriate node and executes the test on the selected node. We can add as many nodes as required based on combinations we want to test as per the cross-browser testing matrix required for testing.

3. What is the URL you need to specify with RemoteWebDriver to run tests on Selenium Grid?

   http://gridHostnameOrIp:4444/wd/hub.

4. Selenium Grid Hub acts as a load balancer: True or False?

True. Selenium Grid Hub distributes tests on multiple nodes based on the availability of the node

Chapter 9

1. How do you initialize a PageObject implemented with PageFactory?

    `PageFactory.initElements(driver, pageObjectClass).`

2. Using which class can we implement methods to validate whether the page is loaded?

    `LoadableComponent.`

3. Which `By class` methods are supported by @FindBy?

    ID, Name, ClassName, TagName, Link, PartialLinkText, CSS Selector, and XPATH.

4. While using PageFactory, if you name the WebElement variable name by the same ID or name attribute, then you don't need to use the `@FindBy` annotation: True or false?

    True. You can declare the WebElement variable with the same name as the value of id or name attribute, PageFactory will resolve it without using the `@FindBy` annotation

Chapter 10

1. What are the different types of Mobile Apps?

    Native, Hybrid, and Mobile Web Applications.

2. Which classes does Appium Java Client library provide for testing iOS and Android applications?

    `AndroidDriver` and `IOSDriver.`

3. What is the command to list the Android devices connected to a computer via USB ports?

    adb devices.

4. What is the default port used by Appium Server?

    Port 4723.

Chapter 11

1. Explain Data-driven Testing.

    Data-driven is a test automation framework approach, where input test data is stored in tabular format or in a spreadsheet format and a single test script reads each row of the data, which can be a unique test case, and executes the steps. This enables reuse of test scripts and increases test coverage with varied test data combinations.

2. True or False: Selenium supports data-driven testing.

    False.

3. What are two methods in TestNG to create data-driven tests?

    TestNG provides two methods for data-driven testing: Suite Parameters and Data Providers.

4. Explain the DataProvider method in TestNG.

    The DataProvider method in TestNG is a special method annotated with the @DataProvider annotation. It returns an array of objects. We can return tabular data reading from any format such as CSV or Excel to test the test case using the data provider.

Other Books You May Enjoy

If you enjoyed this book, you may be interested in these other books by Packt:

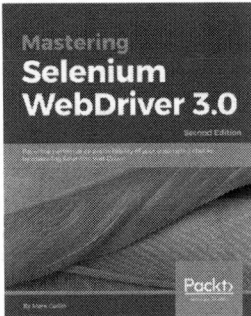

Mastering Selenium WebDriver 3.0 - Second Edition
Mark Collin

ISBN: 9781788299671

- Complement Selenium with useful additions that fit seamlessly into the rich and well-crafted API that Selenium offers
- Use different mobile and desktop browser platforms with Selenium 3
- Perform advanced actions, such as drag-and-drop and action builders on web page
- Learn to use Java 8 API and Selenium 3 together
- Explore remote WebDriver and discover how to use it
- Perform cross browser and distributed testing with Selenium Grid
- Use Actions API for performing various keyboard and mouse actions

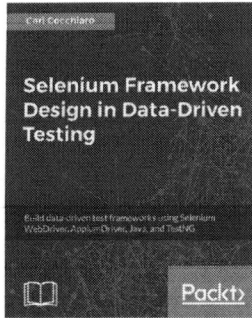

Selenium Framework Design in Data-Driven Testing
Carl Cocchiaro

ISBN: 9781788473576

- Design the Selenium Driver Class for local, remote, and third party grid support
- Build Page Object Classes using the Selenium Page Object Model
- Develop Data-Driven Test Classes using the TestNG framework
- Encapsulate Data using the JSON Protocol
- Build a Selenium Grid for RemoteWebDriver Testing
- Construct Utility Classes for use in Synchronization, File I/O, Reporting and Test Listener Classes
- Run the sample framework and see the benefits of a live data-driven framework in real-time

Leave a review - let other readers know what you think

Please share your thoughts on this book with others by leaving a review on the site that you bought it from. If you purchased the book from Amazon, please leave us an honest review on this book's Amazon page. This is vital so that other potential readers can see and use your unbiased opinion to make purchasing decisions, we can understand what our customers think about our products, and our authors can see your feedback on the title that they have worked with Packt to create. It will only take a few minutes of your time, but is valuable to other potential customers, our authors, and Packt. Thank you!

Index